REPORT

ON

THE OLD RECORDS

OF THE

INDIA OFFICE

REPORT

ON

THE OLD RECORDS

OF THE

INDIA OFFICE

WITH

SUPPLEMENTARY NOTE AND APPENDICES,

BY

SIR GEORGE BIRDWOOD, M.D.,

K.C.I.E., C.S.I., LL.D.

GYAN

Published by

GYAN

Gyan Publishing House
5, Ansari Road
Daryaganj, New Delhi-110002
Phone: 011-47034999, 9811692060
E-mail: books@gyanbooks.com

Distribution Network
gyanbooks.com
India, USA, Canada, UK, Australia

ISBN: 978-93-6208-563-4 (PB)
First Published,1890

2nd Impression 2024

Printed at: Gyan Press, Delhi.

REPORT ON THE OLD RECORDS OF THE INDIA OFFICE
Author: GEORGE BIRDWOOD

REPORT

ON

THE OLD RECORDS

OF THE

INDIA OFFICE;

WITH

SUPPLEMENTARY NOTE AND APPENDICES,

BY

SIR GEORGE BIRDWOOD, M.D.,
K.C.I.E., C.S.I., LL.D.

Ὦ φίλοι, Ἀργείων ὅς τ' ἔξοχος, ὅς τε μεσήεις,
ὅς τε χερειότερος, ...
. . . . . νῦν ἔπλετο ἔργον ἅπασιν.
Iliad, XII. 269-71.

SECOND REPRINT.

LONDON: W. H. ALLEN & CO., LIMITED,
AND AT CALCUTTA

1891.

TO THE VENERABLE

SETT FRAMJEE NUSSERWANJEE PATEL, J.P.,

"THE NESTOR OF THE PARSEES,"

This Volume is Dedicated

IN ADMIRATION OF THE VIRTUES FOR WHICH HE HAS
BEEN HELD IN THE HIGHEST HONOUR
FOR THREE GENERATIONS OF CONTEMPORARIES
IN WESTERN INDIA,

AND IN AFFECTIONATE REMEMBRANCE OF ALL THE
KINDNESSES I RECEIVED
FROM HIM AND OTHER DEAR *SETTIA* FRIENDS, OUR ASSOCIATES
IN THE LOYAL CIVIC LIFE OF

"OLD BOMBAY."

CONTENTS.

ILLUSTRATIONS.

PREFACE TO THE PRESENT REPRINT.

THE present reprint of my *REPORT ON THE* **Old Records** *OF THE INDIA OFFICE* having been undertaken as a business speculation by Messrs. W. H. Allen & Co., Ltd., I thought at first of giving it a more attractive character by the addition of a series of particularly interesting extracts from the documents to which it really is nothing more than a curtly descriptive Index. But the Report having come into demand, not as an entertaining Calendar, but as a comprehensive working Index, I resolved, on second thoughts, to reproduce it exactly as originally printed in 1879, and again in the autumn of last year. One little alteration I have indeed introduced, and that is the relegation of occasional illustrative remarks from the body of the Report to foot-notes. I have also added as foot-notes, both to the Report and the Supplementary Note, some of the Departmental Memoranda on special subjects elucidated by the India Office records, prepared by me subsequent to 1879. Such are the note on Buonaparte at Longwood, at pp. 93–98, and the note on La Bourdonnais at pp. 242–248. The Report is now, therefore, more strictly than ever a bare and, so to speak, short-hand Index to the Supplementary Miscellaneous **Old Records** enumerated in the Statistic and Commerce Departmental List, No. 2,397, and the Lists furnished to me in 1879 by the other Departments of the India Office; and I have been the readier to reduce it to this complexion from a natural desire to avoid using the official facilities I enjoy for the exploration of these **Old Records** to the detriment of less-favoured students of English history, whose researches in them I have in no way forestalled.

The Supplementary Note was originally written merely for my own information and guidance, and was only printed with the Report because the late Sir Henry Yule thought it would be useful to others beside myself. It is nothing but a compilation, copied bodily out of my common-place books on the history of Indian commerce and art, and very imperfect; being disproportionately lengthy where it treats of subjects in which I am interested, and far too brief where they happen to be uninteresting to me. I wished therefore very much to recast it altogether, in the hope of better adapting it for general reading. However, Mr. Quaritch, a very partial friend of mine, and Messrs. Allen & Co. as the responsible publishers of the book, both insisted on the Supplementary Note standing as it first appeared; and so it now reappears, a frequent footnote indicating to the inexperienced where it is particularly defective.

The opportunity has been taken in the present Reprint to correct certain errors, for the most part comparatively trifling, that had crept into both the Report and Supplementary Note; and in a few cases the foot-notes have been amplified and fresh matter introduced. While making these corrections and additions, however, I have been careful to preserve throughout the identical paging of the first reprint; and the two may, therefore, for all practical purposes, be regarded as earlier and later issues of the same edition.

It is a true pleasure to me to here testify to the wonderful improvement that has been effected since 1879 in the order and condition of the India Office records. The credit of this is altogether due to Mr. F. C. Danvers, who in 1884 commenced the first effective attempt to systematically conserve and classify them, and render them promptly and safely accessible to the public. The first step was to procure more space for them than was formerly allowed; and this having been obtained, the many thousands of loose papers that had hitherto been simply tied up in vaguely-assorted bundles were carefully collated with the documents in the better preserved regular series of the records, and bound up with them in chronological order; the volumes comprising each series being consecutively numbered, and placed in distinct ranges of cases.* The royal charters, and other parchment records still in existence, have been unfolded, cleaned, flattened, and, after careful examination, put away in large shallow boxes, shelved on a specially constructed locking skeleton cupboard, standing in the centre of the muniment, provided entirely for these "Parchment Records," as they are now designated, and other special relics of the late Honourable East India Company. The bulk of the documents in the general Record Rooms are distributed in such a way as, in the first place, to best subserve the purposes of the Departments requiring constant access to them. But the convenience of the public has also been considered in the arrangements adopted, and, when they are completed and in full operation, it will be possible for anyone provided with the proper authority to obtain, within a few minutes, any volume that may be wanted from any of the India Office Record Rooms.

The systematic custody of the state records is also being simultaneously provided for in India, in accordance with a parallel and almost identical plan initiated by Professor G. W. Forrest, B.A.; and thus in that country as well as here an immense mass of materials is being rapidly brought within the reach of all those whose duty it is to be fully and correctly informed on the history of the rise and progress of the Indian Empire.

The Government authorities, both at home and in India, have, moreover, long been in the practice of compiling for Departmental or Parliamentary use occasional volumes of "Selections" from Despatches, Letters, Minutes, and other Papers, showing the principles and procedure of various branches of the British Administration in India, and also volumes of "Memoirs," detailing the history and organization of different Departments of the Government. The *Memoir on the Indian Surveys*, prepared by Mr. Clements Markham, C.B., in 1871, is a remarkable example of the latter kind of publications, and a model to which they

* For particulars see Mr. Danvers' interesting "Report on the Records of the India Office," published in 1887 as a Parliamentary Paper [C. 5055].

should in future be always conformed; while of the former class we have a brilliant illustration in Professor Forrest's recently-issued *Selections from the Records of the Foreign Department of the Government of India* [Warren Hastings], 1772–85.

In future the Government might still further promote the diffusion of a thorough knowledge of India by encouraging private enterprise, firstly, in the fac-simile reproduction of such graphic documents in their possession as those photo-lithographed by Mr. William Griggs, of Peckham, in the *Journal of Indian Art* for July last; secondly, in the publication, *verbatim et literatim*, of selected series of the **Old Records**, such as the COURT BOOKS, and ORIGINAL CORRESPONDENCE, after the manner of the publication, in 1886, by Mr. Henry Stevens, of Vermont, of the first volume of the COURT BOOKS [see Appendix B.]; and, finally, by extending the utmost possible assistance and patronage to trained scholars of recognized literary capacity, who would be found willing to re-write the history of British India, or well-determined portions of it, direct from the stored archives of Bombay, Madras, and Calcutta, and the India Office. Only when this is done will the **Old Records** of the India Office have been put to their worthiest and most fruitful service.

I am myself greatly indebted for the help rendered me by Mr. F. C. Danvers, in revising the present volume; and my thanks are also due to Mr. William Foster, B.A., of the Registry and Record Department, for his assistance in seeing it through the press. In this trying work Mr. Foster has served me with the most perfect patience, efficiency, and loyalty, and I cannot too strongly express my obligations to him for his invaluable co-operation.

To those of my readers ignorant of the symbolism of India, it may, perhaps, be as well that I should in conclusion explain the meaning of the ritualistic ornamentation in which I have indulged on the blank leaves at the beginning and end of this volume, and on its binding. The "right-hand *svastika*," stamped in red on the blank leaf facing the title-page, is, among modern Hindus, a symbol of Ganisa or Ganapati, and is commonly placed by them, instead of the image of Ganisa, at the head of invoices and other papers.* It is also the symbol of the male principle in nature, and of the sun of the upper world, that is, in his diurnal course from "East to Occident;" and of the day, and summer, and light, and life, and glory; and it is coloured dominical red, the proper tincture of the East. To the Hindu it is an abbreviated form of the salutation:

OM!
Hail to Ganisa!
Lord of the Hosts of Heaven!
Of Whom are all Beginnings!
Hail!

The "left-handed *svastika*," or *sauvastika*,† stamped in blue on the blank leaf opposite the last printed page of the book is the symbol of Kali, the Indian Mania. It is also the symbol of the female principle in nature; and of the sun of the underground world, that is, in his nocturnal course from "the utmost corner of the West" back to "the fiery portal of the East;" and of the night, and winter, and darkness, death, and destruction; and it is deeply dyed in "nadder blue," the conventional Hindu colouration of the West.‡

Where it is placed it is a graphic reduction of the invocation:

OM!
Wail to Kali!
Leader of the Hordes of Hell!
Of whom is all Consummation!
The Dark Mother of Ganisa!
Wail!

On the cover the little ships placed in alternation between reversely revolving *svastikas* represent the 17th century fleets of the "Old" East India Company, sailing

* Compare our ancient use of the phrase "Laus Deo" in the same manner [see p. 72].

† See Professor Max Müller in Schliemann's *Ilios* [J. Murray, 1880], pp. 346–349.

‡ The Hindu colour for the South is yellow, and for the North white; and these four colours—red, yellow, blue, and white—correctly represent, according to the ritualism of India, the East, South, West, and North, on the ensign of the Peninsular and Oriental Steam Navigation Company.

in their golden progress from the waste "Water of *oblivion*" of the West into the light and life of the rich and gorgeous Kingdoms of the ever illustrious East.

In antiquity, of which India is the last living reservation, blue was everywhere regarded as the colour of the sea, and of the West, and red of the land, and of the East; and in accordance with this ritualistic chromatism the *Odyssey* was, it is said, always wrapped up in blue cloth, and the *Iliad* in red. I cannot therefore help noting in this connection that the change of arms, and particularly in the dominant colours of the arms of the East India Company, as shown in Plates I. and II., foreshadowed its transformation from a mercantile corporation into a great military power. The change of mottoes is still more striking; and there were at the time those who clearly read its inauspicious significance:

"For the *Wise*
"Have a *divining* Soul that never lyes."*

GEORGE BIRDWOOD.

30th November 1890.

---

* These lines, and the phrase, previously quoted, "Water of *oblivion*" [of the West], are from Sir Richard Fanshawe's rugged, and often obscure, but most fascinating version, in "ottava rima," of *The Luciad or Portugals Historical Poem* [1655]. The stanza in which Da Gama thanks the Almighty for his miraculous deliverance from the treachery of "the Moors" at one of the East African ports, concludes with the feeling lines:

What *Care*, what *Wisdom* is of suffisance,
The stroake of *Secret* mischief to prevent,
Unless the SOV'RAIGN GUARDIAN from on high
Supply the strength of frail *Humanity*?

Da Gama's confession, to the Moormen, of his Christian faith is quaintly rendered:

We worship HIM, who is by *every* Nature
(*Invisible* and *visible*) obay'd,
HIM who the *Hemispheres*, and every Creature
(Insensible and sensible) hath made:
Who gave Us *his*, and took on Him *our* feature,
Whom to a shameful death *his own* betrayed;
And *who* from HEAVEN to *Earth* came down in fine,
That *Man*, by HIM, from *Earth* to HEAVEN might climbe.

There is true poetry in the description of an altar-piece representing the Blessed Virgin Mary:

On *It*, the picture of that *Shape* he plac't,
In which the HOLY SPIRIT did alight:
The picture of the *Dove*, so white, so chast,
On the BLEST VIRGIN'S head, so chaste, so white.

And there is no suggestion in Camoens of the magic of the antiphonal repetition: "so white, so chast,——so chaste, so white."

Another happy touch is the line:

The Waters of the *Consecrated* DEEP.

PREFACE TO THE FIRST REPRINT (1889).

By Mr. F. C. Danvers,

Registrar and Superintendent of Records, India Office.

In reprinting the "Report on the Old Records of "the India Office," prepared by Sir George Birdwood in 1878, the detailed classification given to those documents when the Report was first published has been eliminated, as it is no longer applicable to them under the existing arrangements. Since this Report was first issued some few of the documents then missing have been discovered, and wherever this has been the case amendments have been made accordingly. The documents in the First Division described under the heading "Court Minutes," have been found to consist chiefly of the rough Minute Books from which the "Court Books" were most probably compiled;* they, however, were evidently not confined to the rough entries of the proceedings of the Court of Directors at their regular meetings, but they contain also notes of events which occurred between the regular meetings of the Court, and possess, therefore, a greater value than would otherwise have been the case. The "Court of Committees" volumes also appear to contain rough entries only, and from the fact that so few of these now remain, whilst there exists no evidence that fair copies were ever subsequently made, it would appear that they were not intended as permanent records. The proceedings of the Committees of any importance requiring the con-

* See, for instance, the following memorandum in Court Book No. VI., under the date of 26th April 1624:—"Here is a great dispute concerning "the King and the Lord Admiral omitted, *but remains to be seen upon the "original copy.*"

firmation of the Court would necessarily find a place in the Court Books. It is, however, not by any means certain that these missing volumes, as well as those that are wanting from other lists of documents, have not, at some time or other, been sacrificed as waste paper amongst the hundreds of tons of Records so disposed of in former years.

Amongst these Books are two which are particularly valuable as containing, so far as I have been able to ascertain, the only records extant of the separate proceedings of the "English East India Company." These consist of Minutes of the "Court of Directors," the one being the first volume of those Minutes, and commencing the 7th September 1698, or two days after the date of their Charter, and extending to the 20th June 1699. There is then a gap of some years, and the only other volume of the same series bears dates between the 21st July 1704 and the 8th January 1708. There are also four volumes of the Minutes of the "Committee of Managers," extending from the 31st July 1702 to the 13th April 1709. This Committee was a Joint Committee of the two Companies. On the 22nd July 1702 an Indenture or Charter of Union between the two East India Companies passed the great seal, and on the 24th idem each Company did, in pursuance of the said Charter of Union, elect twelve Managers for the united trade of the two Companies. The first Court of Directors of the United East India Company was held on the 23rd March 1709, at which date the union of the two Companies was completed.

In the earlier Records of the East India Company there is almost an entire absence of copies of letters sent by them from this country to their several agents abroad; but it is beyond doubt that these at one time existed. Probably, however, these were very few in the early years of their trade. A book has recently been found containing letters out and other documents up to 1616, after which there is an absence of letters out until 25th April 1653. On the 6th July 1607, at a Court of Committees held on that date, it "was "thought ffitt that all letters from and to India and all "the answers thereof be entered into a book and coated "for future memorie as occasion may fall out." At a Court held on the 6th October 1609 it was further resolved as follows:—

"And for as much as it is esteemed very needfull that "all letters to and from the Company, and also material "writings, be coated and kept in a Register ready for every "occasion, and that some fitt man may be given for that "business or for any other employment of the Company "about his Ma[ties] Court or otherwise. It was now ordered "and agreed that Mr. Eadm[d] Doe do confer and agree "with some fitt and faithful man for the doeing and "effecting of this, or any other the Companie's affaires "wherein he shall be employed."

On the 17th of the same month, "Ffrancis Sadler "was admitted and sworn servant of the Companie for "the registering of sundry letters and other writings fit "to be coated, registered, and kept for the use of the "Company. And further to doe such other their "services upon which they shall think good to employ "him."

The earlier correspondence addressed from abroad to the Company is exceedingly scanty, not more than fourteen documents of date previous to 1610 having been handed down to the present time in the O. C. volumes, besides which there are but very few of an earlier date amongst the loose miscellaneous documents. It appears, however, evident from references in the Court Books that many were received which are not now in existence. From 1610 they become more numerous in each year. Some of the missing documents were probably lost at a very early period. In 1614 "certain journals" were wanted which could not then be found, and it was consequently ordered* that all journals

* Court Minutes, 13th December 1614.

should first be written in the Company's books before being lent to any man, and that none were to use them without the consent of the Committees. The missing journals, which had been lent and could not be found,* were to be searched for. Some months later, in August 1615, a further Resolution† was passed that none of the Company's journals were thereafter to be lent "before "copies of them be entered in their books, whereby the "journals themselves have been lost to the great preju- "dice of the Company, and some things known which are "not fit to be published." After entry they were to be "delivered only to some principal persons of the Company "that shall desire the same." But all other persons wishing to inspect them were to be "satisfied with coming "and seeing them in the Office, or otherwise a copy of "them in the Books."

Besides the defects in these volumes of Indian Correspondence, there are unfortunately considerable gaps in the Court Minute Books. Although the first volume finishes with the 10th August 1603, the second does not begin till the 31st December 1606; there exists, however, one volume entitled "Miscellaneous Court Book," which contains a few entries between these two years. From the latter date until January 1610 the entries are complete; then a hiatus of four years occurs, the third volume beginning with January 1614. The last entry in that book is dated the 17th November 1615, but the next Court Book does not begin before the 19th September 1617. The first missing volume between 1603 and 1606 is perhaps of the most consequence, because the correspondence does not supply the deficiency, which, in a measure, it fortunately does after that date. There are also other gaps in the Court Minutes in later years.

It appears certain that at the union of the "London"

* Court Minutes, 20th December 1614.

† Court Minutes, 30th August 1615.

with the "New" East India Company, the Records belonging to the former were found in great disorder; and there is a Notice, without date, to the effect,—"That "at the dissolution of the Company, meaning when the "Old (or London) was absorbed in the United Company, "great numbers of their Books and Papers were promis-"cuously put together, some of which have since come "to the Trustees' hands, and more are inspecting by "their 'Register,' in order to obtain the necessary infor-"mation for answering Plaintiff Yale's Bill; and that "it will require a deal of care to separate and digest "them."

In 1830 or 1831 an attempt was made to collect all the "Original Correspondence from India, with col-"lateral Documents, originating at any places between "England and Japan" which were then extant. These were carefully bound, numbered, and catalogued, and form what is now known as the "O. C." Records. They extend from 1603 to 1708, and correspond to the volumes of letters from, and proceedings of, the Governments in India of the present day. This collection, however, is sadly deficient, especially in the earlier years, and does not contain all the documents that might have been included, several of which have continued as loose documents, tied up in bundles, to the present day. The great loss of early documents then ascertained naturally excited inquiry, and in 1835 the deficiencies in the Company's Records were brought prominently to notice, and an attempt was made to account for these wherever they occurred, an inquiry, however, which does not appear to have resulted in the recovery of any of the missing documents.

It is greatly to be regretted that the earliest "Marine Records" are missing, viz., the logs, journals, &c., of the first voyages of the East India Company; and this loss is only partly compensated for by the publications contained in "Purchas hys Pilgrimes" and those of the Hakluyt Society. It appears that Mr. Hakluyt was consulted by the Court of Directors of the East India Company from the very commencement of their operations, and by an Order of the Court of the 16th February 1601 certain warrants were ordered to be drawn, including one of £10 to Mr. Hakluyt "for his "travails taken in instructions and advices touching "the preparing of the voyage, and for his former "advices in setting the voyage in hand the last year;" also "30*s*. for three maps by him provided and delivered "to the Company." Mr. Hakluyt was appointed "Historiographer of the East India Company," and he seems to have been entrusted with the custody of the manuscript journals of all the East India voyages from 1601 almost to the date of his decease in 1616. A few years later these documents came into the hands of the Rev. Samuel Purchas, who, instead of publishing them in extenso, formed compilations from them, which he published in "Purchas hys Pilgrimes" in 1625. Purchas died in the following year, and all trace of many of the earliest of these valuable historical records was subsequently lost. There is no evidence that they were ever returned to the East India Company.

In the classification of the India Office Records, now in progress, all the loose documents will be assigned places in accordance with the nature of their subject matter, and be carefully bound, and thus placed beyond all ordinary risk of loss or damage; the O. C. volumes will, however, be left untouched, and the loose documents, which comprise several thousand papers, will be arranged in separate series, according as they consist of Home correspondence, Marine Records, or those relating to the various settlements or factories abroad. It will thus be seen that the arrangement adopted in the present Report is of a tentative nature only, rendered necessary, however, before those documents could be otherwise dealt with and assigned their proper places with the general Records of this Office, in consequence of the chaotic state in which they were found at the time it was made and the following Report on their principal contents written.

On the completion of the new classification, the Records of this Office will be calendared in the same manner as is adopted at the Public Record Office, and they will thus be rendered more readily accessible to any who may desire to consult them. This, however, it must be added, will be the work of some years; but it is intended that volumes containing the calendars of the earliest Records shall be issued from time to time as they may be completed.

F. C. DANVERS,
Registrar and Superintendent
of Records.

India Office,
7th November 1889.

I.

REPORT

ON

The Old Records

OF THE

INDIA OFFICE.

"Qui mare teneat, eum necesse rerum potiri."

CICERO, *Epist. ad Att.*, X.

"And therefore the Sovereignty of the Seas being the most precious Jewell of the Crowne, and next under God the principall means of our Wealth and Safetie; all true English hearts and hands are bound by all possible means and diligence to preserve and maintain the Same, even at the uttermost hazzard of their lives, their goods and fortunes."

Sir JOHN BURROUGHS, Keeper of the Records in the Tower of London, 1651.

"Behold then the true Form and Worth of Forraign Trade, which is:—The Great Revenue of the King; The Honour of the Kingdom; The Noble Profession of the Merchant; The School of our Arts; The Supply of our Wants; The Employment of our Poor; The Improvement of our Lands; The Nursery of our Mariners; The Walls of the Kingdoms; The Means of our Treasure; The Sinnews of our Wars; The Terrour of our Enemies."

Sir THOMAS MUN [*see* p. 22], *England's Treasure of Forraign Trade*, London, 1669.

"Le Trident de Neptune est le Sceptre du Monde."

ANTOINE MARIN LEMIERRE, *Œuvres*, "Commerce," 1810.

REPORT

ON

THE OLD RECORDS

OF THE

INDIA OFFICE.

THE papers submitted to me for classification were the supplementary miscellaneous "Old Records" enumerated in the Statistics and Commerce Departmental List, No. 2,397, and in the Lists furnished by the other Departments of this Office. They have been re-arranged in the "Record Rooms" in the order of the amended List prefixed* to this Report; my object in the re-arrangement of them having been to keep the "Factory Records," and all the documents relating to the Company's Factories, distinct from the other "Old Records" of the Company. All these papers have now therefore been classified under the following five divisions:—

First, the Court Minutes, Committee Minutes, and papers relating to the Legal Affairs of the Company, and to Miscellaneous Matters connected with the Company;

Second, the papers relating to the Shipping, Trading, and General Affairs of the Company;

Third, the papers concerning the Foreign Relations of the Company, many of which it is difficult to really separate from Factory Records, the Company's relations with Japan and China, with the Dutch in the East, and with Persia, having chiefly been in connection with their factories in those countries;

Fourth, the papers relating to the History of the Company in India; and

Fifth, the Factory Records.

---

* This List is omitted from the present reprint of the Report.

I have carefully gone through all these papers with the purpose of coming to an opinion as to their comparative interest and importance; and the opinion I have formed on the point is that every scrap of these papers is of interest and importance, and should be scrupulously preserved.

Quite apart from the extraordinary history of the East India Company, every fact recorded in these papers has its significance for the student of the past. It would be useless therefore to attempt to make a selection from them; for what one enquirer might overlook as of no interest, another would find of the highest importance. For instance, what I have found most interesting in these records are the entries illustrative of the history of articles of trade,—such as the mention made of tea, opium, indigo, gum-lac, gamboge, and kino, and of shawls, carpets, and the like,—which to most persons would seem trivial, if not altogether worthless. The proper plan, therefore, to adopt with reference to these "Old Records," is to keep them in good preservation,—well bound, well arranged, and well classified,—so that whosoever may at any time desire to examine them shall at once know the volumes he wants and where to find them. And someone should be held directly responsible for their charge, and for a general knowledge of their contents; and they should never be lent out of the Office. They have at various times been lent out to persons who have not been sufficiently careful to return what they borrowed; as is evident from the references made in standard works to India Office papers that cannot now be found in the "Record Rooms" here.

In the following description of the contents of the volumes into which the "Old Records" have been sorted, under the five divisions above enumerated, any matters of interest that have struck me in going rapidly, but page by page, through the volumes, are briefly noted.

FIRST DIVISION.

Court Minutes, Court of Committees, and Legal and Miscellaneous Affairs of the Company.

---

*Court Minutes.—26 volumes, from 1690 to 1765.

Vol. 1, 1690–1694, contains a table of the Committees of the Company for the year 1693; namely, "for the Treasury," "for Shipping and *Plantations*," "for Buying Goods," "for Law Suits and Debts," "for Private Trade," "for Secretary's Accounts," "for Surat Factories," "for Surat Warehouses," "for the Coast and Bay" [*i.e.*, Coromandel Coast, and Bay of Bengal], "for the Coast and Bay Warehouses," "for the Company's Books and Accounts," for the *Blew* Warehouse" [*see* Evelyn's letter to Pepys, 23rd September 1685], "for the Pepper Warehouse" [the Company's old Pepper Warehouses, under the Royal Exchange, and the Saltpetre Warehouses, were destroyed in the Great Fire of London, 1666], "for Writing Letters," "for [Ships] Husbands Accounts."

Vol. 2, 1698–99:—appertaining to the "New" or "*English* [East India] *Company*." The first entry is of a Court held September 7th, 1698, "at Mercers' Hall," at which "the Charter for the *English Company*†

---

* *See* Preface, p. 1; and p. 15 *infra*, "General Remarks on Court Minutes."

† The "London East India Company," commonly called the "Old Company," was first incorporated by Queen Elizabeth on the 31st December 1600, under the title of "*The Governor and Company of the Merchants of London trading into the East Indies.*"

Courten's Association of the Assada [Madagascar] Merchants was established 1635, and united with the "London East India Company," 1650; although the Assada Adventurers were not all brought into the Company until 1657.

Evelyn [*see* p. 22], in his Diary, has the following entries relating to the union of the "Adventurers" with the Company:—

26th November 1657. "I went to London to a Court of the East India Company upon "its new union in Merchant Taylors' Hall, which was much disturbed by reason of the Ana-"baptists, who would have the Adventurers obliged only by an engagement, without swear-"ing, that they still might pursue their private trade; but it was carried against them.

"*trading to the East Indies*, and bearing date September 5th, was brought in by Mr. Townsend; and "the first Directors were chosen by a majority of the "Subscribers to the Joint Stock."

Among the directors occur the names of Sir Theodore Jansen and Sir W. Scawen. At a Court held in "Skinners Hall,"* June 20th, 1699, were present,

---

" Wednesday was resolved on for a General Court for election of officers, after a sermon and " prayers for good success. The stock resolved on was 800,000*l*."

27th November 1657. "I tooke the oath at the East India House, subscribing 500*l*."

2nd December 1657. "Dr. Reynolds [since Bishop of Norwich] preached before the " Company at St. Andrew Undershaft, on 13 Nehemiah, 31 ['Remember me, O my God, for " good'], shewing by the example of Nehemiah all the perfections of a trusty person in " publique affaires, with many good precepts apposite to the occasion, ending with a prayer " for God's blessing on the Company and the Undertaking."

10th December 1682. "I sold my East India adventure of 250*l*. principal for 750*l*. to the " Royal Society, after I had been in that Company 25 years, being extraordinary advanta- " geous by the blessing of God."

"*The English Company* [including '*The General Society*,' chartered by William III., 3rd September 1698] *trading to the East Indies*," commonly called "the New Company," was incorporated by William III., 5th September 1698; its charter running to 1714.

The above Company of Merchants of London, and the English Company, were finally incorporated under the name of "*The United Company of Merchants of England trading to the East Indies*" [commonly styled "the Honourable East India Company"] in 1708–9.

The following were the principal charters granted to the "London East India Company":—

1st, of Queen Elizabeth, 31st December 1600, "to 1615"; 2nd, of James I., 31st May 1609, "perpetual"; 3rd, of the Protector, Oliver Cromwell, in 1657, "giving exclusive rights to the United Company": 4th, of Charles II. [" whose word no man relies on"], 3rd April 1661, "perpetual"; 5th, ditto, 5th October 1677, "perpetual," and authorising the Company to coin money at Bombay; 6th, ditto, 9th August 1683, again "perpetual"; 7th, of William III. and Mary, 7th October 1693, "perpetual"; 8th and 9th, of Anne, dated, respectively, the 22nd April and 15th August 1709, to 1726, but actually to 1736. They practically united the "London" or "Old Company" with the English" or "New Company."

Of the above charters, the 1st and 2nd exist at the India Office only as copies; of the 3rd and 6th nothing is known there; and only the 4th, 5th, 7th, 8th, and 9th, with others of the various documents under which the amalgamation of "the Old" and "New" Companies was effected, remain there.

* The Skinners' Hall was originally in Coped Hall, but after "the Great Fire," in 1666, was rebuilt in Dowgate; and there "the New Company" held its General Courts until its amalgamation with "the Old Company"; and they are said to have presented the Skinners' Company with a ship-load of sandal-wood for pannelling the new "parlour" there.

among others, Sir James Bateman, Sir E. Harrison, and Sir Thomas Master.

Vol. 5, 1702–4. Under date October 8th, 1702, a list is given of the Eastern produce to be taken in exchange for the bullion and commodities sent out in the Company's ships, on account of the officers and ship's men. It includes "Cambogium" [*see* p. 27, Joint Stocks, Vol. 2], "Ambergreece," "Assafœtida," "Ammoniacum" [Tavernier mentions it among the exports from Ahmedabad], "Aggatts" ["Achats," *see* Evelyn, May 22nd, 1664, in an account of rarities brought to London by the East India Company], "Goa Stones," [Fryer tells us this once famous medicament was the invention of Gasper Antonio, of the Paulistines monastery at Goa, *circa* 1650], "Roman Vitriol" [*i.e.*, Blue Vitriol, or Sulphate of Copper]. It is added:—"and any other "commodities which the Court shall not reserve for "themselves."

Vol. 14, 1707–8. Contains a copy of the oath taken by the captains of the Company's ships, to be "true and "faithful to the said Company."

Vol. 25, 1760–61, and Vol. 26, 1765, are Index volumes to the Court Books, the latter volume being completed only to the letter H.

General Remarks on the Court Minutes.

The above "COURT MINUTES" are distinct from the "Court Books" or "Court Minutes" ranging from A.D. 1599 to 1858–59, in 191 volumes,*—the earlier of which have been sent to the Public Record Office to be calendared.

The "Original Correspondence" extends from 1603 to 1708, in 72 volumes; and of these volumes also the

---

* Since the present Report was first printed in 1879, the 1st volume of these Court Minutes, 1599–1603, has been printed from the original MS., *verbatim et literatim* [with an Introduction by myself (*see* Appendix B.)], and published by Messrs. Henry Stevens and Sons, St. Martin's Lane, London. 1886, under the title of "*The Dawn of British Trade in the East Indies.*"

earlier have been sent to the Public Record Office.* From 1708 the "ORIGINAL CORRESPONDENCE" has been arranged under the heads of the Presidencies from which it is received.

The "GENERAL COURT MINUTES" [of the Courts of Proprietors] 1700–1858; the "MISCELLANEOUS HOME LETTERS" [from the Secretary to the East India Company], 1700–1859; the "DESPATCHES" to St. Helena, Surat, and other Factories, from 1700; and to Bombay, Madras, and Calcutta, from 1753; the "PROCEEDINGS" of the Governments of Bombay, Madras, and Bengal, and all other Records of the Company, beginning later than the 17th century, are not included in the present Report. But of the unconnected later [*i.e.*, 18th century] records of places of which there are earlier [*i.e.* 17th century] records, the interest in which later records is now languid or obsolete, such as the Angengo, Gombroon, Tellicherry, Tannah, and other unconnected "PROCEEDINGS" of the last century, I have been careful to make a note in this Report under the Fifth, or "FACTORY RECORDS," Division.

COURT OF COMMITTEES.—Six volumes, from 1613 to 1727, the sixth being a volume of "*Advertisements*."

The volume of "*Advertisements*" included under the present head in the re-classified list, is entered separately in the Department List, No. 2,397, p. 11.

Vol. 1, 1613–21. In the Minutes of a Court of Committees, holden the 17th October 1621, the name of a Mr. Halliday occurs as Governour.

Vol. 3, 1634–59, entered, under the present head, in the Departmental List, No. 2,397, was missing when this Report was first printed, but has since been recovered.

Vol. 5, 1701–5. Records the allowances made to the officers and ships' companies in the Company's service,

* Where, together with the Court Minutes, they have been included by Mr. Noel Sainsbury in his invaluable *Calendars of State Papers, Colonial Series, East Indies*, of which four volumes have appeared, extending from 1513 to 1629.

and the oaths taken by the Governours, &c. "At a "general Court of *Adventurers* in the General Joint "Stock to the East Indies, holden the 30th April "1701," among those present were,—Governor Sir T. Cooke, Deputy Sir Sam. Dashwood, Sir Th. Rawlinson, Sir Jonathan Andrews, Sir John Fleet, Sir W. Gore, Sir Henry Johnson, Sir W. Langhorne [Governour of Fort St. George, 1676–8], Sir Richard Levett, Sir W. Prichard, Mr. Vansittart.

Vol. 6, 1709–1727. Contains the "*Advertisements*" of meetings of Courts, with the following list of the London papers in which, apparently, these advertisements were published, viz.:—*The Daily Courant*, *The Postman*, *The Daily Post*, *The Post Boy*, and *The Flying Post*.

LEGAL AFFAIRS OF THE COMPANY.—Twelve volumes, from 1601 to 1782.

A. Ten volumes, from 1601 to 1720, entered under this head in the Departmental List, No. 2,397. Vol. 10, 1720, gives papers in the case of the East India Company *versus* Dubois.

B. A volume, dated 1685 to 1699, of *Petitions*, entered separately under that head in the Departmental List, No. 2,397.

C. A volume of copies of the Company's Commissions to their Governours, Governours-General, Commanders-in Chief, &c., from 1697 to 1782; not entered in the Departmental List, No. 2,397.

Further Remarks on the papers relating to the Legal Affairs of the Company.

Under this head, it will be convenient also to refer to the "East India Documents," 1606–1758, described in my report of April 17th, 1875, Statistics and Commerce, Departmental No. 531. They were calendared by Mr. Noel Sainsbury [*see* Appendix A.], and are deposited in the Library.* They are all original documents, and the most interesting of them is the roll of subscribers to the fund of 2,000,000*l*. raised in 1698. This roll consists of 15 skins of parchment. [*See infra*, "Miscellaneous affairs of the Company," Sub-Section III., "Joint Stocks," Vol. 3, and Sub-Section IV., "Amalgamation of the Two Companies," Vols. 1 and 2.] In the Library there are also preserved 11† other original

---

* They are now in the Record Department.

† These 11 documents were in the India Office Library when this Report was first printed in 1879, but they were subsequently transferred to the re-organized Record Department, excepting No. 7, which must have intermediately been mislaid or stolen by someone who had been allowed to refer to it, for it has disappeared. It was not the treaty of Allahabad itself, which, as above stated, is preserved in the room of the Under Secretary of State, but whether it was a draft, or the official account of the ratification, of the treaty, I cannot, at this distance of time, say. On the transfer of the above enumerated documents to the Record Department, several others were found in the old cases that had been brought from Leadenhall Street and stored in the Library; viz.: 1, Counterpart of a lease of a house in Bishopsgate Street, granted by [Sir] John Massingbird to John Tynte, 19th February 1631; 2, Two decrees in Chancery, Hall and wife, executors of Bostocks, against Leigh and the East India Company, dated respectively the 5th September 1689, and 13th May 1690; 3, Decree in Chancery, Atwood, Halford, and others, against Warr and the East India Company, 19th December 1691; 4, Letters of Administration granted by the Prerogative Court of Canterbury to John Spencer, senior, of the estate of Cæsar Burton, late factor, Angengo, 26th October 1730; 5, Letters of Administration granted by the Prerogative Court of Canterbury to John Spencer, junior, of the same estate, 10th December 1731; 6, Declaration of Trust by the "Old" East India Company as to bonds for 70,000*l*., which by Lord Godolphin's award were deposited in the hands of Trustees appointed by the "New" East India Company, dated 21st March 1709; 7, Charter granting to the "United" Company all the foreign debts due to the "Old" Company, 22nd April 1709; 8, Queen Anne's Acceptance of the surrender of the Charter of the "Old" Company, 7th May 1709; 9, Apparently a record in an ejectment case, dated 8th October 1720; 10, Address to Lord Cornwallis on his leaving Calcutta, dated 5th November 1793 [His Lordship left Calcutta in October of 1793]; and 11, Assignment of Warren Hastings' annuity [*see* No. 8 of above list of 11 documents], in repayment of 36,000*l*., dated 8th April 1796.

Also while searching for No. 7 of the above list [pp. 18–20] of 11 documents I discovered in one of the old cupboards in the Library the following documents:—1, Grant of Arms to the "New" Company, dated 13th October 1698, among the names of members of the Company mentioned in the Grant being those of Sir Henry Furness, Sir Theodore Jansen, Sir W. Scawen, George White, Thomas Vernon, Peter Paggen, Streynsham Master, Samuel Lock, and Edward Allen [*see* page 21, *note*]; 2, Grant of Arms to Haileybury

documents relating to the East India Company, viz.:—1, Act of 6 Anne, for carrying out the award of Lord Godolphin; 2, Grant, of March 21, 1709, from the "Old" East India Company of their debts in Great Britain to Queen Anne, for re-grant to the Trustees of the "New" Company; 3, Letters Patent of Queen Anne, of August 15, 1709, granting Sir Jonathan Andrews and others all sums owing to the "Old" Company before the surrender of their charter; 4, Surrender of the "Old" Company's charter, agreeably to the award of Lord Godolphin, March 25, 1709; 5 Letters Patent of November 17, 1727, called the charter of George II.; 6, Letters Patent of September 19, 1757, granting to the Company a moiety of the plunder taken from the Nawab Nazim [Suraja Daula, "Sir Roger Dowler" of "Black Hole" infamy] of Bengal; 7, Presentation by the titular Mogol, Shah Alam II., of the Dewanee [*diwani*, the office, jurisdiction, and revenues of a *diwan* or Minister of State] of Bengal, Behar, and Orissa, to Lord Clive, 1765; 8, Indenture of April 7, 1796, granting 4,000*l.* to Warren Hastings for 18 years from 25 December 1795; 9, Further loan

---

College, dated 21st March 1807; and 3, Two large folio volumes, of the 1,444 signatures of the subscribers to the 2,000,000*l.* stock raised by the "New" Company, in pursuance of the Act of 5th September 1698, appointing Commissioners to receive the said subscription. These volumes are therefore the legal list of subscribers to the 2,000,000*l.* stock raised in 1698, and the "Roll" of subscribers above mentioned is probably the original rough list of the same. The 1,444 signatures were all taken from the 14th to the 16th July 1698; each page of signatures being attested by the signatures and seals of the Commissioners present; among whom may be noted the names of Samuel Lock, Bartholomew Shilbert, D. Devarenne La Bretonnide, Richard Harrison, John Boyd, George White, James Medlycott, John Paschal, and Thomas Chambers.

[Added 1890.] Since the first reprint of this Report last year [1889], all the documents numbered above, in the text and note [pp. 18–20], have been re-arranged by Mr. F. C. Danvers, in chronological order, and entered in a new "Catalogue of Parchment Records" [which I have printed at the end of this report as Appendix D.], EXCEPTING that Nos. 1, 4, 7, 9, and 11 of the list of 11 documents given above in the text have been omitted from the new Catalogue, as since they were in my hands, in 1879, they would seem to have disappeared.

of 50,000*l*., dated April 10, 1796 ; 10, Grant to the East India Company of booty and plunder in the late war with Tippoo Sahib, dated March 25, 1793 ; 11, Grant to the King's troops of booty and plunder in the late war with Tippoo Sahib. In the room occupied by the Under Secretary of State is preserved the original treaty [in English and Persian] of Allahabad, dated 16th [the date given in the books is the 12th] August 1765, and bearing the signatures of Lord Clive and General Carnac, and the seal of Shuja-ud-Daula [the Nawab Vazir of Oudh]. In the Library Reading Room is hung in a glazed frame the holograph approval, dated 6th November 1657, by Oliver Cromwell, of a petition, of no date or address, from the East India Company, to have "some good Ship and Frigott" sent to "St. Hellena Island" to protect the Company's merchant ships assembled there "from remote parts" against the Spaniards "out of Biskay" seeking to interrupt "our East India trade." The petition is signed among others by Thos. Andrew and [Sir] John Banks.

MISCELLANEOUS AFFAIRS OF THE COMPANY.

I.—THE COMPANY'S SEAL.—*One unbound document*, and two volumes.

The unbound document, dated 1658–60, contains a list of the bonds passed during that period under the Company's seal, and of the dividends declared. *There are* 13 *pages of names of persons.*

Vol. 1, 1667–1706, contains abstracts of bonds to the Custom House, copies of Covenants with Factors, and "An Abstract of several things passed under the Company's Seal."

Vol. 2, 1672–83, contains entries of bonds. *This volume also is full of the names of persons.*

Plate I. ARMS OF THE "OLD" [LONDON] EAST INDIA COMPANY.

[*from the cover of a MS. Record entitled*
Gold and Silver Received and Weighed, 1677].

Plate II. Arms of the "New" [English] East India Company.

[from the original Grant of Arms, dated 13 Oct. 1698].

II.—"ADVENTURERS."—There are 19 volumes, from 1631 to 1707, under this head, all full of the names of persons. *Many of these volumes are stamped with the Company's arms.**

Vol. 1, *undated* [? 1631–42].—"Alphabett to ye "Lidger of ye third Joynt Stock of ye Marchants of "London trading [to] the East Indies." The following names occur:—Sir Morris Abbott, Sir Wm. Acton, Sir Jas. Cambell, Sir Wm. Cooper, Sir Francis Crane, Sir Th. Dawes, Sir Abraham Dawes, Sir Jarvais Elwaies, Sir Henry Garwaie, Sir John Gayer [? father of the Governour of Bombay, 1694–1704], Sir Brian Johnson [cousin

---

* These are the arms assigned to the Company in 1601 [*see* Stevens's *Dawn of British Trade in the East Indies*, p. 171], and they are very beautiful. The shield is divided into two compartments, the upper bearing, between two conventional red roses on a golden ground, an "additionment out of the arms of England," namely, a four-divided square, having, in its first and fourth quarters, a golden fleur-de-lis on a blue ground, and in the second and third, a golden lion, "passant guardant," on a ground of red; and the lower, three quaint-fashioned ships, with streaming ensigns of St. George, in full sail on the tranquil azure of the new-found southern seas. The supporters are blue sea lions, flushed with gold, one on either side; and the crest a sphere celestial, between standards of St. George, and overhung by the motto:—"Deus indicat." Below all is a second motto:—"Deo ducente nil nocet." See Plate I.

After 1708–9, when the United Company was chartered, it received new arms, having for motto,—and there was rue indeed, for all "John Company's" servants, with the difference,—"Auspicio Regis et Senatus Angliæ"; for crest a little lion, "regardant," holding a crown, toward the right, in the paws of its outstretched fore arms, ["the Cat and Cheese" of the old Indian Navy;] and for supporters two big lions, "regardant," each holding in its left paw a St. George's pennon, and resting its right paw on a large white shield, divided boldly by St. George's scarlet cross, and displaying in its right upper quarter the reduced shield of the royal arms of England [English roses quartered with French lilies] surmounted by the imperial crown of the realm.

After this note was written, I discovered the original grant of arms to the "New" Company, dated 13th October 1698 [*see* p. 19, *note*]. They are identical with the arms borne by the late Honourable East India Company, thus affording another proof that the "Old" Company was altogether swallowed up by the "New." See Plate II.

to Sir Henry Johnson, the great shipbuilder of Blackwall], Sir John Jacob, Thomas Mun [author of *England's Treasure of Forraign Trade*], Sir John Nulls (? Knollys), Sir Paule Pinder [our Ambassador at Constantinople when Coryat was there, 1612] and Co., Sir Robert Parkehurst, Sir Wm. Russell, Sir John Watts, Sir John Wolstenholme, Sir George Whitmore, Sir *Ed. Wardour.*

Vol. 2, List of Adventurers, 1675. Among other names occur:—Sir Matthew Andrews [President of Surat, *circa* 1660], Sir John Brownlow, Sir John Banks, Sir Th. Bludworth, Sir Sam. Barnardiston, Sir Francis Burdett, John Bulteele, Sir. Ed. Deering, Sir Jas. Edwards, JOHN EVELYN, Sir Th. Foot, Sir *Gilbert Gerrard*, Sir Mat. Hollworthy, Sir Nat. Herne, Sir Arthur Ingram, Sir Jonathan Keate, Sir Peter Leare, Sir John and Sam. Lethieullier, Sir John Moore, Sir Jas. Oxinden [father* of Sir George Oxenden (or Oxinden), President of Surat, and 5th Governour (1st Company's) of Bombay, 1668–9], Thomas Papillon [Deputy Governor, 1680–81], Sir John Robinson, Sir Robert Vyner, Dr. Wallis.

Vol. 3, 1691, gives, among others, the following names:—The King's most Excellent Majestie (7,000*l.*), Dame Mary Ash [wife of Sir Joseph Ash], Sir *Peter Apsley*, Sir Benjamin Bathurst, The Duke of Beaufort [Henry, 3rd Marquess of Worcester, created Duke of Beaufort 1682], The Earl of Berkley [George, 14th Baron, created Earl of Berkeley 1679], Lady Arabella Berkley, Lady Henrietta Berkley, The Honble. Ch. Bertie, Sir Francis Bridgman, Sir *Edward des Bouverie*, Lord *Chandos* [James Brydges, died 1714], Sir Job Charlton, Sir Francis Willoughby [decd.], Sir Thos. Willoughby [decd.], Sir Thos. Chambers, Sir JOHN CHARDIN, Dame Mary Clayton, Sir JOSIA CHILD [author of *A New Discourse of Trade*], Sir J. Cropley, Sir Thomas Cooke, Sir W. Coventry [decd.], Dame Anne Coulston, Sir T. Davall, Sir Rob. Ducking-

* Sir James Oxenden, through the marriage of his daughter Anne with Richard, son of Sir Edward Master [1574–1640], was the grandfather of Sir Streynsham Master [1640–1724], Governour of Madras, 1678–81.

field, Sir Stephen Evance [the celebrated jeweller and banker], Sir Th. Grantham [knighted for his services in suppressing Capt. R. Keigwin's mutiny at Bombay, 1683–84], Sir R. Geffreys, Sir W. Goulston, Sir W. Godolphin, Sir Joseph Herne [a sea-captain of the Company's; and son of Sir Nathaniel Herne], Sir W. Hedges* [Governour and Agent in Bengal, 1681–2], Wm. Hewer, Sir Roger Hill, Sir Hele Hooke, Sir Abraham Jacob, Sir Wm. Langhorne, Philip Earl of Leicester [grandson of Robert Sidney, Viscount Lisle, and grand-nephew of Sir Philip Sidney], Dame Susanna Lear, Sir Simón Lewis, Sir T. Littleton, Sir Rich. Loyd, Sir John Matthews, The Honble. Baptist May, Mrs. Marg. Massingbird, Sir John Micklethwaite [decd.], Sir John Morden, Sir Peter Parrivicine, Sir Thos. Rawlinson, Sir Jeremy Sambrooke [nephew of Jeremy Sambrooke, senior, and at one time in the Company's service at Madras, where he was imprisoned during the usurped Governourship of Sir Edward Winter [1665–8], Dame Jane Smith, Sir W. Turner, Sir H. Tulce, Sir Jas. Ward, Sir Edmond Wiseman, Sir Joseph Williamson [principal Secretary of State in 1676].

Vol. 4, 1693, contains, among others, the following names :—Sir Stephen Anderson, Sir Rowland Aynsworth, Sir Wm. Barkham, The Honble. Rob. Boyle [decd.], Sir Wm. Cronmer, Sir Humphrey Edwin, Thos. and John Elwick, Sir John Fleet, Sir William Gore, Sir John Goldsborough [another of the Company's sea-captains, appointed, on the death of Sir John Child, 1689, "Superviser, Commissary-General, and Chief Governour in East India," with Sir John Gayer as his Lieutenant-Governour, died 1693], Sir George Meggot, The Honble. Charlotte Mordaunt, "Their Majesties the King William and Queen Mary" [down for 7,000*l.*].

Vol. 5, 1693, an account of the additional stock paid in May and June. The same names as before.

---

* Since this report was first printed the *Diary of William Hedges*, with extracts from the India Office Records, edited by the late Sir Henry Yule, has been published in 3 vols. by the Hakluyt Society.

Vol. 6, 1694. Among other names, the following occur:—The Countess Dowager of Anglesey, "Junior," [Lady Elizabeth Manners], Sir Th. Abney, Sir Cornwall Bradshaw, Viscount Colchester [Richard Savage], The Earle of Devonshire [William Cavendish, 4th Earl of Devon, created Marquess of Hartington and Duke of Devonshire, 1694], John Danvers [afterward Sir John Danvers, of Culworth, 3rd Baronet], Sir Jas. Etheredge, Sir Humphrey Edwin, Sir Basil Firebrace, Sir Edward Frewen, Sir Henry Furnese, Sir Abraham Jacob, John Earl of Marlborough [the great general and diplomatist, created Baron Churchill, 1685, Earl of Marlborough, 1689, and Marquess of Blandford and Duke of Marlborough, 1702], Sir Ch. Meredith, Sir Th. Millington, Sir John Parsons, The Duchess Dowager of Richmond and Lennox [Frances Theresa, grand-daughter of Walter, 1st Lord Blantyre], Sir Leonard Robinson, General Trelawny, Charles, 4th Marquess of Worcester [who married Rebecca, daughter of Sir Josia Child, and died 1698].

Vol. 7, 1695.

Vol. 8, 1696.

Vol. 9, 1699. "The King's most Excellent Majesty," 7,166*l.* 5*s.* 0*d.* [Queen Mary had died December 28, 1694.]

Vol. 10, 1701. "The King's most Excellent Majesty," 7,166*l.* 5*s.* 0*d.*

Vol. 11, 1702. "The Queen's most Excellent Majesty," 7,166*l.* 5*s.* 0*d.* [King William died March 8th, 1702, and Queen Anne succeeded.]

Vol. 12, 1703.

Vol. 13, 1707. This volume includes the following names, among others:—Sir Lambert Blackwell, Sir Sam. Blewitt, Sir Jas. Eyton, Sir W. Fazackerly, Sir W. Humfreys, Sir Solomon de Medina, Moses de Medina, The Honble. W. Montague [decd.], Sir Isaac Rebow, The Lady Elizabeth Savage.

III.—Joint Stocks.—Five volumes, from 1671 to 1709.

Vol. 1, 1671, gives the valuation of the Joint Stocks at that date.

The first entry is "Good debts owing to the East India "Company, the 30th April 1671, by the bookes appeare "136,735*l.* 19*s.* 0*d.*"

The next entry is "Desperate debts owing the East "India Company, 30th April 1671, as by the bookes "appeare,* 65,542*l.* 17*s.* 2*d.*"

The next entry is "Stocke in shipping . . . . . "17,709*l.* 18*s.* 8*d.*"

---

* The East India Company at this time banked with Alderman Edward Backwell, a banker in a large way of business in the days of Charles II., who likewise kept the accounts of His Majesty the King, James Duke of York, Prince Rupert, the Duke of Orleans, and all the principal nobles and merchants of the time.

In the year 1670 the East India Company had large transactions. Sums of money were paid into Backwell's bank on the Company's account by such merchants as Rodriques of Berry Street, John Houblon of Threadneedle Street [the first Governour of the Bank of England], Fransia of Leadenhall Street, Peter Barr of Austin Fryar's [*sic*], Da Costa, Alderman [Sir Benjamin] Bathurst, Claud Hayes of Fenchurch Street, Michael Dunkin, Vandeputt, Alderman Allington, and Frederick and Co. of Old Jewry, and others. Michael Dunkin appears to have been the most important depositor. Several bankers and goldsmiths also appear as paying in large sums to the credit of the Company, such as Sir Robert Vyner, G. Snell, Thomas Row, Thomas Kirwood, Jerry Snow, &c.; and the sums thus deposited probably represented the respective shares of the contributors in the Company's ventures to the East Indies.

From March 1670 to March 1671 the receipts were 237,900*l.* In the month of August 1670 the receipts amounted to 44,000*l.* In the months of September, October, November, and December the receipts were 190,250*l.*, of which sum 175,000*l.* rested in Backwell's hands until March 23, 1671, when gold and silver bullion was purchased to the amount of 182,000*l.*, and between January and March 7,000*l.* was paid in to meet this sum. The East India Company made the following yearly gifts to Backwell: 25 lbs. of pepper, 2 lbs. of nutmegs, 1 lb. of mace, 1 lb. of cloves, and 1 lb. of cinnamon.

Edward Backwell, who lived at the Unicorn in Lombard Street, was ruined in 1672 by the closing of the Exchequer [in which the bankers of that time deposited their surplus cash as a loan to the King at high interest] by Charles II. These accounts are all to be seen in the old ledgers kept at "Child's Bank" in Fleet Street, and I am indebted to Mr. F. G. Hilton Price, F.S.A., F.G.S., for the above extracts from them.

The next entry is "Goods remaining on hand . . . "313,255*l*. 11*s*. 6*d*." Among the goods are named "Guiny [*i.e.*, *juta* or "jute," the fibre of Corchorus capsularis and C. olitorius, used by the Hindus chiefly in the manufacture of *goni* or "sacks" and "sacking"] Stuffes," "Jappan Gownes," "Ginghams," "*Blew* Long-cloth," "Punia [? "Pina," *i.e.*, pine-apple fibre stuffs, called also "Pinascos"] Silke," "Pertian [Persian] Yarnes," "Thea"* [valued at 20*s*. per lb.].

* Tea had been introduced into England some years previously. The first mention of it by any English writer, so far as I can find, is in Pepys's Diary, 25th September 1660,—"I did send for a cup of *tee* (a China drink), of which I had never drank before." In the same year, by Act 12 of Charles II., chh. 23 and 24. a duty of 18*d*. is imposed on every gallon of chocolate, sherbet, and *tea*, made for sale; coffee being charged only 4*d*. Waller's lines,—

"The best of Queens, and best of herbs, we owe
To that bold nation which the way did show"

—to India, are well known. The East India Company purchased and presented 2 lbs. of tea to King Charles II. in 1664, and 23¾ lbs. in 1666. The first order for its importation by the Company was in 1668;—"Send home "by these ships 100 lbs. weight of the best *tey* you can gett": and the first consignment of it, amounting to 143½ lbs., was received from Bantam in 1669. The generally received story is that Lords Arlington and Ossory were the first to introduce tea into this country in 1666 from Holland.

The earliest mention of tea in the Old Records of the India Office is in a letter from Mr. R. Wickham, the Company's Agent at Firando, in Japan [*see* page 52], who, writing, 27th June 1615, to Mr. Eaton at Miaco, asks for "a pot of the best sort of chaw."

How highly a present of tea was prized in England during the 17th century may be judged from the following pertinent extracts from the earlier "Court Books" of the Company:—

22 *August* 1664. "The Governour acquainting ye Court that ye Factors haveing in every place failed ye Company of such things as they writt for to have presented his majestie with and that his ma[tie] might not finde himself wholly neglected by ye Company, he was of opinion if ye Court thinck fitt that a silver case of oile of cinnamon which is to be had of Mr. Thomas Winter for 75*l*., and some good Thea, be provided for that end, which he hopes may be acceptable, ye Court approved very well thereof."

This entry refers to the present of 2 lbs. of tea made to Charles II. in 1664.

3 *July* 1666. "The Court now left itt to the governour and deputie to dispose of the value of about 10*l*. in Thea to some gentlemen where they see reason to place itt."

Writing also to Madras, 13 Feb. 1684/5, the Directors say:—

"In regard Thea is grown to be a commoditie here, and we have occasion to make presents therein to our great friends at Court, we would have you send us yearly five or six canisters of the very best and freshest Thea; that which will colour the water in which it is infused most of a greenish complexion is generally best accepted."

Then follows this entry: "Remaining at Surratt, and "the factories subordinate," among which are named "Amadavad," Agra, "Bombay Island," Rajapore, and *Lucknow*.

Vol. 2, 1685, a similar book. Almost every denomination of cotton and silk goods in which the Company traded is to be found in this volume. It is invaluable. I here note only "Theas damaged" [*see supra*, under Vol. 1, 1671], "Shawles Carmania," "Cambodiam" [the first mention of Gamboge is in Vol. 3, "Court Books," under date October 13, 1615], "Lapis Tutia" ["Tushy-stone," or Tutty, an artificially prepared argillaceous oxide of zinc, obtained from Persia*], "Carmania Wooll," "Tanna Stuffs" [silks]. The volume closes with a list of all persons to whom the Company was then owing money, and with a statement of the total of the Company's estate. It appears that they owed the Almshouse at Poplar 4,200*l.*

Vol. 3. First entry, July 14, 1698, records the appointment of Commissioners to receive the subscriptions to the English Company. The Governor and Company of the Bank of England were disqualified to act as Commissioners. The copy of the subscription list follows. The original list, which fills 15 skins of parchment, is fully described in my Report of April 17, 1875 [*see* Appendix A.], and is now in the India Office Library† along with the other parchments described in that Report. [*See supra*, Section, "Legal Affairs of the Company."] Among the subscribers are to be found:—The King, Robert Cecil [brother of James, 4th Earl ("the Catholic Earl") of Salisbury], The Earl of Montague, The Earl of Ranelagh, Lord Herbert of Cherbury, John Cowley, The Earl of Oxford [Aubrey de Vere], Charles Fox, Thomas Vernon [? brother of

---

* Called also "Cadmia factitia" and "Cadmia fornacum." There are three salts of this oxide commonly found in Indian bazaars: [1] *nila tutiya*, *i.e.*, blue vitriol, or sulphate of copper; [2] *hira tutiya*, green vitriol, or sulphate of iron; and [3] *safed tutiya*, white vitriol, or sulphate of zinc.

† They are now, 1889, in the Record Department.

James Vernon, the father of Admiral Vernon], Lord Portland [Hans William Bentinck, created Baron Cirencester, Viscount Woodstock, and Earl of Portland, 1689], The Duke of Shrewsbury [Charles Talbot, 12th Earl, created Marquess of Alton, and Duke of Shrewsbury, 1694, and died 1717 without heirs to the Marquessate and Dukedom], The Duke of Devonshire.

Vol. 4, 1707–1709. The old East India Company's interest book from 12th April 1707 to 17th March 1708/9. *It contains about* 9,000 *names of persons.*

Vol. 5, 1708. Balance of the Company's books of interest, taken the 30th June 1708. Contains a perfect list of names, beautifully written; among others those of Sir Thos. Rawlinson, Dame Mary Rawlinson, and Honour Rawlinson.

IV.—Amalgamation of the two Companies.— Five volumes, from 1708–1746.

Vol. 1, 1708:—

First entry.—Copy of award of the Lord High Treasurer concerning both Companies [*i.e.*, the "London" or "Old" East India Company, and the "English" or "New Company"], signed "Godolphin" [Sidney, 1st Earl].

Second entry.—Agreement between the two Companies about Saltpetre.

Third entry.—Old East India Company's Declaration of Trust.

Fourth entry.—The schedule mentioned in the above declaration.

Fifth entry.—The Grant from the Old East India Company of their debts to the Queen, with schedule, which apparently gives *the names of all the Writers and Factors then in the Company's service, and a list of all the debtors to the Company.* Among other names in the schedule of Writers and Factors occur the following:—Gulston Addison [brother of Joseph Addison, and died Governour of Fort St. George, in 1709], Factor; Mathias Aram,

Writer; John Bulteel, Writer; James Bruce, Factor; *John Child,** Factor; Daniel Dubois, Factor.

Sixth entry.—Re-grant by the Queen of the Old East India Company's debts to trustees for the United Company, giving at the end *a list of about* 900 *names of persons under covenant or obligation to the Company.*

[Compare the entries under the above six sub-headings with the Section on the "Legal Affairs of the Company" and "Further Remarks" on the same, *supra.*]

---

* I do not know whether the above John Child was a son of Sir John Child or not. The family of Sir John's great brother, Sir Josia Child, became extinct in 1784, with the son of his second son, Sir Richard Child, created Viscount Castlemaine in 1718, and Earl Tylney in 1731; and through Catherine Tylney Long, a descendant of Sir Richard's daughter, Lady Long, "the fortune of the Childs," says Sir Henry Yule [*Diary of William Hedges,* Vol. II., pp. 112–13], was carried to William-Pole-Tylney-Long-Wellesley, afterwards 4th Earl of Mornington. It is to this devolution of the fortune of the Childs that allusion is made in the lines from the *Rejected Addresses*:—

"Bless every man possessed of aught to give:
Long may Long-Tylney-Wellesley-Long-Pole live!"

Although the families of Sir Josia and Sir John Child banked, until they became extinct, at "Child's Bank," no connection has ever been established between them and the family of Sir Francis Child, the founder of the Bank. Sir Francis Child, Lord Mayor of London, 1698–9, and Member for the City in the 1st Parliament of Queen Anne, was the son of Robert Child, of Headington, co. Wilts. He was born in 1642, and, after serving his apprenticeship as a goldsmith to William Hall, London, went into the business of his uncle, William Wheeler, at the Marigold, in Fleet Street. On his uncle's death he married his daughter, and entered into partnership with Robert Blanchard, the firm taking the name of Blanchard and Child. Sir Francis had several daughters and sons, and those of the latter who entered the Bank were Sir Robert Child, Alderman of Farringdon Without, Sir Francis Child, Lord Mayor of London, 1732, and Samuel Child. The last named married and had two sons, Francis and Robert, both of whom became partners in the Bank, which, on the death of the latter, took the name of Child and Co., which it has ever since borne; its present head being the Earl of Jersey, the great-great-grandson of Robert Child, through the marriage of his daughter, and only child, with John, 10th Earl of Westmoreland, at Gretna Green.

Seventh entry.—An Index of Contents to "This Book" (Vol. 1, 1708), and of "Court Book."

Eighth entry and last.—Copies of some orders of Courts of the Old East India Company relating to the trustees of the said Company.

Vol. 2, 1708–9. Almost a duplicate of Vol. 1.

Vol. 3, 1723–27. Copies of letters to the trustees of the Old East India Company, among whom are named,—Edward Gibbon [the great historian's grandfather, 1666–1736], Thos. Bowdler [? father of the Editor of the *Family Shakespeare*], Charles Du Bois [formerly of the Madras Council], Arthur Moore.

Vol. 4, 1727–29. Ditto.

Vol. 5, 1737–49. Minutes of meetings of the trustees, signed in autograph by Charles Du Bois, and by "Edward Gibbon, Junior" [father of the historian and M.P. for Petersfield 1734, and for Southampton 1741], Hester Gibbon, Edward Elliston, and Joseph Taylor—who all sign as executors of the aforesaid Edward Gibbon.

V.—Offending and Defaulting Servants of the Company.—Two volumes, one of which is bound in black calf, 1624–98.

Vol. 1, 1624–54. Contains "Extracts out of the "Court Booke of the East India Companye, concerninge "the errors and misdemenours of their servants, kepte "accordinge to order of Court, the 8th of December "1626, and beginninge from September 1624." *Full of "names of persons.*

Vol. 2, 1687–98. "A book of charges against *Com-"manders* of ships, *Factors*, and others, Anno Domini "1687." *Full of names of persons.* The following names of places also occur in this volume:—Amoy, Bombay, Bencoolen, Carwar, Decca [Dacca], Fort St. George, Indapoora, Pattana [Patna], Syam, St. Helena, Surratt.

These two volumes were evidently the *Black Books* of the Company's "bad bargains," and are of very curious interest to the pursuer of the scandalous chronicle of society. In the first volume "Fraunces Day" is handed down to infamy for being "the first projector of the forte of St. George"! [*See* p. 216.] The last entries in the Index to the second volume, are—"Zinzan, Mr., blamed, for opening letters, &c."; "Zinzan, Mr., totally dismissed"; "Zinzan, Mr., deceased." This is the Mr. Zinzan who was on Sir John Child's Council at Surat during the suppression, by Sir Thomas Grantham, of Capt. R. Keigwin's mutiny at Bombay, 1683–84; and who for some time remained at Bombay as Governour after Sir Thomas Grantham had sailed home with Keigwin in 1685.

VI.—Ostenders.—One volume only, A.D. 1731–32.

Contains copies of documents relating to the Ostend Company,* also to the trade between *Sweden* and the

* The *Portuguese*, who were the first Europeans to visit India by way of the Cape of Good Hope, doubled by Da Gama, November 22nd, 1497, never put their Eastern trade into the hands of an incorporated Company, except in the year 1731 only, when the King gave permission to *one* ship, to the exclusion of all other ships, to make *one* voyage to Surat and the Coromandel Coast. Except in this solitary instance, the monopoly of the Portuguese East India trade was always, until it was abolished in 1752, vested immediately in the Crown. However, various important articles still continued subject to royal privileges.

"*The Dutch East India Company*" was formally instituted in 1602, by the union of the funds of various rival companies, that had sprung up in Holland in consequence of the success of Houtman's voyage in 1596–97.

The first *French* East India Company was formed in 1604. The second in 1611. The third in 1615. The fourth [Richelieu's], 1642–43. The fifth (Colbert's), 1644. The sixth was formed by the French East and West India, Senegal, and China Companies, uniting under the name of "*The Company of the Indies*," 1719. The exclusive privileges of the Company were, by the King's decree, suspended in 1769; and it was finally abolished by the National Assembly in 1790.

The first *Danish East India Company* was formed in 1612, and the second in 1670.

In 1617, Sir James Cunningham obtained from James I. a patent for the establishment of a *Scottish East India Company*, but the concession was withdrawn in the following year. In 1695 William III., anxious to ingratiate himself with the Scotch, and to obliterate the tragical memories of Glen Coe, sanctioned the incorporation of "*The Company of Scotland trading to Africa, and the Indies*," for 21 years. The Company, however, miserably failed in its

East. There is a letter dated Whitehall, April 6th, 1731, signed "Holies Newcastle" [Thomas Pelham Holles,* Duke of Newcastle, married Lady Henrietta, daughter of Francis, 2nd Earl of Godolphin], addressed to the Governour of the Company [*i.e.*, *our* Company, not the Swedish] regarding an English merchant who

---

very first venture, and, to appease the cruel disappointment of the subscribers, it was stipulated at the Union of Scotland with England, in 1707, that their capital should be returned to them, with interest at 5 per cent. *per annum* from the date of the incorporation of the Company [*see* p. 232, *note*].

"*The Ostend Company*" was incorporated by the Emperor of Austria in 1723. their Factors being chiefly persons who had served the Dutch and English East India Companies; but the opposition of the maritime powers forced the Court of Vienna in 1727 to suspend the Company's charter for seven years. The documents in the above volume relate to this period. The Company, after passing through a very trying existence, prolonged through the desire of the Austrian Government to participate in the growing East India trade. became bankrupt in 1784, and was finally extinguished by the regulations which were prescribed on the renewal of the "Honourable East India Company's" Charter in 1793.

When the *Ostend Company* was suspended a number of its servants were thrown out of employment, of whose special knowledge of the East Mr. Henry Koning, of Stockholm, took advantage, and obtained a charter for the *Swedish Company*, dated June 13th, 1731. It was supported chiefly by smuggling tea into Great Britain, until the British Parliament in 1784 lowered the tax on tea, when the *Swedish Company* was immediately annihilated.

The Spanish "*Royal Company of the Phillipine Islands*" was incorporated in 1733, in defiance of the treaty of Munster [1648], re-chartered in 1785, and again in 1803, and came to an end with the French conquest of Spain in 1808.

The Prussian "*Asiatic Company*," founded in 1750, like the Swedish, principally occupied itself in the China trade, and died out about 1803–4; and the Prussian "*Bengal Company*," founded in 1755, came to its untimely end in 1756.

The Austrian "*Imperial Company of Trieste for the Commerce of Asia*" was founded by William Bolts, an ambitious and discontented servant of the "Honourable East India Company," in 1775–81, and failed in 1785, entirely through Bolts being too much carried away by the dashing speculative spirit characteristic of the intellectual "Company promoter."

* It was to his predecessor in the title, "John Holles, Duke of Newcastle, Marquis and Earl of Clare, and Baron Houghton," that John Fryer [1698] dedicated his *New Account of East India and Persia*.

had been attempting to obtain from the *Grand Duke of Tuscany, liberty to trade with India*, and was stopped by Mr. Coleman, Her Majesty's "Residence" at Florence.

VII.—The Swedish Company.—Two volumes, 1732–33 and 1733–34.

Vol. 1, 1732–33. Copies of letters relating to the Swedish Company. In the account of the sale of piece goods at Gottenbourg, February 23rd, 1732, the following are named,—"Jaunes," "Verts," "Bleues," "Rouges," "Vert de peroquette," "Aurora," "Escarlate," "Vert enfonce," or "French Grain." Further on is a statement of the method of computing the Company's tonnage, and *an alphabetical list of all the goods in which they at this time traded.*

Vol. 2, 1733–34. Complaints by the Swedish Company against the French and the English.

The first entry is a declaration by Benjamin Bonnet, Notary Public of London, certifying the correctness of the translations contained in the volume. This declaration is stamped with impressed stamps, of the value of sixpence each, which are of a very beautiful design; namely, a Tudor rose surrounded by the Garter, with its legend, and surmounted by the Imperial Crown of England, of the flattened Georgian style.

VIII.—Unclassed papers relating to the Miscellaneous Affairs of the Company.

Under this head are included the following volumes:—

A. The volume entered at page 13 of the Departmental Record List, No. 2,397, under the title of "*Parliamentary Proceedings*," 1710–11, and 1717.

The first entry is a petition "To the Honourable the "Knights, Citizens, Burgesses in Parliament assembled, "the humble petition of the *Clothiers* of the county of "Gloucester," to the effect that the East India Company had bought cloth at low prices and forced their bonds on the petitioners; "and at the same time have "entered out very considerable quantity of silver" [to the East]. The petition was referred to selected members, "and to all that serve for the countys of "Gloucester, Worcester, Wilts, Somerset, Cornwall, "York, and *Southamptonshire.*" Dated "Sabti die, "17 Feb. 1716."

B. The volume entered p. 13, List No. 2,397, under the title of "*Home Letters,*" 1668–75. It contains matters relating to the ship *Leopard*, to the Hugly Factory, and to Gombroon.

C. A worthless *Index*, only to P, without title, and not entered in any list.

D. The volume entered page 11 of the Departmental List No. 2,397, under the title of "*Commissioners to India,*" 1769–70. The volume contains :—

First, the appointment of Henry Vansittart, Luke Scrafton, and Francis Forde, Commissioners* authorised, notwithstanding any powers granted to the Company's "Presidents and Council, to superintend, direct, con- "trol, manage, and transact all the business and affairs "of the Company in and through all parts of India, "during the good will and pleasure of the Company, "reserving nevertheless, &c." This document is dated September 15th, 1769.

---

* These Commissioners constituted the well-known "Board of Supervisors." Their appointment was opposed with great vehemence by all who were interested in the corruption of the Company's servants; but was carried at length by a General Court of the proprietors, disgusted by the failure for so many years of their covetous dreams of extortionate dividends. The "Supervisors," with their "Instructions," were put on board one of the King's frigates for India, but through what seas she sailed, or to what bourn, is unknown. The frigate, and the Supervisors, and their letter of Instructions were never seen nor heard of more. Such was the strange dismal end and perdition of all that acrimonious demand for investigation and reform. O si sic semper et ubique!

Second, the Instructions to the same Commissioners, of the same date.

They are instructed to *restore peace* to India upon a solid and permanent basis, to that end providing effectually for the honour and security of their faithful ally "Mahomed Ally Cawn of Arcot" [the Nawab Mahomed Ali, styled "Prince of the Carnatic"].

If *war be necessary*, they are to direct the operations of the three Presidencies upon one uniform plan of action, "*always bearing in mind that the preservation and security of*" *Bengal is of all others the most important object and conside-*" *ration to the Company.*"

Bassein and Salsette are to be obtained under a solid right of title.

The blank "Phirmaund" [Persian *ferman*, *i.e.*, "order" or "concession"] of the Deccan is to be returned to the King, "*being a grant improperly ob-*" *tained.*"

They are to remove unworthy civil and military officers, "*but with great tenderness and circumspection.*"

[In para. 20 the Mogol Government is spoken of as "*the Moorish Government.*"]

In para. 21–22, they are instructed:—"The channels " of *trade* should be in every respect *free* and uncon-" strained; no undue influence or exertion of power " should be used over the manufacturers; for by fair " means only we wish to have the preference of the " markets obtained for them. *Every degree of restraint is*" *contrary to the fundamental principles of trade and*" *commerce*, which therefore are found to thrive the " most among a free people, for the number of manufac-" tures will always increase in proportion to the encourage-" ment and protection they meet with."

They are to encourage the export of silk, yarn, and opium.

To inquire whether the *scarcity of silver* is general, and whether it is owing to exportation "*or to the fatal conse-*" *quences of the gold coinage.*"

All monopolies are to be discouraged, particularly in cotton, and they are to inquire into the abuses in the exclusive trade in *Betle Nut*, *Tobacco*, and *Salt*.

To inquire also into the fortunes made by the Company's servants in private trade.

And also " into the enormous increase in the Company's " Military Establishments," &c.

Third, a letter to same Commissioners of the same date, sent after them by the *Aurora* frigate.

Fourth, a letter to same of September 26th, 1769, addressed to them " whilst at Portsmouth."

Fifth, to same of November 10th, per *Houghton*.

Sixth, to same, January 6th, 1770, per *Bridgewater*.

Seventh, to same, March 23rd, per *Morse* and *Lord Mansfield*.

Eighth, to same, June 17th.

Ninth, to same, November 30th.

SECOND DIVISION.

Trading and Shipping, and General Commercial Affairs of the Company.

I.—SALES AND DELIVERIES.—19 volumes, from 1643 to 1722, being the books of the sales and deliveries of goods in London.

Vol. 1, 1643–52, marked outside "First Voyage" and "Second Voyage." It is the account of "*callicoes*" delivered to sundry persons, to the value of over 28,000*l*. The detailed accounts are highly interesting, both on account of the names of persons given, and of the denominations of piece goods, such as "Synda cloth" [Scinde cloth], "Dymitty," "Synda dimities," "Baftas" [a kind of Calico, so called from *bafta*, "woven"], "Broderas" [Baroda cloth].*

* A proclamation of Charles I., in 1631, enumerating the imports and exports of the East India Company in that year, affords a good idea of the nature of the trade between Europe and the East Indies at this period. As quoted in Bruce's *Annals*, the EXPORTS were:—"Perpetuanoes [strong "('long-enduring') woollen cloths, much affected by the Puritans, originally "imported into England from the Netherlands] and drapery [broad cloths, "&c.], pewter, saffron, woollen stockings, silk stockings and garters, ribbands, "roses edged with gold lace, beaver hats with gold and silver bands, felt "hats, strong waters, knives, Spanish leather shoes, iron, and looking-glasses." And the IMPORTS:—"Long pepper, white pepper, white powdered sugar, pre- "served nutmegs and ginger preserved, myrabolums, bezoar stones, drugs of "all sorts, agate beads, blood stones, musk, aloes soccatrina, ambergrease, "rich carpets of Persia and Cambaya, quilts of sattin, taffaty, painted cali- "coes, benjamin, damasks, sattins and taffaties of China, quilts of China "embroidered with gold, quilts of Pitania [Patania] embroidered with "silk, galls, worm-seeds, sugar candy, China dishes, and porcelain of all "sorts."

In the *Treasure of Traffike* published by Lewis Roberts, London, 1641, we have a succinct survey of the English textile manufactures of the same period, arranged under the head of the natural staples employed for the purpose:—"as are [1] Cotton Wooll and Yarne, of which is made Vermil-

Vol. 2, 1657–59. "Guynie stuffs" and "Guinea stuffs" [for Gunny stuffs].

Vol. 3, 1659–64/65. "Warehouse book of the New "General Joynt Stock, begun 29th July 1659." "Ducka [? Dacca] Dutties" [*? dhotis*], "Topsails" [elsewhere "Tapseiles," evidently some denomination of cotton or silken stuff], "Small Pintadoe [(hand) 'painted'] "Quilts." This volume contains an invaluable list of piece goods.

Vol. 4, 1664. Sale book for the 29th of March 1664. This is the book in which the entries were made during the actual sale on this day. They will be found clean copied into the previous volume 3.

Vol. 5, 1665. Sale book of March 20th.

Vol. 6, 1666. Ditto, April 20th.

Vol. 7, 1669–71. Account of deliveries of goods sold.

Vol. 8, 1669–72. Delivery book. Contains an invaluable list of names of persons and goods sold. It is in perfect condition.

Vol. 9, 1696–98. Accounts of sales.

Vol. 10, 1699–1707. Accounts of sales of *Red Wood* [Pterocarpus santalinus, *ruckta-chandana*, "Red Sandal Wood" or "Red Sanders"] and Saltpetre.

Vol. 11, 1704. Accounts of quarterly sales, made up

"lions, Fustians, Dimities, and such others; also [2] Fleece Wooll, of which "is made woollen-cloth, Sayes, Sarges, Perpetuanas, Bayes, and sundry other "sorts comprehended under the name of 'new drapery' with us; also [3] "Grograme [*gros-grain*]-Yarne, of which is made yarnes, Grograms, Durettas, "silk-mohers, and many others late new invented Stuffes; [4] Flaxe, Hempe, "and the yarne thereof, of which is made all sorts of Linens, fine and coarse, "all Ropes, Tackles, Cables, and such like used in shipping; [5] all raw "silke and throwne, whereof is made all manner of Silke-Laces, Sattins, "Plushes, Taffetas, Cally-mancoes, and many others."

I take this paragraph from *The Drapers' Dictionary*, by S. William Beck, published at *The Warehousemen and Drapers' Journal* Office, Aldersgate Street, E.C. It is an admirable work, accurate and scholarly, and should never be allowed to pass out of print. The above term "Cally-mancoes" occurs in every European language, but no satisfactory etymology of it is to be found.

Plate III. THE OLD EAST INDIA HOUSE, circa 1638–85.

(from a Dutch print in the British Museum).

Plate IV. THE OLD EAST INDIA HOUSE, circa 1714–26.

(from William Overley's Trade Card, in the British Museum).

of the printed bills of sale, afterwards pasted into this volume, and the names of purchasers added in red ink. The sales were held at various places.

First sale, March 28, at the East India House.* Pepper, Jambee; Pepper, Light; Pepper, White; Pepper, Black; "*Scummings and Flaggs;*" Quicksilver; Stick Lack.

Second sale, at the *Blew* Warehouse, in St. Helens. Cubebs, *Vermillion*, Copper, Mother of Pearl, Tortoise Shells, Quicksilver, Stick Lack, Safflower, *Indico* [the Company in its first trade with India inquired chiefly for Indigo, which had from the earliest ages been exported from Cambay], Green Ginger, Sugar Candy, Cassia Lignum, Aloes *Epatica*, Anacardium, Benjamin, "*Charranoyl*" [? some preparation of *charras*, *i.e.*, Cannabis sativa, or "Indian hemp"], Sago, Gallingall, Cowries, Tincal [Sanskrit *tankana*, crude Borax, imported from Thibet], Nux Vomica, Long Pepper, Cotton Yarne, Tea, Cake Lack, Elephants' Teeth, Shellack,† Gunnys.

---

* The first "Assemblie," on the 25th September 1600, of the subscribers to "the Old" East India Company was held in "the Founders' Hall," then situated in Founders' Court, Lothbury, but afterwards transferred to St. Swithin's Lane; and the Company used the Founders' Hall for its meetings continuously from March 1601 to September 1602. For some time after this date it is said to have occupied rooms in the Nag's Head Inn, but I am unaware of any adequate authority for the statement. From 1604 to 1621 its business was carried on in the house of its first Governor, Sir Thomas Smith, in Philpot Lane; from 1621 to 1638 its regular offices were in Crosby Hall, Bishopsgate Street, then belonging to Lord Northampton; in 1638 the Company moved to the house of Sir Christopher Clitheroe, at that time Governour, in Leadenhall Street, and in 1648 to the house adjoining, then belonging to Sir William Craven; in 1726 a new front was put to this house, which was entirely reconstructed by Jupp in 1796. When the unrivalled dominion of the Company was sequestrated to the Crown in 1858, the India Office was removed to the Westminster Palace Hotel in 1860; and finally to its present pretentious [in their internal decorative details] premises in St. James's Park in 1867. *See* Plates III. to VI.

† Lac is a resinous exudation produced in India and Further India on the twigs and branches of certain trees, particularly the *pipal* or "sacred fig" [Urostigma religiosum], by the puncture of a species of kermes or cochineal insect called Coccus Lacca. These minute insects swarm in countless

To be seen at "Bartolph Warfe":—Cowries, Red Saunders [*see Red Wood*, vol. 10 above], Sappan [Cæsalpinia Sappan, *patanga*, or, in Malaya, *sapang*, à species of "Brazil Wood"].

To be seen at "Leaden Hall":—China Raw Silk, Bengal Raw Silk, "Floretta" yarn [? Flos-silk].

To be seen at the East India House:—*China Ware*, both Nankeen Blue, and Painted Porcelain—an immense quantity; also *Japan* ware.

To be seen at Leaden Hall:—Piece Goods, among which, Ginghams, "*Herba* Lungees" [Longcloth of rhea or ramie fibre, *i.e.*, China-grass; *see* p. 26, "Pinascos" or stuffs of pine-apple fibre], "*Herba* Taffaties" [Taffety (from *tafta*, "woven"), of same; compare "*Herba* Bengalo"].

To be seen at the "*Blew* Warehouse," St. Helens:—"*Blew* Longcloth," Damasks, Satins, Persian Taffaties, Velvet, Diapers, Chintz, "Painted Pelongs" [*i.e.*, "Palampores" *i.e.*, *palang-posh*, or "bed-covers," hand-painted], Gold Gauze, Chawools [Shawls].

---

numbers on the extremities of the trees attacked by them, and hence the common Indian denomination of this substance, *laksha* in Sanskrit and *lakh* in Hindustani, meaning "a hundred thousand." From this word come our words "lac," "lacquer," a varnish of lac, and "lake," the red pigment [consisting of the bodies of the female Coccus Lacca embedded in the resin exuded about them], extracted by boiling it out from the "raw lac." Lac as produced on the trees from which it is gathered we call "stick lac," and the Hindus *kham-lakh*, *i.e.* "raw lac," corrupted by us and other European peoples into "*gum*-lac," as a generic designation of all commercial forms of lac; none of which, however, contain any admixture of gum with the native resin. The resin in the granular state to which it is reduced in washing out the colouring matter from it is "seed lac:" when this granular lac has been liquified over a fire, and allowed to consolidate in cakes, it is "lump lac": and when again melted, and clarified, and run into thin flakes, it is the "shell lac," used so largely by hatters; or, if run out in bright little drops, it is the "button lac" used in the preparation of sealing-wax and varnish. The term "shell lac" is translated directly from the Hindustani *chapra-lac*; and an old commercial name for it was "Spanish-wax." "Lake lac," "lac-lake," or "lac-dye" is crude lake formed into little lumps like those of indigo. What the *Lac Tigridis* of Evelyn's *Diary* [22nd June 1664, quoted on p. 220, *note*] may be, I do not know, and have never seen the appellation elsewhere. It may be corrupted from an Indian name of lac; or it may have been used in

Plate V. THE OLD EAST INDIA HOUSE, circa 1726–96

[*from an engraving in the British Museum.*]

Plate VI. The Old East India House, circa 1796–1858.

(from an engraving published by Colnaghi, Sala & Co.)

Vol. 12, 1704.
Vol. 13, 1704.
Vol. 14, 1705.
Vol. 15, 1705.
Vol. 16, 1705.
Vol. 17, 1707.

These are all Sale Books, similar to Volume 11; and these seven volumes, 11 to 17 inclusive, are invaluable records of the Company's trade at this period. I have not here copied out the names of all the denominations of piece goods entered in these important volumes, as they have been already published in the "Official Handbook to the British "Indian Section of the Paris Exhi- "bition of 1878." Very complete lists of them are also given in Milburn's *Oriental Commerce*, 1813; and in Sir Henry Yule's *Hobson-Jobson* [article "Piece Goods"], 1885.

Vol. 18, 1715–28. Accounts of sales.

Vol. 19, 1722. A Sales Book, similar in character to volumes 11 to 17, but very dilapidated.

II.—Gold and Silver.

One volume, 1677–97, being accounts of gold and silver received and weighed.

III.—Dyeing and Packing Cloth Bills.—One volume, 1704–1708.

Among entries,—"Canvis Buckerams," Scarlets, "*Camblets*," and Camlets, "Auroras," "*Glosters Popinjays*."

Evelyn's day to discriminate Kermes [*i.e.*, the Arabic *kirmij*, "insect" (specifically the female Coccus ilicis), whence "carmine" and "cramoisce," and through *vermes*, "vermillion," "vermeil," *et cetera*], the "scarlet grain" of Asia Minor, from the *Lac Sumatri*, the "lake lac" or "lac-lake" of Further India. The best "lac dye" or "lake" comes from Pegu, Siam, and China, and the best "lump lac" and "shell lac" from Bengal.

IV.—Invoices of Goods to and from India.—Two volumes, from 1664 to 1675, invaluable records of the Company's trade at this date.

Vol. 1, 1664–68.

First entry.—Rules and directions for keeping the East India "Accompts" in England, August 12th, 1664.

The first account is the invoice of the ship, "*Constantinople Merchant*," burden 300 tons. The last line of this invoice runs—"Some totall of this cargo, which God "prosper, 1,494*l.* 13*s.* 10*d.*"

The invoices of the following ships are also given:—*American*, *St. George*, *Retourne*, *Dorcas*, *Charles*, *Bantam*, *Coast Frigatt*, *London*, *Richard and Martha*, *Loyall Merchant*, *Rainbow*, *Unicorn*, *Blackmore*, *Loyall Subject*, *Rebecca*, *Constantinople Merchant*, *John and Martha*, *Morning Starr*, *Crowne*, *Antelope*, *Bombay Merchant*, *Humfry and Elizabeth*, *Sampson*.

Vol. 2, 1674–75, contains invoices of *London*, *Cæsar*, *Massingberd*, *Ann*, *Bombay Merchant*, *Unity* [Fryer's ship], *Eagle*, *Mary*, *Falcon*.

The *Falcon* was from Surat, and among the piece goods she brought were "Dolkas," "Nunsarees," "Deboys," and "Cambaja Brawles."

These are all the names of towns [Dholka, Nansari, Debhoy, and Cambay]; and the list shows that nearly every town and village of India in the 17th century manufactured piece goods, which generally received their commercial denominations from the places of their production.

V.—Home Petty Cash.—Four volumes, from 1657 to 1709, of no general interest.

Vol. 1, 1657–60, almost perished out of existence.

Vol. 2, 1659–69, in good condition.

Vol. 3, 1666–74, in good condition.
Vol. 4, 1705–1709, in tolerable condition.

VI.—Private Trade.—Five volumes, from 1768 to 1782.

Vol. 1, 1768–69, contains lists of goods *sent out* in the following ships :—*Anson*, to Coast and Bay ; *Britannia*, ditto ; *Cruttenden*, China ; *Duke of Albany*, St. Helena and Bencoolen ; *Devonshire*, to Coast and China ; *Deptford*, Bombay ; *Duke of Kingston*, Coast and Bay ; *Duke of Grafton*, ditto ; *Duke of Cumberland*, Bombay ; *Essex*, Fort St. George and Bombay ; *Earl of Lincoln*, Fort St. George and Bombay, and China ; *Earl of Ashburnham*, ditto ; *Europa*, Coast and Bay ; *Fox*, Bombay ; *Grenville*, Fort St. George and Bombay ; *Glatton*, China ; *Harcourt*, China ; *Hector*, China ; *Hampshire*, Bombay ; *Havanna*, Coast and China ; *Houghton*, Coast and Bay ; *Lioness*, Coast and Bay ; *Lord Holland*, ditto ; *Lord Camden*, Bombay ; *Lapwing*, Bengal ; *Marquis of Rockingham*, Bombay ; *Norfolk*, Coast and Bay ; *Nottingham*, ditto ; *Neptune*, ditto ; *Ponsborne*, Fort St. George and Bombay ; *Pigot*, Coast and China ; *Plassey*, ditto ; *Prince of Wales*, Coast and Bay ; *Royal Captain*, Bombay ; *Royal Charlotte*, Coast and Bay ; *Salisbury*, ditto [her cargo included "*Bulgar Hydes*," *i.e.*, Russian leather] ; *Speke*, St. Helena and China ; *Speaker*, Bombay ; *Triton*, Coast and China ; *Valentine*, Coast and China ; *York*, Fort St. George and Bombay.

Vol. 2, 1769–71. Vol. 3, 1770/1–73. Vol. 4, 1772–75. Vol. 5, 1779–82.	Full of similar lists of goods sent out in the Company's ships.

These five volumes are invaluable for the complete view they give of the Company's export trade to India and the East for the included period. Many of them are stamped with the arms of the United Company. [*See* p. 21, *note*.]

Shipping Papers.—Various, from 1610–11 to 1703–4.

A.—*Diaries.*

(1.) Sir H. Middleton's ship, sixth voyage, 1610–11.

(2.) Sir W. Morris, on his voyage to India in the *Harwich*, 1699–1700.

(3.) Ship *Vlaardeng.* Journal written in Dutch, 1663–64.

(4.) Ship *Adventure.* Diary of Captn. Goodlad, 1684–86.

(5.) Ship *Samuel and Anna.* Orders to Captn. Reddall, 1702–5.

(6.) Ship *Edward and Dudley.* Orders to Captn. Lambert, &c., 1703–4.

B.—*Various Shipping Papers.*

(1.) *Inventories of Ships' Cargoes.*—Vol. 1, 1611–13. Vol. 2, 1638–40. Vol. 3, 1708, is missing. I have put up in this bundle the "Loyall Cook's" account, entered separately in the Statistics and Commerce Departmental List, No. 2,397.

(2.) *Index to Mariners' Books.*—"Alphabet for the Mariners' Book," 1626; an Alphabetical List, apparently, of the sailors in the Company's service.

(3.) *Mariners' Wages.*—Vol. 1, 1665–68. Vol. 2, 1669–74. Vol. 3, 1675–76. Full of names of sailors.

(4.) *List of Stores*, 1639, being a *Steward's* Book; marked outside "Jonah's Booke."

(5.) *Inventories and Wills.*—Vol. 1, 1639. Vol. 2, 1660–61. Vol. 3, 1664–65. Full of names of sailors.

Other Shipping Papers.

Besides these shipping papers, there are the "SHIPS' JOURNALS" preserved in the Military [Marine] Department,* of which Mr. Clements Markham, C.B., has given a list† at the end [pp. 263–77] of *The Voyages of Sir James Lancaster to the East Indies*, published by the Hakluyt Society in 1877.

Remarks on the Company's earlier Voyages.

The earlier voyages of the Company are distinguished as the "*Separate Voyages*" and the "*Joint Stock Voyages*." Stimulated by the discoveries of the Spaniards and the Portuguese, the English began as early as the reign of Henry VII. to endeavour to participate in the trade of India. They first attempted to reach India by the North-West and North-East Passages; and they attempted these roundabout ways to the East in order to avoid the Portuguese. But, on the Dutch in 1598 boldly sending out their four ships under Houtman direct to the East by the Cape of Good Hope, the fuel of jealousy was added to the commercial ardour of the English to seize their share in the wealth of "Ormuz and of Ind," and the London East India Company was at once projected. In the first flame of avaricious rivalry the list of subscribers to the adventure was readily filled up, but the calls of the Committee upon them for the payment of the instalments of their contributions were imperfectly obeyed, and the Company, therefore, to avoid all risk to themselves, instead of trading to India in their earlier voyages on the terms of a Joint Stock, arranged that the subscribers should, individually, bear the expense of each voyage, and reap the whole profits. It was under these regulations that the first so-called "Separate Voyages" were fitted out. But after 1612

* They are now [1889] in the Record Department.

† To this List may now [1889] be added the "Journal of the Eighth Voyage," under Captain John Saris, in 1611, mentioned at page xiii. of Mr. Markham's Preface as being then [1877] in the possession of the War Office, but which has since been restored to the India Office.

it was found very difficult to compete successfully on the footing of individual ventures against the Portuguese and Dutch, and then the Company resolved that the voyages should be on the Joint Stock account, hoping thus to give a more efficient organization to the trade of England with the East.* This, however, only served to intensify the opposition of the Dutch, the most

---

* Although all the "Separate Voyages," excepting the Fourth, were prosperous, the clear profits hardly ever being below 100 per cent., and in general reaching 200 per cent. on each voyage, they did very little to develope the trade opened by them with India, which never, during the period covered by them, became of any great national importance. The aggregate capital raised for these twelve voyages was no more than 464,284*l.*, or an average of 38,690*l.* for each voyage; which sum was, according to Milburn, invested in the following manner:—

	£
In merchandise	62,411
Bullion	138,127
Shipping, stores, provisions	263,746

and gave a profit, one voyage with another, of 138 per cent.

With the institution of the "Joint Stock Voyages," all this was changed, in spite of the antagonism of the Dutch, which reduced the profits on the four voyages on the first "Joint Stock" account to 87½ per cent. on the subscribed capital. Nevertheless, when in 1617 the second "Joint Stock" was opened, the sum of 1,620,040*l.* was at once raised, the 954 contributors to it including 313 merchants, 214 tradesmen, 25 foreign merchants, 15 dukes and earls, 82 knights, 26 doctors of Divinity and Medicine, 13 ladies of title, 18 "widows and virgins," and 248 undescribed persons; and from this date the Company's trade became an imperial concern. In 1621 the Company presented to Parliament "the estate of their trade from the beginning thereof in "1600 to the 29th November 1621," from which it appears that in this period they had "sent forth to the Indies" 86 ships; of which 36 returned home safely laden; 9 were lost; 5 worn out by long service from port to port in India; 11 captured by the Dutch; and 25 "do remain in India or on their "homeward passage." By their license the Company might in this period have shipped 910,000*l.* in foreign coins to India; but "in all the said time, "upon all the said ships" they had "laden away," "as well out of these "Realms, as out of the Downs, Holland, and other places," no more than 613,681*l.* And together with this money they had "shipped out of the "Realm, in woollens, lead, tin, iron, and other wares, to the value of 319,211*l.*, "making together 932,892*l.*" "And of all the before-mentioned monies and "goods sent into the Indies, there have been employed the value of 375,288*l.* "for the [un]-lading of 36 ships, which are returned home with sundry sorts "of wares, all of which wares have produced here in England by sales "2,004,600*l.*"

formidable antagonists the English ever had in the East, our trade with which from this date gradually languished until the massacre of Amboyna [17th February 1622/3] roused the patriotic spirit of the whole country in support of the interests of the Company. The massacre of Amboyna is, indeed, the turning-point in the history of the rise and progress of the British Empire in India.

"*The Separate Voyages.*"

First Voyage, 1601–3, under "General" James Lancaster, on board the *Mare* [commonly written *Malice*] *Scourge*, re-christened *Red Dragon*. The "Vice-Admiral," the *Hector*, carried John Middleton, who died at Bantam, 1603. The other ships completing the squadron were the *Ascension*, the *Susan*, and the *Guift* [commonly written *Guest*]. John Davis, who had already made the voyage to the East Indies, with the Dutch fleet under Houtman [1598–1600], embarked on the *Red Dragon* as Chief Pilot under Sir James Lancaster. [See also Appendix B.]

Second Voyage, 1604–6, consisting of the *Dragon*, *Hector*, *Ascension*, and *Susan*, was commanded by Henry Middleton.

Third Voyage, 1606–9, commanded by Captain Keelinge

Sir Josia Child, in his *Discourses on Trade*, published in 1670, treating of the gain to this country by the Company's trade with India, points out that, it provided us with "25 to 30 of the most warlike ships of the kingdom, with "60 to 100 mariners in each"; and supplied us fully, and at first hand, instead of through the Dutch, with pepper, cloves, cinnamon, nutmegs, mace, saltpetre, indigo, and calico, as well as with muslins, lawns, and cambrics previously obtained from Flanders and Germany; and furthermore with excess of pepper, and with cowries, and "painted stuffs," to the amount of 300,000*l.*, for carrying on our trade with France, Spain, Italy, and Guinea.

The "most warlike ships," referred to by Sir Josia Child, were of the then fast increasing type of the *Loyall Merchant* [*see* p. 42], built for the Company by Captain Millet in 1660, with three decks, and carrying 30 guns, being the first three-decker launched in England, and designed for the protection of the Company's merchandise against the pirates of Algiers, or "Turkish rovers" as they were then called.

in the *Dragon*, with William Hawkins in the *Hector*, and David Middleton [brother to Sir Henry] in the *Consent*.

Fourth Voyage, 1607–9, consisting of the *Ascension*, commanded by Captain Sharpeigh or Sharpey, and the *Union*, by Captain Richard Rowles, was unfortunate.

Fifth Voyage, 1608, commanded by David Middleton of the *Consent*, the only ship sent.

Sixth Voyage, 1610, consisting of the *Trades Increase*, commanded by Sir Henry Middleton, the *Peppercorn*, by Captain Nicholas Downton, and the *Darling*.

The *Trades Increase* was by far the biggest merchant ship yet built in England.* She was of 1,100 tons burden, and was launched at Deptford, in the presence of King James I. and his Court, who were entertained on board by the Company with a splendid dinner, all served on dishes and plates of Chinaware, then a great rarity in England. It was her disastrous fate to run aground in Bantam Roads, where, while being repaired, she careened over, and was set on fire and totally destroyed by the Javanese, in 1613; Sir Henry Middleton dying soon afterward of grief for her loss.

Seventh Voyage, 1611, commanded by Captain Anthony Hippon of the *Globe*, the only ship sent. [Did Hippen's (now Prince's) Island, in the Straits of Sunda, derive its old name from Captain Hippon ?]

Eighth Voyage, 1611, consisting of the *Clove*, *Hector*, and *Thomas*, all under the command of Captain John Saris.

Ninth Voyage, 1612, commanded by Captain Edmund Marlowe of the *James*, the only ship sent.

Tenth Voyage, 1612, consisting of the *Hoseander*, *Hector*, *James*, and *Solomon* [James I., 1603 to 1625, Sully's "wisest fool in Christendom," the "English

---

* For the tonnage of English war ships at this period, *see* pp. 74–6 of *A Life of John Davis*, by Mr. Clements Markham, C.B. George Philip and Son. 1889.

Solomon" of his flatterers], commanded by Captain Thomas Best.

Eleventh Voyage, 1612, was that of the *Solomon* in Best's Fleet, as the *ninth* was that of the *James*.

Twelfth Voyage, also 1612, was that of the *Expedition*, commanded by Christopher Newport.

The *Expedition* was commissioned chiefly to carry back to Persia Sir Robert Shirley [nearly always written Sherley in the India Office Records], Ambassador from Shah Abbas to King James I. Sir Robert, born 1570, had accompanied his brother Sir Anthony to Persia in 1598; and was sent as Ambassador to England in 1612, and again in 1623; and died at Casbin, 13th July 1628. The two brothers made a most favourable and abiding impression in Persia, and Mr. Caspar Purdon Clarke, C.I.E., Keeper of the India Museum, South Kensington Museum, has several deeply interesting contemporary Persian water-colour paintings* of either the brothers Shirley or members of their English retinue.

"*The Joint Stock Voyages.*"

The *First Voyage*, 1613, consisting of the *New Year's Gift*, *Hector*, *Merchant Hope*, and *Solomon*, all under the command of Downton, is the only one on the Joint Stock Account of general historical interest. Peyton commanded the fleet which in January 1614/15 took Sir Thomas Roe [on board the *Lion*] to India, as Ambassador from James I. to the "Court of the Great Mogol" [Jehangir, 1605–27] at Agra. Captain Benjamin Joseph commanded the fleet, consisting of the *Charles*, *Unicorn*, *Globe*, *Swan*, and *Rose*,

---

* These water-colours are also interesting from being done in the Tartaresque style of painting prevalent in Persia down to the reign of Shah Abbas [1585–1628], when the great change to the present Italianesque style of Persian painting was brought about through the influence of the young Persians sent by Shah Abbas to learn painting in Italy "under Raffael" [1483–1520], according to the tradition, as Mr. Caspar Purdon Clarke informs me, of modern Persian artists, and certainly under masters of the school of Raphael.

which in February 1615/16 took out Edward Terry [on board the *Charles*] as "Chaplain to the Right Honble. Sir Thomas Row, Knt." Sir Thomas Herbert went out with the fleet which sailed from the Downs "upon Good Friday," in the year 1626; and John Fryer with the fleet of 1672, composed of the *London*, *Massengberd*, *Bombaim*, *Unity* [Fryer's ship], *President*, *Ann*, *East India Merchant*, *Sampson*, *Cæsar*, and *Antelope*, all commissioned as men of war, the English being at the time "at open defiance against the Dutch." John Ovington sailed from Gravesend 11th April 1689 in the *Benjamin*, sent to Surat "as an advice-ship of "that wonderful Revolution whereby their Sacred "Majesties [Mary and William III.] were peaceably "settled in the Throne." Mr. Markham has pointed out that William Baffin served in the fleet, consisting of the *London*, *Hart*, *Roebuck*, and *Eagle*, which sailed in February 1619/20 under Captain Shillinge. The latter was killed in an encounter with the Portuguese fleet off Ras Jashk, at the entrance of the Strait of Ormuz, in January 1620/21, and Baffin died on the 23rd of January 1621/22 of a wound received at the siege of a Portuguese fort on the island of Kishm, where he lies buried, a few miles due south of the island of Ormuz. Shillinge was buried near the town of Jashk. John Davis, Mr. Markham also notes, sailed as pilot on board the *Tiger*, in Sir Edward Michelborne's independent voyage, in 1604, to China and Japan, and was slain in an encounter with a Japanese junk off Bintang, in the Straits of Malacca, 27th December 1605.

THIRD DIVISION.

Foreign Relations of the Company.

Persia.—1621–30, two volumes.

Vol. 1, 1621–22. Copies of letters from Ispahan, Ghilan, "Kharistan"? [? Laristan, ? Faristan, ? or Khusistan], Laur [Lar], Minaw [Minab], Gombroon [Gamrun or *Bandar Abbasi*], Jiyone or Jeroon [a name for Ormuz, *i.e.*, Hurmuz, the famous island opposite Bandar Abbas], Kustack, Costack, and Chostack [Jasques, *i.e.*, Jashk].

Vol. 2. Firmans and other documents from "Sawal [Shawal] A.H. 1036" [A.D. 1627] to "Zilkada [Zu-ul-Kaida], A.H. 1039" [A.D. 1630]. The firmans are of the 42nd year of the reign of Shah Abbas [succeeded to the throne of Persia, 1585], and the 1st and 2nd years of the reign of Shah Safi [succeeded 1630]. Both volumes are of historical value.

China and Japan.

These volumes do not correspond with the entry at p. 1, Statistics and Commerce Departmental List, No. 2,397. The entry there is of the 4 vols. [viz.: Vol. 1, 1672; vol. 2, 1685–86; vol. 3, 1699–1759; vol. 4, 1721–1723] classed by me under the sub-section D of this Section. And besides these 4 volumes I found a series of volumes of "China Materials," numbered from 1 to 9 [sub-section A], of which volume 8 is missing; and two supplementary volumes [sub-section B], one of which relates to Japan; and a separate volume on Japan [sub-section C].

A.—"*Extracts towards a History of the Rise and Progress of the Trade with China.*"

The extracts are from the Court's Letter Books and other records in the India Office, and from "Purchas, his Pilgrimes."

Vol. 1, 1596–1675. Vol. 3, 1682–1686.
Vol. 2, 1673–1683. Vol. 4, 1684–1699.

The above 4 volumes were lent to the Record Office for examination, and have been duly returned.

Vol. 5, 1694–1701. Vol. 8, missing.
Vol. 6, 1699–1702. Vol. 9, 1712–1725.
Vol. 7, 1702–1704.

B.—*Supplement to China Materials.*

Vol. 1, 1600–1702, relates really to Japan.
Vol. 2, 1606–1699, China.

C.—*Japan.*

One volume, 1614–1616, belonging apparently to a set entitled "Japan Miscellanies." This volume consists of copies of letters from Richard Wickham, the Company's Factor at Firando. He makes the earliest mention of tea ["chaw"] in the Company's Records, in his letter of 27 June 1615, to Mr. Eaton at Miaco [see p. 26, note].

D.—*Tonquin, Amoy, Canton, and Chusan.*

Vol. 1, 1672. Tonquin Journal and Register:—"Begun June ye 25, and December ye 7 ended." Apparently received *ex Eagle*, and recorded in London 13th April 1675. A most interesting record of the Company's first trade in the *Tonquin* river.

Vol. 2, 1685–86. History of the attempted settlement at *Amoy*.

Vol. 3, 1699–1759. History of attempts to acquire and establish a trade at *Chusan.*

Vol. 4, 1721–23. Consultations and Diary of James Nash and others, supercargoes of the four ships *Eyles, Lyell, Walpole,* and *Emilia,* at *Canton.* The cargo taken at Canton included "Gorgarons," *i.e.,* silks, "Poises?" "Tutenague" [from *tutiya,* "oxide of zinc," and *nak,* "like," tutenag being an amalgam of zinc, copper, and iron, largely exported from China to India, until superseded by Silesian spelter].

These are four invaluable volumes on the early trade of the Company with China. *The impression of the Company's arms has been filched from the cover of vol.* 2.

[The China "PROCEEDINGS" in the next century extend from 1721 to 1840.]

"The Dutch in the East."

A. Five volumes, entered under this heading, "*The Dutch in the East,*" in Departmental List, No. 2,397. Vols. 1 and 5 are important historical records.

Vol. 1, 1622–24, and 1650–54, contains proceedings before the High Court of Admiralty, and before the Commissioners; evidence in Latin supporting the Company's complaint against the Dutch, 1622–25; and documents relating to *Paulo Roon* and *Lantore,* 1616–1620; *Jaccatra,* 1619; Pepper; "The Massacre of *Amboyna,*" 1622/3; and to the Dutch trade in the *Persian Gulf.*

Vol. 2, 1625. "Lemmens to the Dutch East India Company," being the "Translate" of a Remonstrance made by Francis Lemmens to the Dutch East India Company, in 70 paras., and also extracts of articles out of above remonstrance.

Vol. 3, 1651–54. Complaints of the English East India Company against the Dutch East India Company.

Vol. 4, 1684–85. Transactions touching *Bantam*, between the English and Dutch Commissioners, 1685.

Vol. 5, 1685–86, ditto.

B. Five additional volumes, not in any previous list; all of great interest and value.

Vol. 1, *no date.* Marked on the back, "Connection "with the Dutch in the Eastern Seas," being "A statement of the States and Princes in the Eastern Seas "with whom the Dutch appear at any time to have had "connection, showing the nature and extent of that "connection. Compiled chiefly from two volumes of "copies and extracts of treaties bearing dates from the "year 1596 to 1797, which were extracted from the "Dutch Records at *Batavia* by a committee especially "appointed by the late British Government at Java for "that purpose, and transmitted by the Bengal Government to the Court of Directors in 1818, together with "such collateral information as has been collected "from the earlier records by the East India Company, "and from earlier authorities." *This is an invaluable volume.*

Vol. 2, 1773. *Palembang Records.* A few pages only.

Vol. 3, 1785.} Bencoolen Records.
Vol. 4, 1791.}

Vol. 5, 1813–20. Dutch Memoranda relating to Sir Stamford Raffles's period. *An important volume.*

General Remarks on the Dutch in the East.

Besides the above records relating to the Dutch in the East, there are the papers catalogued in the "Printed Lists of Records," No. 1 and No. 2, bearing date the 8th November, 1875, and the 9th February 1876, respectively, enumerated separately in my confidential "Memorandum on the Records in the India Office on the Dutch in the East," of January 17, 1878 [Statistics and Commerce Department, No. 3,049], prepared for the Intelligence Department of the War Office.

There are also "the Mackenzie MSS." in the Library, of which those relating to the Dutch are very important. *See* also, *infra*, Fifth Division, under "Damaged Papers," Bundle A, the reference to the *packet marked "The Dutch."**

---

* The organization of the administration of their trade with the East by the Dutch was followed in almost every detail by the English East India Company.

Their Civil Service took precedence of all others, and was divided into 13 grades, viz.,—1st, that of *Schrijver*, or "Writer," recruited from the deserving soldiers of the Dutch Guards, pay, 9 to 14 *guilders* a month; 2nd, of Under Assistant, 20 *guilders* a month, and 4 *rix dollars* for table money; 3rd, of Upper Assistant, Book-keeper, or Secretary, 28 to 36 *guilders*, and 4 *rix dollars* table money; 4th, of *Onder-Koopman* [*Anglicè*, Copeman; *cf.*, chapman, copesmate, Copenhagen, Chippenham], or "Under Merchant," 36 to 45 *guilders*, and 8 *rix dollars* table money; 5th, of *Koopman*, 50 to 65 *guilders*, and 8 *rix dollars*; 6th, of *Opper-Koopman*, 80 to 120 *guilders* a month, with 12, and at Ceylon and Batavia 13, *rix dollars* table money; 7th, of *Kommandoor* [from the Portuguese *Commendadôr*, and the origin of the English Company's old Civil Service title of "Commodore" *], 150 *guilders*, and 20 *rix dollars* table money; 8th, of *Direktoor* [the origin of the English Company's official title of "Directore," now spelt Director], 200 *guilders*, and 30 *rix dollars* table money; 9th, of Governour, with the same salary and table allowance; 10th, of Members of the "Extraordinary Council of India," with the same salary and table allowance; 11th, of the "Ordinary Council of India," at Batavia, each 350 *guilders* a month, and 100 *rix dollars* table money; 12th, of "The Director General," or "Second at Batavia," with 600 *guilders* a month salary, and 100 *rix dollars* table money; and 13th, of "The Governour General of Batavia," with 1,200 *guilders* a month salary, and 200 *rix dollars* table money, and every time he visited the Fleet, which was always done upon a Fleet's departure for Holland, a "gratuity" of 1,500 *rix dollars*. Also, the Governour General's allowances included wine and other liquors, and provisions of every description, without limitation; and all others down to the Assistants were allowed monthly, liquors, spices, oil, wood, rice, vinegar, candles, each

---

* Even after the abolition of the English East India Company's Warehouses, on the withdrawal of its trading privileges in 1834, when with the other warehousemen "the Commodore of the Blues" [*i.e.*, Indigo], "the Commodore of the Peppers," *et cetera*, were all pensioned off, this quondam Civil Service title continued to be borne by a certain grade of India Office Messengers, and two of these "Commodores of Messengers" are still living one as a pensioner, and the other in the active service, but no longer under his old denomination, of the Secretary of State for India. Under the Company the Superintendent of "the Maids" of the India House also bore the title of "Commodoress."

according to his grade. Thus, the Upper Copeman's allowance was 20 Canadars of *Spanish* wine *per mensem*, besides "Mum" [*mumme*, strong German beer. Tavernier notes that it was the principal delight of the Dutch at Batavia "to see new drinkes arrive, especially English beer, and that which they call *mom*, which comes from Brunswick"], "White Wine, and other "liquors, 24 *li* of Wax for Candles, Corn for Poultry, Rice for Slaves, &c. "So that the Diet Money allow'd them is only for Fresh-Provisions."

The Military Service of the Dutch Indies was divided into only six grades,—1st, of Private, with rank and pay of Under Assistant of the Civil Service: 2nd, of Sergeant, with rank, pay, and allowances of Assistant; 3rd, of Ensign, with rank, pay, and allowances of Under-Copeman; 4th, of Lieutenant, with rank, pay, and allowances of Copeman; 5th, of Captain, with rank, pay, and allowances of Upper-Copeman; and 6th, of Major, with rank, pay, and allowances of Commodores.

The officers of the Dutch Colonial Navy were also divided into six grades.—1st, of Able-bodied Seaman, with rank and pay of Under Assistant: 2nd, of Third Mate, Gunner, and Boatswain, with rank, pay, and emoluments of Assistant, only that the Ship's Carpenters of this rank received from 40 to 50 *guilders* a month; 3rd, of Second Mate, with rank, &c., of Upper Assistant; 4th, of Chief Mate, with rank, &c., of Under-Copeman; 5th, of *Schipper*, with rank of Copeman, and 60 to 100 *guilders* a month; and 6th, of *Kommandoor*, ranking as Civil Commodore, with from 100 to 150 *guilders* a month, besides "Ship's Allowance," and "Road-Money" when in harbour at Batavia.

The Chaplains were divided into Dominees, or Visitors of the Sick, with the pay and rank of Assistant, and Predicants, or "Preachers," with the pay and rank of Upper-Copeman. The Surgeons also had the pay and rank of Upper-Copeman.

All military, naval, and other officers gave place to Civilians of the same rank.

It is thus quite clear that the exclusive spirit of the Indian Covenanted Civil Service is based, not on Brahmanical traditions, but on the strictly mercantile organization of the administration of the Dutch Indies. It is clear, also, from the close care taken of their sick and disabled officers, and of the widows and orphans of their officers, by the Dutch, that it was from them that the English East India Company learned to make such methodical provision for the families of its officers; both, in this respect, affording an example which, on account of their great worldly success, will be for ever memorable, not only of the pious observance of that part of Christian justice due from all masters to their servants, but also of the soundest commercial prudence and the highest public economy.

FOURTH DIVISION.

The History of the Company in India.

THE FRENCH IN INDIA.—Two volumes, 1749–59.

Vol. 1, 1749–59. Extracts from the East India Company's advices regarding the conduct of the French on the coast of Coromandel, and the "country government there."

The *First Letter*, dated Fort St. David, August 30, 1749, and received May 10, 1750, that is eight months afterwards, was sent *viâ Bussorah*, as likely to reach London sooner than if sent round the Cape.

At pp. 329-37 are letters from Admiral Watson, Clive's loyal coadjutor, giving an account of his victorious operations in the Hoogly [Hugli], 1757.

At p. 341 is Clive's own account of the decisive victory won by him, 23rd June 1757, on the "plain of Placis" or Plassey [*i.e.*, Palasi, so called from the *palas* trees, Butea frondosa, growing on it].

This is a volume of the highest interest. It is in perfect order and preservation, and quite worth publishing separately.*

Vol. 2, 1754–55. Further correspondence.

General Remarks on the French in India.

There are innumerable papers on the French in India among the papers catalogued in the "Printed Lists of Records," Nos. 1 and 2, referred to above, under *General*

* Since this Report was first printed, Sir W. Wilson Hunter, K.C.S.I., C.I.E., has, in his work entitled *The Indian Empire, its History, People, and Products*, Trübner & Co., 1886, quoted direct from the above interesting original account of the battle of Plassey.

Remarks on "the Dutch in the East." *See* "Printed Lists of Records, Nos. 1 and 2," *infra.* The "CARNATIC COMMISSION" Papers extend from 1773 to 1839.

MYSORE.

One volume, 1779–1782. Narrative of the second war [1780–4] with Hyder Ali. A very complete compilation.

General Remarks on Mysore.

There are many papers relating to Mysore in the "Printed Record List," No. 2. *See infra.*

Addendum.

The papers referred to in the three following paragraphs are not included amongst the "Old Records" treated of in this Report, and are here referred to simply to direct attention, in the present connection, to the fact of their existence.

1. The papers in the "Printed Lists of Records," Nos. 1 and 2, relating to the French and other foreigners in India and other parts of the East.

2. The papers in the "Printed Lists of Records," Nos. 1 and 2, relating to the history of the Company in India, apart from the French and other foreigners.

3. "MOGUL COURT PROCEEDINGS," 1714–1717; the "CLIVE PROCEEDINGS," 1757–1766; the "WARREN HASTINGS PROCEEDINGS," 1775; and the "BENGAL SECRET PROCEEDINGS," 1772–1779.

BENGAL, BEHAR, AND ORISSA.

One volume, dated on the back 1676. On the first page is written — "Specimen of Collections for an

"History and Description of the Provinces of Bengal, "Behar, and Orissa." At page 106 and onwards is a very interesting letter on the piece goods made at Ballasore: Ginghams, "Herba Taffaties," "Herba Lungies," "and other Herba goods." It is noted that "the waters of the Casharry [? Koinsari] give the most "lasting die to them" [the said fabrics], "and within "two days journey of this place" [Balasor]. At p. 125 and onwards is an interesting letter on raw silk, &c., and on the manufacture of "Taffaties" at Cossimbazaar. At p. 137 is described "the manner of providing cloth at Dacca."*

---

* The muslins of Dacca, chequered, striped, spotted, flowered, and finest of all, the plain, which have been famous from Roman, and, as would now seem, from even Babylonian and Assyrian times, were first imported direct by the East India Company into England between 1660 and 1670; when the total export of these fabrics from Dacca amounted, in value, to 1,000,000*l*. The Company greatly fostered their manufacture, but their doom was sealed when in 1785 the use of the mule jenny in weaving was first introduced at Nottingham, and two years afterward 500,000 pieces of muslin, in imitation of the coarser Dacca denominations, were rolled off the power looms of Great Britain. The cry then was to protect the British manufacturer from the competition of the Dacca weavers, and a duty of 75 per cent. was imposed on all Indian cotton goods. In consequence, the exportation of Dacca muslins to this country, the value of which in 1787 stood at 30 *lakhs* of rupees, gradually fell to 8½ *lakhs* in 1807, and 3½ *lakhs* in 1813, until it ceased altogether in 1817, when the Honourable East India Company's Commercial Residency at Dacca was abolished. And although in 1825 the duty was reduced to 10 per cent. *ad valorem*, this had little effect in reviving the manufacture of Dacca muslins, as about this very time English mule twist began to be largely imported for weaving into India, where its consumption rose from 3,063,556 lbs. in 1827 to 6,624,823 in 1831, to the almost entire exclusion of the use of native thread, from which alone the finer varieties of Dacca cloths can be made. Melancholy indeed, and a bitter rebuke to the people of England, is the contrast between the prosperous condition of Dacca under the East India Company in the last century, and the impoverished state to which it was reduced when, at the beginning of the present century, the Imperial Parliament began to seriously interfere with the Company's administration in India. The terrible story is fully told in Surgeon James Taylor's admirable *Sketch of the Topography and Statistics of Dacca*, "printed by order of Government," at Calcutta, in 1840. Still more sad and humiliating is it to reflect that the desolation which then swept over Dacca also more or less overtook every one of the ancient polytechnical cities of India, and everywhere as the result of the disadvantages we so unrighteously enforced

against them in their already unequal competition with the rising manufacturing towns of Nottingham, Warrington, and Glasgow. But in the fateful year 1857 a steam loom mill was opened at Bombay; and now [in 1887–88] India again exports cotton manufactures to the annual value of Rs. 27,988,540. Thus the whirligig of Time brings in his revenges! Dacca also still continues to export small quantities of its hand loom flowered muslins to Persia, Syria, Egypt, and Turkey.

The East India Company, in the days of its comparative freedom from Parliamentary interference, not only succeeded in confirming the prosperity of the indigenous manufactures of India, but was also the beneficent means of naturalizing in that country a new one, which has in some places become of considerable local value. They were compelled latterly to export large quantities of English woollen cloths to Bombay, Surat, Fort St. George, and Calcutta; and some of these, the "Auroras," "Salisbury flannels," "Popinjays," "Shalloons" [*ras de Chalons*], &c., of the "Old Records," were of very beautiful bright colours, rose, ivory white, French green, scarlet, "Telmont yellow," Mazarine blue, Turkey red, emerald green, Neapolitan yellow, black, &c., which made them universally popular, and at length led to their successful imitation in many parts of India.

FIFTH DIVISION.

Factory Records.

It is impossible to note everything I would of the contents of these voluminous records. All that I have done, as a rule, is, to indicate as briefly as possibly the general character of the contents of each volume, or collection of volumes. Further than that I only notice facts of universal interest. At the conclusion of the division, however, a concise account will be given of the history of our Factories, and early territorial acquisitions in the East.

ABSTRACTS OF LETTERS FROM VARIOUS FACTORIES.—Under this head twelve volumes are entered in the Departmental List, No. 2,397, from 1617 to 1722. Volumes 10, 11, and 12 are of Letters from the Company to their Factories.

Vol. 1, 1617–32, contains many letters from Thomas Baker in Persia. This is an exceedingly valuable volume, comprising abstracts of at least 114 letters which are not to be found elsewhere.

Vol. 2, 1669–80, missing.

Vol. 3, 1699–1707. Letters from the Bay of Bengal, the Coast of Coromandel, Surat, Borneo, and China. A list is prefixed of the Establishment of Merchants, Factors, and Writers at the above five Factories at the dates included.

A.—"*Bay of Bengal.*"—*Merchants*, among others, Sir Edward Littleton, Chief, under the "Old Company," of the Kazimbazaar Factory, 1679, and President, under the "New Company," for the "Bay of Bengall," 1698—1704–5.

Factors, among others, Fulk Lacy, *Surgeon*. This is Dr. Fulke Lacey, "who died on board the *Antelope*, 10th September 1699"; as did also, in the following December, Dr. Thomas Pendleton, "Our [*i.e.*, the New Company's] designed Chyrurgeon in the Bay" of Bengal.

Writers, among others, Mulis Lamb.

B.—*China*.—Among *Factors*, William Travers.

The letters as usual all relate to the details of the Company's mercantile transactions.

Vol. 4, 1716–22.

Vol. 5, 1663–72.

Vol. 6, 1675–95. Letters from various places subordinate to "Surratt." Very interesting.

Vol. 7, 1696–1707.

Vol. 8, 1664–76, missing [in 1878, but since found].

Vol. 9, 1677–1706, missing [ditto].

Vol. 10, 1658–73. From London. Standing rules of the Company to be observed in their several Factories. *This is a volume of the highest interest*, in perfect preservation, and completely indexed.

Vol. 11, 1672–79. Under date of London, December 13th, 1672, is an order for goods, in which occurs this entry: "Salloos, made at Gulcundah, and brought from "thence to Surat, and go to England."

Vol. 12, 1702–6. Letters from London. Orders for investments of cargoes, &c.

Despatches and Letters to India from the Directors.—Nine volumes, 1655 to 1741.

Vol. 1, 1655–59, contains copies of letters to Surat, &c., *viâ* Aleppo, from "the Committee of Adventurers in the "ships *William*, *Benjamin*, and *Hopeful*." [*See Bruce's Annals*, vol. I., p. 508.]

Vol. 2, 1703–6. In one letter mention is made of

"Slabs of Totanague" [*see* p. 53]. *At pages* 220 *and* 286 *are long lists of commodities.*

Under the lists of goods to be provided at Surat, page 220, are the following:—"Chintz, Persia, to be of "lively *brisk* colours, and no blacks, 5,000 pieces." "Chelloes, 4,000." "Tannah stuffs, of all colours and "stripes, 500." "Indigo, Agra and Lahore." "Car-"mania wool, red, and other goods to be received from "Persia." The order concludes, "Send more or less as "procurable at encouraging prices."

Under the list of goods to be provided in China, p. 286, are the following:—"Poisies" [?], "Goshecs" [?], "Hockins" [?], "Paunches," "Pelongs," "Gelongs." They are all evidently silk goods.

The list of goods to be provided at Fort St. George, p. 321, includes "Izarees," "Morees," "Bettelles," "Saserguntees," "Callawaypose," "Sadarunchareеs," "Goaconcherulas," "Allegaes." These names, each under many forms of spelling, constantly occur. They are the names of piece goods, and, judging from the names of those goods sent from the Surat Factory, are generally to be traced to the names of the places of their production. *A list of ships is given at p.* 234.

Vol. 3, 1706–7, a similar book. *List of ships*, p. 145. *Lists of goods*, pp. 157–158.

Vol. 4, 1707–8, a similar book, written up to p. 67 only.

Vol. 5, 1730–32.
Vol. 6, 1732.
Vol. 7, 1732–34.
Vol. 8, 1734–36.
Vol. 9, 1736–41.

} Five volumes of demi-official and semi-private letters from the Secretary of the Company to various of their servants. Vol. 8 contains a letter of November 28th, 1735, from *Cavendish Square* to Mr. Lethieullier.

Miscellaneous.

Under this head I include the entries of 11 volumes at page 4 of the Departmental List, No. 2,397, A.D. 1675 to 1786.

Vol. 1, 1675–76. Copy of Puckle's Diary, Metchlipatam [Masulipatam] and Fort St. George.

Vol. 2, 1675–77. Copy of Streynsham Master's Diary, from London to Fort St. George. Sir Streynsham Master [continually spelt Masters] was Governour of Madras [1678–81] in succession to Sir William Langhorne [1670–8].

Vol. 3, 1678. Record of proceedings of the Court of Judicature at Fort St. George; containing a list of houses taxed to pay for the cleaning of the "Black [also called "Christian," meaning native Christian] Town" of Madras. [*See*, *infra*, Angengo, Vol. I.]

Vol. 4, 1679. Statement of the gold "coyned" by Mr. Richard Mohun [dismissed in 1680 for defalcations in his accounts as Chief of Masulipatam], and in his absence by Vincent Sayon.

Vol. 5, 1687. Copy of the Charter of James II. establishing a Municipality and Mayor's Court at Madras. Missing [in 1878, but since found and incorporated with the "Parchment Records." *See* Appendix D.].

Vol. 6, 1703–4.} Letters from various places in India
Vol. 7, 1704–5.} to Fort St. George.

Vol. 8, 1716. } "Translates of Phirmaunds." Im-
Vol. 9, 1716. } portant.

Vol. 10, 1729. Catalogue of the Library of Fort St. George. *Very interesting.* The reading of the century in India was limited, but solid, and very feeding:—The Bible, Buchan's Domestic Medicine, Johnson's, Walker's and Sheridan's Dictionaries, Taplin's Farriery, Hoyle's Book of Games, Fanny Burney's, and the-then-equally-popular-but-now-utterly-forgotten-save-by-the-curious Charlotte Smith's, novels, the Sporting Dictionary, Brigg's, Glass's, and Farley's Cookery Books, Macpherson's Ossian, Don Quixote, and Gil Blas, *Persian*, and *Arabic*, even more than Hindoostanee Dictionaries, Bell's British Theatre, Shakespeare, Gibbon, Robertson, Hume and Smollett,

Langhorne's Plutarch, Gilchrist's East India Vade Mecum, Ainslie "on Cholera Morbus," and Struensee [not J. F.] "on Field Fortification." These were the works, in the order of the demand for them, carried out in every ship to India, at the end of the last century, and beginning of the present, before the time of Scott and Byron. Also, always, "all new books for "children."

Vol. 11, 1786. A list of the English and other European captives at Mysore. *An invaluable record of names.*

Twenty-seven Combined Volumes.—27 volumes [found since my first examination of these Records], 1623 to 1708.

Vol. 1, 1623–25. Consultations at Batavia, Surat, Amboyna, and Gombrone.

Vol. 2, 1626–35. Ditto Surat, Batavia, Jambee, Bantam, Ispahan letters, and letters to Persia. A letter to "The Viceroy and Principals of the Portugall Nation in "Goa," in which the Viceroy is styled "The Padre Pro-"vincial," and "Your reverent Fatherhood."

Vol. 3, 1634–59. Surat, Bantam, Fort St. George. The volume contains a letter from Sir John Massingbird, *with two perfect seals on the back.* Also a letter marked "Copia out of French."

Vol. 4, 1659–66. Madraspatam, Bantam, Macassar, Bengal, Metchlipatam [Masulipatam].

Vol. 5, 1666–69. Bantam, Balasore.

Vol. 6, 1669–72. Bombay, Jambee, Metchlipatam, Bantam, Golconda, Ceylon, Bengal.

Vol. 7, 1672–75. Bombay, Metchlipatam, Japan, Bantam, Ballasore.

Vol. 8, 1675–76. Bantam, Madras, Tonquene.

Vol. 9, 1676–79. Tonquin, Fort St. George, Cossimbazaar, Metchlipatam, Amoy, Tywan [Formosa], Hugly.

Vol. 10, 1677–81. Tywan, Amoy, Bantam, Bombay, Tonqueen, Siam, Hugly.

Vol. 11, 1681–82. Cossimbazaar, Hugly, Maulda, Engleswad, Syam.

Vol. 12, 1682–83. Bantam, Syam, Dacca, Fort St. George, Batavia, Tonquin, Surat, St. Helena.

Vol. 13, 1682–85. Macao, Amoy, Batavia, Bombay, Pattana, Metchlipatam, St. Helena.

Vol. 14, 1685–87. Conimero, Bombay, Fort St. George, Balasore, Fort York, Madapolam, Cuddalore, Porto Novo.

Vol. 15, 1686–90. Bengal, Metchlipatam, Bombay, Fort St. George, Bencoolen, Fort York, St. Helena, Canton.

Vol. 16, 1691–92. Bombay, Surat.

Vol. 17, 1692–93. Fort York, Fort St. George, Bombay, Surat, Chuttanuttee.

Vol. 18, 1693–94.

Vol. 19, 1693–94; 1699–1701.

Vol. 20, 1693–97. Acheen, Tonquin.

Vol. 21, 1695–97. Fort St. George, Tonquin, Fort St. David.

Vol. 22, 1697–98.

Vol. 23, 1699. Bombay, Fort York, Surat.

Vol. 24, 1699–1700. Fort St. George, Metchlipatam, Fort York *or* Tryamong, Surat.

Vol. 25, 1699–1701. Fort St. George, Metchlipatam, Fort York, Fort St. David.

Vol. 26, 1701–3. Cossimbazaar, Macao, Canton, Batavia.

Vol. 27, 1702–8. Amoy, Fort William, Fort St. George, Calcutta, Surat.

The "I.P. [*i.e.*, Injured Papers] Volumes."

Vol. 1, contains loose and injured papers of various dates, 1608, 1613, 1622, 1626, 1677, 1681, 1692, 1696, &c., relating to Batavia, Surat, Fort St. George, Chuttanuttee, Madapolam, Metchlipatam, Balasore, Hugly, Tonqueen, Dacca. Most of the papers are in the old Court hand.

Vol. 2, contains loose papers of all sorts from Pulicat, Surat, Maha (?), Bombay, Fort York, Armagaon, Hugly, dated from 1602 to 1682.

Vol. 3, contains all sorts of loose papers from 1629 to 1723. Among others, the Hugly Diary, from December 2, 1681, to June, 1682. Copies of letters from Bantam, written in 1629–37. Minutes of Consultations at Bantam, in 1679. Memorandum dated Anno 1677, at Tonqueen. Minutes of Consultations at Fort St. George, 1681. Copies of letters from Surat to the Factors at Broach, 1698. Letters from [Sir] Jno. Gayer from Swally, to various, 1700–1. Consultations and letters to and from Englesvad, Hugly, Scingee? [? Gingi], 1681 and other dates. Consultations, Fort St. George, 1693. Diary, dated 1701, of some Factors in China. Copies of letters, 1699. Consultations at St. Helena, in original, 1733.

The "D.P. [*i.e.*, Damaged Papers] Volumes."

These are not entered in the Departmental List, No. 2,397, and are contained in four bundles, A, B, C, and D.

Bundle A.

Fragments of miscellaneous documents on trade, ships, commissions, the Dutch, law, accounts, invoices, remainders, valuations, bills of lading, policies of insurance, customs lists, and all sorts of odds and ends of correspondence,—just such a sack-full of torn papers as might have been gathered out of the waste paper baskets of the Company's offices in Crosby Hall, or the Leaden Hall, at any time during the seventeenth century. The following documents may be noted :—

A letter from Samuel Boyle, Bantam, dated January 13, 1614/5, and endorsed "No moment."

A letter from James Bagg, Junior, Plymouth, of December 29, 1618.

Letter from "Messieurs Cartwright and Cooper," on board the Dutch ship *Agreement* at "Taxell," bound for Bantam, dated 26th and 31st August 1619.

A letter from John Clant, on board the *Bull*, Portland Bay, bound for Bantam, August 10th, 1619.

A letter from George Kempe, Plymouth, of May 29, 1621. *The seal is perfect.*

A letter from Adrian Roquigny, Rouen, January 30, 1637.

Letters from Henry Whitaker, Amsterdam, July 25, August 15 and December 9 and 16, 1644, and July 9 and 16, 1646.

Letters from Francis Townley, Hamburg, November 21 and 27, 1646.

Letters from "Signors Gault and Isaac Van der Vort," Venice, June 19 and July 26, 1647.

Letter from Jer° Williamson Aschman, Middleburg, July 19, 1650.

Letters from Ephraim Skinner, Robert Balle, and Francis Gosfright, Livorno, August 25 and September 1, 1674, advising purchase of coral.

Letter from Wm. Berry, "Bourdeux" (Bordeaux), 1st November 1683.

Letters from various Factories in India, 1613 to 1645.

The packet marked "THE DUTCH" contains, among other papers :—

The Company's petition in 1617 to the King, complaining "of the manifest and insupportable wrongs and abuses "lately done by the Hollanders unto Your Majestie and "your Majesties said servants."

"An Account General" with the Dutch [1620–21] for ships, goods, &c., taken by them, and unrestored.

A copy of the States' letter to His Majestie [French], dated the Hague, August 20, 1619.

The "*Treaty of Defence*"* of July 7, 1619. Irreparably damaged; endorsed, "There is a perfect copy in "'List of Papers relating to the Dutch,' taken from the "Law Presses No. 5;" but nothing appears to be known of it.

"The state of the question [between the English and "the Dutch Companies] concerning restitution in the Low "Countries of goods brought thither, propounded by the "English and answered by the Dutch Commissioners in "Holland" [? January 7, 1621/22]. A most important historical document.

"Minutes of that which passed at the Council Table "between the Dutch and English Commissioners "touching restitution," 10th July 1622.

"Complaint to the King of the protraction of the nego-"tiations for restitution by the Dutch Commissioners, and "of the Dutch Company having, since the publication of "the Treaty, seized the islands of Lantore and Pulo "Roon," dated 28th July 1622. [The islands were seized in 1620, immediately after the proclamation of the Treaty of Defence, and the English people on them treated with merciless inhumanity.]

"Copy of Sir Henry Marten's discourse [Counsel's "opinion] of the *Black Lyon*, with Mr. Birde's opinion in "concurrence," 1622.

---

* This was the well-known Act of Amnesty and Oblivion between the Dutch and English ["London"] Companies for the disgraceful injuries done us by the Dutch in the East Indies. The treaty was to be binding for ten years, and on its ratification King James promised not to grant another charter to any person whatsoever during the term of the above treaty. The Dutch, however, continued to carry on their excesses against us just as arrogantly and ruthlessly as before, until at last, on the 17th of February 1622/3, they barbarously massacred the whole establishment of the servants of the English Company at Amboyna.

The Dutch reply (in Latin) to Sir Henry Marten, 1622.

"The Company's answer to the propositions of the "Netherlands East India Company, which they desire to "be inserted into the rule and order for reglement of both "Companies," 1622.

"The present state of the business between the "English and Dutch Companies," 1622.

"Copy of a letter to the *Maiores*" [Heads] "of "the Dutch Company," [? 1624 or 1625]. Much damaged.

"Letter to the *Mayors* of the Dutch Company," January 24, 1624/25.

"Order of the Dutch Ambassador in a dispute "between the Dutch and English Companies," May 23, 1629.

"Letter of the English Ambassadours to the Prince of "Orange; in the camp at Boxtel," July 17, 1672.

The packet marked "Accounts" contains, among others, the following papers:—

"Abstract of the Stock adventured by the Company "from 1601 to 1619, as well in their Distinct" ["Separate"] "as Joint Voyages." Endorsed in red "Very important." *It is in perfect preservation, and is a most important paper.*

"The profit and loss of the second Joint Stock from its "formation." 1615–39.

"The nature and qualities of several Adventurers "behindhand in their subscriptions to the second Joint "Stock," 1620. Not a name can be read.

"Account of the Subscriptions yet overdue," 1622. A much damaged fragment.

"Note of the Adventurers yet unpaid for the Second Joint Stock," June t, 1624. *All the names can be clearly read*, and the following are noteworthy:—Thomas Erle Arundell [died at Venice 1646], William Aleyn, Anne Archer, Sir George Abercromy, George Duke of Buckingham [*i.e.*, George Villiers,* assassinated by Felton, 23rd August 1628], Francis Benbowe, Theophilus Cope, Sir Lyonell Cranfeild [Lord High Treasurer 1621–24], William Coxe, Sir Edward Cockett, Sir Dudley Diggs [son of the astronomer, Thomas Digges, author of *A Defence of Commerce*, and supporter of the impeachment of Buckingham], Sir Thomas Dale, William Dyke, minister, Lady Lettice Danvers, Sir Clement Edmonds, Sir W. Garway & Co., Sir Edward Harwood, GEORGE HERIOTT [James I.'s "Jingling Geordie"], Sir Laurence Hide, Nicholas Hide, Lodwick Duke of Richmond and Lenox [Lodowick Duke of Lennox, created Earl and afterward (1623) Duke of Richmond by James I.], Sir W. Lovelace, Phillip, Erle Montgomery [Philip Herbert, second son of

---

* When the Company's business was taken over by the Imperial Parliament in 1858, one of the first acts of the new masters of the India House in Leadenhall Street was to make a great sweep out of the old records that from 1726 had been preserved there with scrupulous solicitude. They swept 300 tons of these records out to the Messrs. Spicer, paper makers, to be boiled, bleached, and bashed into low class paper pulp; and from one of the cartloads of them, on their way to the Messrs. Spicer's tanks, a paper was blown off by the wind, and picked up by a passer by, of whom, on my accidentally making his acquaintance some years afterwards, I purchased it for 5*l.* It is addressed, "To my loving friends the Governours and Company of the East India Merchants;" and endorsed, "November 28th, 1619. My "Lord of Buckingham about resigning his interest in my Lord of Warwick's "goods. Recd. Dec. 1, 1619." And it runs:—

"After my heartfelt commendations. Whereas his Majesty by his former letters, about the beginning of the last summer, signified unto you that he was pleased to bestow upon me that part which belonged to him of the forfeiture incurred by the Earl of Warwick [Robert Rich]: Yet since he hath likewise pleased to write also in my Co: of Warwick's behalf, I have thought fit to signify unto you that I do willingly remit to him likewise all my interest and [an *obliteration] that I had therein by his Majesty's said warrant. And so I rest your very loving friend.

[Signed] G. BUCKINGHAM.

"Newmarket, 28 November 1619."

The paper is sealed with the Duke's [Felton's man] own seal, the beautiful impression of which is as fresh as when made on the above November day, just two hundred and seventy years ago. *See* also *The Athenæum* of 22nd February 1873, page 247.

---

* The obliteration here is probably of the word "pretence"; *i.e.* judging from the Court Minutes" of 1st December 1619, recording the receipt of this letter.

Henry Earl of Pembroke, created Earl of Montgomery 1605, succeeded his brother William as Earl of Pembroke 1630, and died 1652],* Sir John North, William Erle Pembroke [brother of aforesaid Philip Herbert Earl of Montgomery], Henry [Wriothesley] Erle Southhampton, Henry Whitaker, John Westley, John Wiseman, Sir Henry Yelverton [Attorney-General 1617–21].

There is also a supplementary *list of names of defaulters* to the Second Joint Stock.

" Abstract of the Estate in the Indies of the 3rd, 5th, " and 11th voyages." *No date, but in good order.*

Under date 1613, I find the, apparently, "Bazaar Account" of someone living at Narsapoor. The form of the pages is that of the bazaar books still used by English housekeepers all over India.

Under May 1632, is, apparently, the Surat Factory cash-keeper's accounts with the Native Broker, Gourdas.

August 27, 1663. "Account of cash and goods deli-" vered to Henry Aldworth for presents and expenses, at " his going to Hugly with the Salt Petre boats."

March 4, 1606/7, a paper headed—

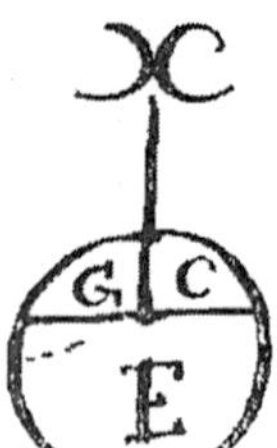

"Laus Deo, in London, the 4th March, " Anno Domini 1606." "Cargazon of the " money and goods laden on the *Dragon*, " *Hector*, and *Consent*, in the third voyage " to Bantam." *A most interesting paper.* It bears the mark here copied by me, which was the "general mark" adopted by the Company 31st Dec. 1600.

Dated 1606. "A cargozon or proportion for a bark of " 44 tons for the parts about Cumina, with [what] money " the commodities will cost, and what is like to make of " them severally, set down in peazes and rials." *Very interesting.*

Dated 1610. "Account of cloth purchased for the " eighth voyage of ships *Thomas*, *Hector*, and *Clove*."

---

* It is to his son, Philip, that Sir Thomas Herbert's *Travels into Divers Parts of Africa and Asia the Great* [1665] are dedicated.

Bantam, 1614/5, January 15. "Cargazon" of "*Purslane*," [Porcelain?] and "*Camboja*" [Gamboge] shipt in the *James* for the eighth voyage.

Patanie, July 25, 1614. Invoice of goods landed from the *James*, ninth voyage.

1622, July. "Contents of a *Chest of Chirurgery*, for "Jaccatra House, laden upon the *Abigail*." *A very interesting list of Materia Medica.*

1630, April 12. Cargazon of *Charles*.

1643/4, March 23. Abstract of goods sent to Mocha "on a Jounk of Suratt."

1647/8, January 6. Invoice of goods laden on the *Antelope* from Surat. It bears the mark here copied.

According to Fryer "the Company's Mark upon all their Goods, Bales, and Parcels," shipped from Surat, "Ahmedavad," "Bombaim," &c., in India, was this, here copied.

1650/1. "Generale carga van de negen Oost Indische "schepen namentlijck," &c., &c.

1656/7, January 20. Swally. Invoice of ship *Benjamin*.* It bears the mark here copied. *A most interesting invoice.*

---

* *See page* 62.

1659, May 6. Account of goods laden at Gambroon on the *Mayflower*, bound for Metchlipatam.

The MAYFLOWER with the English Pilgrim Fathers, from Delft Haven, Southampton, and Plymouth, landed at Plymouth Rock, New England, December 25, 1620. Could it have been the same ship as the Company's *Mayflower*?*

---

* This heedless question, although some good came of it, has been the cause also of considerable confusion, as may be most conveniently shown by reproducing the following extract from a letter addressed by me to the Editor of the *Daily Telegraph* on the 24th October 1889:—

"Sir Edwin Arnold, addressing his distinguished audience [Harvard University], asks, 'Do you know that the *Mayflower*, which brought your ancestors hither, went down in Indian waters off Masulipatam?' The *suggestio falsi* in this interrogation originated in the following manner:—

"In 1878 I reported on the supplementary miscellaneous 'Old Records' of the India Office, and as wherever I put in my thumb I pulled out a plum, instead of contenting myself with a cut-and-dried official description of them, for the mere purposes of classification, I put all the plums I found into my report, which, on account of its consequent interest, was published by Her Majesty's Printers for general circulation. One of the biggest of these plums, as I then thought it, was the following extract from the 'D. P. [Damaged Papers] bundle':—'May 6, 1659. Account of goods laden at 'Gambroon on the *Mayflower*, bound for Metchlipatam (*i.e.* Masulipatam).' On this extract I asked: 'Could this have been the same ship as the Pilgrim 'Fathers' *Mayflower*?' On the report going out to India it was there discovered that a Company's ship of the name of *Mayflower* had, about the same date, foundered in 'the Bay' (*i.e.* of Bengal), and on the supposition, based merely on my question, that the two were identical, numerous newspaper articles appeared connecting the foundered *Mayflower* with the immortal ship of the Pilgrim Fathers. Again, the late Mr. Henry Stevens, of Vermont, of the publishing house of Henry Stevens and Son, London, an enthusiastically patriotic American, became deeply interested in my extract and question about the Company's *Mayflower*, and being convinced that she was the same *Mayflower* as that of the Pilgrim Fathers, determined to publish every document in the India Office naming the sacro-sanct vessel. This resolution led to his publishing, as a commencement, the first volume of the "Court Minutes" of the East India Company, extending over the years 1599 to 1603, simply because a ship called *Mayflower* is constantly referred to in it. By the time that the volume was ready for publication I had begun to have serious misgivings of the identity of any of the *Mayflowers* belonging to the Company with *the Mayflower*, and in the introduction to Mr. Stevens' volume relegated my reference to the subject to a foot-note. Soon after its issue I was satisfied that there was no connection between them; and in reviewing *The Dawn of British Trade to the East Indies*—as Mr. Stevens named his book —in the *Athenæum* for October 15, 1887, I remarked:—'Mr. Stevens was

No date. Abstract of Pinnace *Lannaret*'s cargo for Bussorah.

No date [? 1614]. Invoice of goods laden upon the *Advice* for 'Jappan,' for the first voyage.

Bantam, 1613. Remainder in Bantam on account of the 3rd, 4th, 5th, and 11th voyages. *Unfortunately much damaged, or otherwise would have been invaluable.*

1629, November 20. "Amadavad," "household stuff," remaining in the factory, with their weight, &c.

1629, December 6. An inventory of the "household stuff" at Surat.

The packet marked "Bills of Lading," contains, *inter alia*, the following entries:—

Bantam, 1614/5, January 1. Bill of lading in the *James* for the "*Purslane*" [porcelain ?].

1633/4, March 25. Bill of lading in the *Palsgrave*, from London to Surat. It bears the mark here copied by me.

The packet marked "Policies and Insurance," contains, *inter alia*, the following entries:—Under date February 16, 1656/7, insurance of goods shipped on

---

'allured into his patriotic undertaking by the romantic fancy that the *May-'flower* mentioned in this volume, as one of the ships inspected for the 'Company's "first voyage" to India, was the veritable *Mayflower* that carried 'the Pilgrim Fathers to America. *Mayflower* was a common name for a ship 'in those days, and the one examined for the Company in 1600, and the 'other possessed by the Company in 1659, which is believed to have subse-'quently foundered in the Bay of Bengal, must both have been larger ships 'than the little craft of the Pilgrim Fathers. The *Mayflower* of 1600 must, 'moreover, have ceased to exist in 1620, and that of 1620 long before 1659. 'Only ships built of Indian teak could have kept the sea from 1600 to 1659, 'like those used by the Phœnicians at Tylos, which Theophrastus tells us 'had continued sailing for 300 years." This question has now [1890] been finally set at rest by the discovery of an entry proving that the Company's *Mayflower* was of 280 or 300 tons burthen, whereas the historical *Mayflower* was of only 180 tons.

the *Three Brothers*, homeward bound from Macassar, Bantam, &c.

The packet marked "Customs House List" contains, *inter alia*, the following entry:—

A printed list of goods imported into and exported from London, dated February 5, 1667/8, No. 28, and of goods exported by certificate.

From *Amsterdam* were imported silk, organzine silk, quicksilver, caraway seed, "*Ozenbrigs*," "*Harfords*," madder, safflower, argoll, castoreum, varnish, smallwares, drest bristles.

From *Middleborough*, silks, linseed, clover seed, canary wine.

From *Rotterdam*, nutmegs, mace, silk, hair stuffs, safflower, hemp, madder, "*Tarras*" or "*Tattas*," gally-tiles, snuffers, iron wire, thread.

From *Lubeck* ? "*Hinterlands*" goods are shown to have been imported from Ostend, Flushing, Harlem, Roan [Rouen], Deipe [Dieppe], Nants [Nantz], Civill [Seville], Rochell [Rochelle], Norway, Barbadoes.

The places named to which goods were exported from London are Hambro, Rotterdam, Porto [Oporto], Lisbon, Cadiz, Dunkirk, Amsterdam, Bridges? [Bruges?], Bremen, "Straits" [of Gibraltar], Tangier(s), St. Valery, Bilboa, "Bermoodos" ["the still vexed 'Bermoothes'" of Shakespeare's *Tempest*], "Legorn," Guinea, France, Ostend, Dieppe, "Burdaux," Middleboro', "Roan" [Rouen], Virginia, Barbadoes, New England, Canaries.

The packet marked "Miscellaneous" contains, among other papers, the following:—

1606. *First page of Captn. Keelinge's Journal*, of the "Third Voyage."

1615 or 1615/6. Document endorsed "Contentions about Oxwick in Acheene."

1626, September 8. Letter to Mr. Bagwell in Holland, to buy 2,000*l.* worth of "Rials;" stating also that the goldsmiths had been disappointed in their expectation to enhance the value of British coins by a Proclamation of the King to the contrary.

1631. Acceptance by the Commissioners for repairing St. Paul's *Church*, of Mr. Smethwick's offering.

1643. "A draught of the South Land* lately discovered;" a rough sketch, much damaged, and only kept together by being backed with goldbeater's skin.

1642/3, January 17. Copy of Company's bonds to Sir Peter Ricault, knight.

1653, November 2. Letter from V. Markham, Auditor to the Company, recounting his services.

Paris, 1664, May 26. Printed paper, being the fragment of an address to the French nation in favour of an East India Company [*i.e.*, Colbert's Company]. The articles are complete. This is a very interesting document.

1706, and 1707, and 1708. Order for payment of gratuities to the Governour, Deputy, and Members of Committees.

1720–23. The journal, in French, of the French ship of war, *Le Content*.

No date. Mr. Sambrooke's argument in favour of a Joint Stock.

No date. Abstract of the Earl of Devonshire's estate.

No date [?1637]. Instructions from Charles I. to Nicholas Wilford, sent on a mission to the "Emperor of Persia" to collect antiquities, take drawings of ancient buildings, and to procure information regarding "Madagascar, by reason of its propinquity to Persia."

---

* This must be a draught either of Van Diemen's Land, discovered by Tasman 24th November, 1642, and named by him after Maria Van Diemen, the beautiful daughter of the Dutch Governor of Batavia; or of New Zealand, also discovered by Tasman in 1642. Owing to the prejudice which was found to deter English emigrants, the name of Van Diemen's Land, or *Demon's* Land as they called it, was changed about 40 years ago to Tasmania in honour of its susceptible and romantic discoverer. It was not known to be an island until explored by Flinders, who, with Bass, discovered Bass's Strait in 1799.

No date. Particulars of [? the Company's] charitable gifts in Stepney, Poplar, &c.

No date. Commons' Declaration and Impeachment against the Duke of Buckingham.

No date. Supposed objections in Parliament against the Company answered.

In the packet marked "Commissions" there are, among others, the following papers:—

Circa 1613–14. A book marked "*Downton's Voyage*" [1st Joint Stock], also "instructions in the voyage of the *Hector, New Year's Gift*, &c., 4 shipps."

No date. Copy of King Charles's Commission to Captain Quaile of the *Sea Horse* to capture the ships of Spain in the East Indies.

1640, 24 July. Commission of the King of France to Captain Digard of the *Rose of Diepe*.

London, 1662, July 11. Commission to Captain Egmont of the *George and Martha*.

[? 1671, 20 Sept.] Commission of the Company to the Rear-Admiral of the Fleet bound to Bantam.

In the packet marked "Ships" are, among others, the following papers:—

1613. "Roll of the dead men out of the *Clove, Hector*, and *Thomas*." [Eighth voyage under Saris.] *An interesting list of dead men's names.*

No date. Proceedings to recover gold plundered from the *Morning Star* by an Algerine pirate.

In the packet marked "Minutes" there is, among other papers, the following:—

November 7, 1705. An order, in original, for Blood Money.

In the packet marked "Trade" there are, among others, the following papers:—

Sir J. Sambrooke's Report on the Progress of the East India Trade, begun in 1600.

1620/1, February 22. Account of the bullion and goods exported by the Company since 1600.

These are two important records.

About 1640. Declaration of the grievances which discouraged the East India Company.

1697, August 3. A packet of *patterns from Persia*, received overland, *viâ* Aleppo, of *silks and dyes. Very interesting.*

No date. Papers giving prices of various articles in Persia, Arabia, and India. *Very interesting.*

No date. Barloe's remonstrance against military expenditure on fortifications, &c., and regarding the great profits on inland trade in India.

The packet marked "Diary" contains a diary from Dacca, 1678.

The packet marked "Law" contains, under the date 1621, copy of a bill filed in Chancery against Richard Chamberlyn and others by Benjamin Deicroe, the agent of the Company for discovery of new trades in Russia and Muscovy.

Bundle B.—"Wilks's Collection."

This is a miscellaneous collection of damaged papers, like those already noted, sorted by Mr. Wilks, a clerk in the old Examiner's Office, and put up by him into leather cases.

The leather case marked "Various Dates" contains, among other papers:—

A packet marked "Dutch," being copies of papers from 1672 to 1742, and 1807 to 1819, relating to the Dutch in the East.

Also a list of papers collected by the Committee of Bombay, appointed in 1797 for procuring information for the Company's Historiographer, and received by Mr. Bruce in 1802. The list is copied on *paper of the date of* 1825.

In the leather case marked "Time Charles 1st," are the following papers:—

1st. "Courten's Association," special grant of Charles I.

for settling a trade at Goa and other parts of the East Indies.

2nd. "Extracts of memorable passages encountered by ship *Dragon*, and Captain Weddell's Fleet." [The China Fleet of 1637.]

3rd. Captain Weddell's relation of his China voyage [1637].

4th. "Translate of the Mocha Phirmand, laid before the Committee of Correspondence, Oct. 21, 1789."

In the leather case marked "Bengal Firmands," are the following papers:—

1st. "Translate of Sultan Shauh Shujaes Neshaun [Sultan Shuja, Governour of Bengal, 1639–60] letters patent to the English in India," in Heg. 1066 [A.D. 1655], being the 28th year of the reign of Shah Jehan.

2nd. Account of trade at Balasore, Patna, Maulda, and Metchlipatam, 1670–76.

3rd. "Translate of Ruffee *Chauns* [Rafi Khan], Nabob "of Orissa, his order or grant for confirmation of the "English privileges in said kingdom." In the 13th year of Aurungzebe [A.D. 1671].

4th. "Translate of Nabob Shausteth *Cawne* [Shaista "Khan, Governour of Bengal, 1664–77], Lord of the "Noblemen, his confirmation of the English privileges "in the kingdom of Bengala." In the 15th year of Aurungzebe [A.D. 1673]. This is the Cha-Est-Kan to whom Tavernier sold his great American pearl, the "biggest pearl that was ever carried out of Europe into Asia."

5th. "Translate of a letter from Shausteth *Caukne* "[the same Shaista Khan], Lord of the Noblemen, "*Prefect of Bengala*, in answer to one from Wares Cawne, "Great Chancellor of the Province of Bearra [Behar] "about the English." In the 18th year of Aurungzebe [A.D. 1676].

6th. Complaint, dated Fort St. George, March 10, 1686/7, to the Great Mogol, of hindrances to the Company's trade.

7th. Extract of treaty of peace with Nawab, or Governour [Shaista Khan, 1680–9,] of Bengal, 1687.

8th. Copies of letters, accounts, &c. laid before the Committee of Correspondence, 1790.

List C. Papers [not a Bundle].

A rubbishy Index, indicating nothing.

Bundle D.

Contains, *inter alia*, fragment of the Journal of Peter Williamson Floris, a Dutchman in the Company's Service, for the 7th voyage [*Globe*, Captain Hippon, 1611]. It relates to Masulipatam, "Petapoli," and "Paleakate" [Pulicat].

Cranganore, March 10, 1615/6. The Zamorin's letter to James I. [relating to the treaty obtained by Captain Keelinge, to trade and settle a Factory or House of Trade at Cranganore, and to expel the Portuguese from Cochin]. This is in triplicate.

1625/6, March 1. Papers relating to the first Settlement of Armagaon.

1632, November. "Translate of the 1st *Masulipatam Firman*."

1633/4, February 21. Translation of the *Golconda Firman*.

1633/4, February 26. Translation of the *Matterable Firman*.

Articles of Agreement with the King of Porqua.

1668, September 12. Articles of Agreement with the King of Carwar. In duplicate.

[? 1669.] Project of a Treaty with the Rajah of Canamore for the settlement of a factory at *Biliapatam*.

1699, July 20. General Perwanna [Persian *parwana*, "permission," "pass," "concession,"] by the Nawab of Golconda to the Company.

1711, October 23. Account of our first Settlement at Fort St. George.

1716, November 13. Grant of "Divy Islands."

1750/1, January 1. Agreement with the King of Tanjore.

[Received, 1756, November 9.] "Translate of 12 letters from the Nannah [Nana Farnavis], received from Govin Sewram Punt at Ghereah"; that is, Gheria [*i.e.*, "the Enclosure"], otherwise called Vijayadrug [*i.e.*, "Fort Victory"], the stronghold of the pirate chief Tuloji Angria, captured by the English sea and land forces under Admiral Watson and "Colonel Clive," acting in concert with the Peishwa's ships and troops, 12th April 1756.

1667–1702. A packet of fragments of copies of letters, abstracts, and extracts, of which I can make nothing. *Sivajee* [Sivaji, founder of the Mahratta nationality, 1627–80,] is mentioned.

1670–71. Grants on account of services against *Sivajee*.

1671–81. Extracts, &c. *Sivajee* mentioned.

Finally, a rough memorandum, dated 1817, regarding the posts of *Registrar of Indian Records* and *Historiographer*, —"abolished."

The Factory Diaries and Consultations.

I.—Surat Records [including "Swally," *i.e.*, Suwali, the roadstead north of the mouth of the Tapti].

A. Twenty volumes of "Consultations," from 1631–32 to 1702–4.

Vol. 15, 1679. This is a typical volume, clearly written and in good condition.

At page 5 is a petition to the Right Honble. Thomas Rolt, "Governour of Bombay, *President of India*, *Persia*,

Arabia, &c." Rolt was third Company's Governour of Bombay, 1677–81, in succession to Gerard Aungier, 1669–77, and Sir George Oxenden, 1668–69; and in precession to Sir John Child, 1681–90.

At page 6 is a letter from JOHN FRYER asking to be made surgeon to the Surat Factory.

At page 7, instructions are asked as to how the President and Council at Surat were to comport themselves in the strife between "Sevagee" and the King of "Vizapore" [Bijapur, *i.e.*, Ali Adil Shah, 1656–72, whose chivalrous general, Afzul Khan, was assassinated by Sivaji, on the hill side of Pertabghar, 1659].

At pages 23, 24, 25, lists of commodities.

At page 69, notice of "Sevagee" fortifying "Hendry Kendry," the twin islets, now called Henery [*i.e.*, Vondari, "Mouse-like"] Kenery, [*i.e.*, Khandari, *i.e.*, "Sacred to Khandaroo"], at the entrance of Bombay Harbour, to the southward. It was in 1679 that Sivaji's admiral took possession of Kenery, when, after a vain attempt to dislodge him by the English supported by the Sidi [Saed] of Jinjira, we occupied Henery.

At page 86, details of proceedings with "Sevagee."

Sivaji first looted Surat in 1664, and again in 1669–70. After this the Mahrattas, or "Seevagees," as they are sometimes termed in the India Office records, renewed their raids on it almost every year, down to 1676, when the wall of defence, begun in 1664, was completed, and the city thenceforward rendered safe against these predatory attacks. Streynsham Master took part, under his uncle, Sir George Oxenden, in the defence of the Company's Factory in 1664; and again, in 1670, the new President [in succession to Oxenden, who died at Surat in July 1669], Gerard Aungier, deputed him, with a small party of seamen, from Swally, to occupy the Factory at Surat, which he successfully held against Sivaji. It was for this latter service that Sir Streynsham Master received from the Company in 1672 a gold medal, bearing on one side the arms of Master, and on the other those of the

Company, with the Latin inscription, "PRO MERITIS CONTRA SEVAGEUM APUD SURATT, 1670." *See* Sir Henry Yule, under "Master," pp. 225–6, "*Diary of William Hedges,*" Vol. II.

Vol. 20, 1702–4. A very different volume from the rest in size, but full of the same particulars of the daily routine of the Company's trade at Surat. Under date of January 26, 1702/3, mention is made of "*Olibanum Sahaar.*"

B. Forty-six volumes of letters from Surat, from 1635/6 to 1706/8.

In Vol. 5, 1662, p. 12, is copy of the letter containing the Duke of York's instructions to the Earl of Marlborough* for taking over the Island of Bombay from the Portuguese. At page 40, in a long letter to London, the prices of various commodities, "Allum," "Tynn," "Rough Amber," "Corrall," "Vermillion," are stated.

---

* This was James Ley, third Earl of Marlborough, the eminent mathematician and navigator. He was slain in the great sea fight with the Dutch, June 3, 1665; and his body lies in Westminster Abbey. He had arrived in India on the 18th of September 1662, with a fleet of five ships, to take possession of the Island of Bombay as part of the Infanta Catherina's dower on her marriage with Charles II. The Portuguese in Bombay having refused to give up the Island, Marlborough landed the 500 soldiers with him under Sir Abraham Shipman, on the small Island of Anjeedeva, 12 leagues to the south of Goa, where having left them, he sailed away to England. The consequence was that Sir Abraham Shipman and most of his men miserably perished on this unhealthy spot of exposure during the rains of 1663–4. The 100 survivors formed the cadre of the Honble. Company's 1st European regiment or Bombay Fusileers, afterward the 103rd Foot. The other regiment raised at the same time became known as "Kirke's Lambs," afterward the 2nd or "Queen's" Regiment.

Under date the 15th May 1663, Pepys writes:—"The Portugalls have "choused us, it seems, in the Island of Bombay in the East Indys, for after "a great charge of our fleets being sent thither with full commission from "the King of Portugall to receive it, the Governour by some pretence or "other will not deliver it to Sir Abraham Shipman, sent from the King, nor "to my Lord of Marlborough; which the King takes highly ill, and I fear "our Queen will fare the worse for it." And under date of September 5, he speaks of "the disappointment of the King by the knavery of the Portugall "Viceroy, and the inconsiderableness of the place of Bombaim even if we "had had it."

C. Forty-one volumes of letters to Surat from various sub-factories and other places, from 1628 to 1704–5.

Vol. 3, 1655–56. Letter from Ispahan, giving list of prices there.

Vol, 5, 1659–60. Letters from "Rajapore."

Vol. 6, 1662–63, contains a narrative of the siege and capitulation of Cochin, p. 39; and the articles of agreement with the King of Porqua, p. 87.

The Surat "PROCEEDINGS" extend from 1700 to 1804.

Surat was a Presidency of the East India Company from 1612 to 1678; and again from 1681 to 1685–87, when the Presidency of Western India was finally transferred to Bombay. Between 1629 and 1635 Surat was the chief seat of Government over all the Company's possessions in the East.

Thomas Coryat, the author of "*His Crudities*," died at Surat in December 1617: "killed with kindness," writes Fryer, by the English merchants, "who laid his rambling brains at rest." He was buried on the hill near Swally.

II.—Bombay Records.

A. Seventeen volumes of Diaries and Consultations, from 1669 to 1702–3.

B. Forty-five volumes of letters from Bombay, from 1672 to 1708–10.

C. Forty-two volumes of letters to Bombay, from 1673–74 to 1703–4.

[The Tannah "PROCEEDINGS" extend from 1777 to 1799.]

Bombay was transferred to the East India Company in 1669; and their first Governour was, as above stated, Sir George Oxenden, 1668–9. The previous four Governours of Bombay, appointed by the Crown, were Sir Abraham Shipman, his Secretary, Mr. Humfrey Cooke, who first took possession of the Island in 1665, Sir

Gervase Lucas, who succeeded in 1666, and Captain Henry Garey, who officiated in 1667–8.

III.—Angengo Records.—Two volumes.

Vol. 1, 1717–22. Extract of letters as to the estate of late W. Gyfford.

William Gyfford was Governour of Madras 1681–7, in succession to Streynsham Master, 1678–81 [*see supra*, under "Miscellaneous," Vols. 2 and 3], who had instituted a tax for cleaning the Black Town of Madras and building up a wall for its defence on its north and west sides. When Master left the inhabitants petitioned against it, and "our too easy Agent Gyfford," elsewhere written of as "that heavy President Gyfford," abolished it. The popular memory of the opposition to this imposition, which led to open riot in 1684, is still preserved in Madras in the name of "Wall Tax Street" leading along the remains of the west wall. He was succeeded in the Governorship of Madras by Elihu Yale, 1687–92, who established the Factory at Cuddalore, and became a great benefactor of Yale College, U.S. Gyfford was possibly a descendant of Philip Gyfford, Deputy Governour of Bombay, who died 1676.

Vol. 2, 1727. *A most interesting account of the place, written on thin India paper,* WHICH IS FAST PERISHING. The story of "Gunner Ince's" heroical defence of Angengo,* some time prior to 1717, is worthy of a place beside Clive's defence of Arcot, about 50 years later.

The Angengo "PROCEEDINGS" extend from 1774 to 1804.

The East India Company built a factory and fort at Angengo [Attinga, *i.e.*, *Anju-tenga*, "Five Cocoa-nut Trees"] in 1695, but abandoned it in 1810, when the station was subordinated to their Political Resi-

* Since the publication of the first edition of the Report this has been published in the *Times* of 27th July 1886.

dent at Trevandrum. Angengo was the birth-place of Robert Orme, "the British Thucydides," and "father of Oriental History." He was born here in 1728, and died in England in 1801. It was also the birth-place of Mrs. Daniel Draper, Sterne's [and the Abbé Raynal's] "Eliza"; who died in Bristol 1778, aged 35. "Eliza's Tree" at Masulipatam was swept away by the great cyclone of 1864.*

IV.—Fort St. George [Madras] Records.

A. Twenty-three volumes of Diaries and Consultations, from 1662–63 to 1705.

B. Twenty-six volumes of letters from Fort St. George, from 1661–62 to 1704.

C. Twenty-one volumes of letters to Fort St. George, from 1672–73 to 1703–4. Vol. 13, 1687–88, is missing.

Fort St. George was founded by Francis Day in 1639–40, in subordination to Bantam; and in 1653 was raised to the rank of an independent Presidency.

V.—Fort St. David Records.†

A. Diaries and Consultations, four volumes, namely, for 1696, 1698, 1702, and 1704.

B. Letters from Fort St. David, one volume, namely, for 1692–93.

C. Translates of "Phirmans," dated from 1689 to 1751, in two volumes.

Fort St. David [Cuddalore] was built on a site purchased from the Mahrattas in 1690, and after the capture of Madras, in 1746, became for a time the chief settlement of the East India Company on the Coromandel coast.

VI.—Metchlipatam [Masulipatam] and Madapollam Records.

A. Thirteen volumes of Diaries and Consultations, from 1675 to 1685.

---

* The Abbé Raynal's apostrophe to Eliza Draper in his *History of the Settlement and Trade of the East and West Indies*, begins:—"Anjengo, thou art nothing, but thou hast given birth to Eliza!"; and it goes on in this absurd way for five 8vo. pages, in pica, every paragraph beginning with 'Anjengo,' or 'Eliza.'

† *See* also Cuddalore Records, p. 89.

B. Thirteen volumes of letters from the above Factories, from 1640 to 1686.

C. Eleven volumes of letters to the above Factories, from 1670–71 to 1685.

The Metchlipatam [*i.e.*, Machlipatam, "Fish-town"] or Masulipatam* Factory was founded in 1611 under Captain Anthony Hippon, who commanded the *Globe* in "the Seventh Separate Voyage." The English expelled by the Dutch from the Spice Islands found a refuge here in 1622. The place was taken by the Dutch in 1686, but was re-occupied in 1690 by the English; to whom it was finally assigned after its recapture from the French [by Colonel Forde], in 1766.

VII.—Conimero Records.

Four volumes of Diaries and Consultations, namely, for 1682–83, 1683, 1684, and 1685. One volume of letters from Conimero [also Conimere, Conimeer], 1684, and one volume of letters to Conimero, 1684.

VIII.—Pettipollee Records.

Four volumes of Diaries and Consultations of 1683, 1684, 1685, and 1686–87. Two volumes of letters from Pettipollee, for 1682–84 and 1685, and one volume of letters to Pettipollee, for 1684–85.

---

* There is no certain etymology of the name of Masulipatam, the Μαισωλία of Ptolemy and *Μασαλία* of the *Periplus*; but it is strange that, from the time of the *Periplus*, Masulipatam has been famed for its muslins, and other artistic cotton textures, and that the word muslin is derived from Mosul [*i.e.*, Mausul or Mausil], the Arabic name of the city which occupies part of the site of Nineveh, *i.e.*, "Fish-Town"; and that while on the coasts of Southern India *masoli* and *masuli* mean "fish," and *masola* on the Coromandel Coast means "fishing-boat," *mahsul* in Arabic means "a tax," and *mahsuli* "a revenue station." There used formerly to be an intimate connection between the countries in the Persian Gulf and Masulipatam; and the characteristic fabrics manufactured there are still exported to Persia and Syria.

The Pettipollee [Pettapollee, Pottapolle] factory, established by Captain Hippon and Peter Williamson Floris, is generally identified with Nizampatam, near Ellore, the name being derived from the neighbouring village of Pedapali.

IX.—Cuddalore Records.*

Two volumes of Diaries and Consultations for 1685 and 1686. One volume of letters from, 1684; and two volumes of letters to, namely, for 1684 and 1685.

The East India Company first settled at Cuddalore [Kudalur, "(the town at) the-Junction-of-two-Rivers"] in 1682, erecting Fort St. David for the protection of the place about 1690–1.

X.—Vizagapatam Records.

Three volumes of Diaries and Consultations for 1692–93, 1693–94, and 1694–95.

The Company's Factory at Vizagapatam [Visakhapatam, "the City of Visakha," *i.e.*, Mangala, or Karttikya, the Hindu Mars] was established in 1668; was seized by the Mogols in 1689; and restored to the Company in 1690.

XI.—Coromandel Coast Records.

One volume, being a collection put together in 1788, relative to various Factories, "Tangore," "Armagaon," &c., from 1624 to 1681.

Armagon, or Armeghon, the Company's first Factory on the Coromandel Coast, was built on the site of Chenna Kuppam, near Durgarayapatnam, in the Nellore District of the Madras Presidency, and was named after Arumugam Mudaliar, who greatly aided the Company in settling here in 1625. But the place was not very suitable for trade, and it had to be abandoned in 1638 in favour of Madras.

---

* *See* also Fort St. David Records, p. 87.

XII.—Calcutta [including Chuttanuttee] Records.

A. Eleven volumes of Diaries and Consultations, from 1690 to 1806.

The volume [5th] for 1698–99 entered in the Departmental List, No. 2,397, is missing;* while I have found a volume for 1697–98, not entered in the said Departmental List. In the Consultations Volume for December 1694, reference is made to the wreck of the *Royal James and Mary*, which is thus described in a letter to the Company from Chuttanuttee, dated the 14th of that month (O.C. 5949):—

"*The Royal James and Mary* [James II. and Mary of " Modena] arrived in Balasore Road from the West Coast " in August, with 286 Behar and 415 lbs. of Pepper, and " Redwood 268 candy 16 maunds, which she took in at " Madras; but coming up the river of Hugly on the 24th " of September she fell on a sand on this side Tumbolee " Point, and was unfortunately lost, for she immediately " overset and broke her back, with the loss of four or five " men's lives."

This shipwreck of the *Royal James and Mary* is obviously the origin of the name of the *James and Mary Sandbank*, which has hitherto been supposed, by people in Calcutta, to be an Anglo-Indian corruption of either *jahaz-mara* " [the place where] the ship struck," or *jal-mari*, " dead water."

B. Ten volumes of letters from Calcutta to Chuttanuttee, from 1690 to 1704–5.

C. Eight volumes of letters to Calcutta and Chuttanuttee, from 1677–78 to 1703–4.

In 1686, the English retreating from Hugli established themselves under Job Charnock at Chatanati. The new settlement gradually extended itself to Kalikata [Calcutta] and Govindpur; and from 1689 became the chief seat of the East India Company in Bengal. Fort William was

---

* This volume has since been found.

originally built in 1696; and the three villages of Chatanati, Kalikata, and Govindpur were finally assigned to the Company in 1700. "The 24 Parganas," forming the sub-urban [Calcutta] "District" of the "Presidency Division" of Bengal, were ceded to the Company by Mir Jafir, our puppet Nawab Nazim of Bengal, 20th December 1757.

XIII.—Hughly Records.

A. Four volumes of Diaries and Consultations, namely, for 1676–77 and 1677-78, the volumes for 1678–79 and 1679–80 being missing [in 1878, but since found].

B. Four volumes of letters from Hugly, namely, for 1678–79, 1679–80, and 1680–82, the volume for 1684 being missing [in 1878, but since found].

C. Four volumes of letters to India, namely, for 1678–79, 1679–80, 1682–83, 1683–84.

The East India Company's Factory at Hugli was established in 1640, in order to provide them with a better port for trading with Lower Bengal than Pippli in Orissa, where they had a factory from 1624 to 1642.

XIV.—Cossimbazaar ["Castle Bazaar"] Records.

Eight volumes of Diaries and Consultations from 1676–77 to 1684–85.

The East India Company's first commercial agent at Kasimbazar was appointed in 1658.

XV.—Maulda and Englesvad Records.

Five volumes of Diaries and Consultations from 1680 to 1690–93.

The East India Company had a factory at Maldah as far back as 1686. Angrez-abad, *i.e.*, "English-town," corrupted by us into Englesvad, and "English-bazaar," gradually in the 17th century grew round the English Factory at Maldah, and is now the chief town of the District.

XVI.—Pattana Records.

Four volumes of Diaries and Consultations from 1680–81 to 1683–84.

Patna [*i.e.*, Pattana, "the City"], the ancient Pataliputra, the Palibothra of Megasthenes, was the seat of one of the Company's factories in Bengal so early as 1620.

XVII.—Dacca Records.

One volume of Diaries and Records for 1689–91.

Dacca [Dakha, and so called from the *dakh*, or Butea frondosa, trees of the neighbourhood] was occupied by flourishing Dutch, English, and French factories in the 17th century.

XVIII.—Balasore Records.

Three volumes of Diaries and Consultations for 1679–80, 1680–81, and 1686–87.

The right to establish a factory at Balasore [Bal-Eshwar, "Strength of God"] was granted to the Company in 1642; and in 1645, and 1646, in return, as the story goes, for medical services rendered to the Great Mogul [Shah Jehan, 1627–58], and to his viceroy the Nawab of Bengal [Sultan Shuja, 1639–60], by Surgeon Gabriel B(r)oughton of the Company's ship *Hopewell*, additional privileges were awarded to the Company in respect of their factories at Hugli and Balasore. It was to Balasore that the Pippli factory was transferred in 1642.

XIX.—Records relating to Fort York, Fort Marlborough, Java, Siam, and Macassar.

A. *Fort York.* Four volumes of Diaries and Consultations from 1695 to 1701–3. Three volumes of letters from Fort York for 1685–6, 1701–2, and 1702–3, and one volume of letters to Fort York for 1701–3.

B. *Fort Marlborough*. Instructions relating to ship *Duke*, and diary, 1740–41. [The Fort Marlborough "PROCEEDINGS" extend from 1704 to 1818.]

C. *Java*. Two volumes of letters from Bantam, 1649–50, 1666, and one volume of letters to Bantam, 1659–60.

D. "Three extra volumes."

E. *Siam*. One volume of Diaries and Consultations for 1683.

F. *Macassar*. One volume, 1613–74.

XX.—St. Helena Records.—Four volumes of Consultations, &c.

Vol. 1, 1676.
Vol. 2, 1694–95.
Vol. 3, 1695–96. } Consultations.

An odd volume, dated 1677–1714. Copies of the laws and ordinances of St. Helena. This is one of the most interesting volumes of the Old Records.

The Dutch, who first occupied the Island of St. Helena in 1645, abandoned it in 1651, when it was at once taken possession of by the English. The Dutch expelled us from it in 1673, but we immediately retook it, and in December 1674 it was formally granted by the Crown to the East India Company, by whom it was held until 1834, when the island was re-invested in the Crown.

The St. Helena "PROCEEDINGS" date from 1704 to 1835.*

* I had in 1880 to determine whether there was any documentary evidence in support of a suggestion of Longwood having been conveyed to the Emperor Bonaparte, and the following extracts from the St. Helena Proceedings in the India Office, made by me in the course of my search, are of sufficient interest to warrant my printing them here as a foot-note.

The St. Helena Proceedings kept in the India Office extend, as above shown, from 1704 to 1835,* and therefore cover the whole period of the

* After this was written several additional volumes were found, carrying these "Proceedings" back to 1676.

There are no special separate Factory Records of the

Emperor Bonaparte's captivity, viz., from 1815 to 1821. They fill five long quarto volumes of MS. I looked through all these volumes page by page, and found that, while they contained many interesting allusions and references to Bonaparte, there was not a word in them of any conveyance of Longwood to the Emperor; on the contrary, they afforded presumptive evidence of no such conveyance ever having been made or contemplated. They contain occasional reports on the Company's farms on the island, and in these reports Longwood is also mentioned, showing that to the last it continued to belong to the Company.

I will now detail some of the entries relating to the Emperor which I have noted in the volumes.

A.—*St. Helena Council Volume for* 1815–16.

1. Government Order of 11th September 1815:—

"A royal salute to be fired immediately in honour of the decisive victory obtained by the Duke of Wellington over Bonaparte in person, with the capture of 214 pieces of cannon. A festival for the garrison, with the usual allowance of wine, to be prepared and issued on Thursday.

"(Signed) T. H. BROOKE, Secretary."

2. A Proclamation of 17th October 1815, setting forth that whereas H.R.H. the Prince Regent had been pleased to command that "General Napoleon Bonaparte" should be detained on the Island of St. Helena, and the Hon. Court of Directors have been pleased to issue orders consequent on this determination, the inhabitants of the island are warned from aiding or abetting the escape of the "said General Napoleon Bonaparte, or that of any of the French persons who have arrived here with him"; and are interdicted from "the holding any communication or correspondence with him or them," on pain of expulsion from the island.

3. A Government Order of 17th October 1815, directing, under orders from the Prince Regent, that "General Napoleon Bonaparte" is to be "respected and considered on all occasions as a General." "The respective "officers of this garrison, therefore, whenever the said General Bonaparte "may pass, or they may in any way meet with him, are to turn out guards, "and otherwise show him the same marks of respect precisely as a General "in His Majesty's service [not in chief command] would be entitled to."

4. Under the same date an entry is made to the effect that, Rear-Admiral Sir George Cockburn having signified his wish that the house at Longwood, hitherto the residence of the Lieutenant Governour, should be prepared for the reception of "General Bonaparte,"* it had become necessary that

---

* The Emperor landed on the island 16th October, and slept the night in James' Town. The next morning he rode out to see Longwood, which was to be set in order for

following places, but only "PROCEEDINGS": Tan-

---

another house should be provided for the Lieutenant Governour, "the rent of which together with all expenses" are to be charged to the account of His Majesty's Government, in obedience to the fourth paragraph of the Court's letter of 1st August 1815.

5. Under date of 24th October 1815 is a letter from Mr. Secretary Brooke to Mr. Joseph Luson, Acting Agent of the Hon. East India Company at the Cape of Good Hope, in which, *inter alia*, it is stated that, the arrival at the island of General Napoleon Bonaparte having led to the importation of regular and ample supplies of live stock and other necessaries from the Cape of Good Hope, for the use of the troops and squadron stationed at St. Helena, "it becomes a question . . . whether the services of the St. Helena schooner will be any longer required here."

6. Under date of 30th October a Minute in Council allots compensation to His Excellency Rear-Admiral Sir George Cockburn for his removal from Longwood. This Minute is confirmed by the Council under date of 6th November following.

7. Under date of 9th November is a letter from the St. Helena Council to His Excellency the Earl of Moira, Governor General in Council, Bengal, pointing out how, owing to the residence on the island of "General Napoleon Bonaparte," and the other State prisoners who have followed his fortunes, and the consequent "large augmentation to our garrison besides naval armament," they were suddenly called upon to provide for an increased consumption of food, the supply of which was all the more straitened because of the circumstance of all ships, except those of the King's Government and the East India Company, being prohibited from touching at the island during the detention there of General Bonaparte; and they request, therefore, that their indents on the Government of Bengal for provisions may be punctually complied with.

8. Under date of 14th December is a long Minute by Admiral Cockburn on the privations he had endured through giving up Longwood to Bonaparte. It reads very like the record of an "aboard of ship" quarrel. It is very petty, and possibly throws light on Admiral Cockburn's treatment of Bonaparte while the latter was at the Briars, of which Las Casas complains.

9. Under date of 6th December, Admiral Cockburn transmits for the consideration of the Governor, Mr. Wilkes, "some regulations which I deem "necessary to be forthwith established for the better security of General "Bonaparte and his followers at Longwood." In consequence of the above

---

his reception; but on his way back, having noticed the house called the Briars, and being very loth to return to the rooms which had been assigned as his temporary residence in James' Town, Sir George Cockburn at once allowed him to change his quarters to the Briars. He continued to live there until the 10th December, on which day he removed to Longwood.

jore, 1771–1803; Tellicherry, 1777–93; Patna, 1714–17; and Gombroon, 1708–63.

GEORGE C. M. BIRDWOOD, M.D., LL.D.,
Special Assistant,
Statistics and Commerce Department.

India Office,
1st November 1878,
and
17th November 1889 [date of first reprint],
30th November 1890 [date of second (present) reprint].

---

a Proclamation was issued on the same day giving effect to Admiral Cockburn's regulations.

10. Under date of 11th December is another long letter from Admiral Cockburn, about his Longwood grievances.

B.—*St. Helena Council Volume for* 1816–17.

1. Under date of 30th March 1816 is a Proclamation to the inhabitants of St. Helena, informing them that "a letter addressed to one of the "foreigners detained in the island was some time since received under an "enclosure addressed to an inhabitant," and warning them that any of them who might receive such letters, and did not within twenty-four hours inform Sir George Cockburn, or whoever might be thereafter in custody of General Bonaparte, of the same, would be dealt with according to the spirit of the Proclamation of 17th October 1815, above noted.

2. Under date of 22nd July is a letter from the St. Helena Council to the Earl of Moira, pointing out how the demand for labour had risen in consequence of the island having been adopted as the residence of General Bonaparte, and asking for 350 labourers from China.

3. Under a Resolution of Council of 7th September, Lieut. Nagle is allowed 270*l.* for building his premises at Longwood.

4. Under 30th September is a report on the Company's farms on the island, including Longwood.

5. Under date of 9th December commence the Council's interminable proceedings with their Farm Superintendent, Mr. Breame, for depredations at Longwood, and other misconduct connected with that and the other farms. Mr. Breame was probably the most truculent subordinate the long-suffering East India Company ever had in their service, and the only motive the Council of St. Helena could have had in putting up with him for so many years must have been as a resource against *ennui.*

C.—*St. Helena Council Volume for* 1817–18.

1. Under date of 10th March 1817, a letter from Mr. Secretary T. H. Brooke to Mr. Joseph Luson, Agent to the Hon. E. I. C., Cape of Good

Hope, indenting for articles "for the Governor's use, Regimental Messes, Purveyor to General Bonaparte's Establishment," &c.

2. Under date 17th August W. Balcombe, Purveyor to General Bonaparte, solicits that his disbursements on account of the establishment at Longwood may be met by bills on England instead of by cash payments in dollars. The order on this application is finally confirmed under date of 15th September.

3. Under date of 10th November is a long letter from Mr. Secretary Brooke to Sir Hudson Lowe, the new Governor, about Mr. Breame and Longwood.

4. Under date of 15th December is the "Information of Mr. Bigger" regarding Mr. Breame's misconduct in connection with Longwood farm: "I have known him [Breame] to kill cattle for Longwood establishment, "and fill that establishment at the rate of 1*s*. 6*d*. a pound, and reserve one "third himself and charge it only at a shilling. Some time ago he killed a "veal calf which might have weighed about 50 lbs., or half a hundred, and "sold 35 of it to the Longwood establishment, and the rest he kept "himself."

D.—*St. Helena Council Volume for* 1818–20.

Nothing to note in present connection.

E.—*St. Helena Council Volume for* 1820–21.

1. Under date of 7th December 1820, 125*l*. granted to Mr. Wills, and 100*l*. to Mr. Robinson, as compensation for any diminution in the supply of water on their lands from which they might have suffered since Longwood and Deadwood were drained in the year 1809.

2. *On* 11*th December* 1820 *the storekeeper paid in the sum of* 105*l*. *on account of* 48 *dozen champagne rejected by General Bonaparte.*

3. Under date of 14th May occurs the entry:—"Saturday, the 5th, died General Napoleon Buonaparte." The date in books, by an obvious misprint, is 3rd May.

4. Under date of 11th June the Island of St. Helena is again announced to be opened to all British ships, and those of all nations in amity with Great Britain.

This is all that is said of the passing away of the great Emperor, the greatest military genius that the world has known since Julius Cæsar and Alexander the Great; and the above are, I have little doubt, nearly all th entries relating to Bonaparte and Longwood in these volumes. But the Proceedings all through refer to other correspondence, which probably still exists in the India Office in Departmental compilations of which I am ignorant, and which would probably fill up the gaps in the history of Bonaparte's residence at Longwood as set forth in these volumes of the Proceedings.

There is a great deal of other interesting matter in the volumes. Besides the correspondence with Mr. Breame, there is, under date of the 9th of July 1821, a voluminous indictment of the Chaplain, Mr. Boys, for a sermon he preached at the Plantation House Church on Matthew xxi. 31, "Verily I say "unto you, that the publicans and harlots go into the kingdom of God "before you;" which sermon the Governor in his Minute, which is concurred in by his Council, declares was directed against himself and his colleagues on the Council Board.

Next, under 16th July, Mr. Brooke, now Member of Council, complains of a sermon delivered *extempore* by Mr. Boys the previous evening on the text, in Psalm xviii. 40:—"Thou hast also given me the necks of mine enemies; that I might destroy them that hate me." Mr. Brooke is certain, from the tenor of the sermon, and from Mr. Boys's gesticulations, that it was directed against himself and the rest of the Council.

Under 10th July 1815 is a public notice that *all persons found smoking cheroots in the streets* will be considered as infringing the regulations *prohibiting fire being carried about the streets*, and fined in a sum not exceeding 5*l*.

Most interesting of all is the Proclamation of 24th August 1818, abolishing slavery on the island:—"Whereas by the universal concurrence of the "inhabitants, and slave populations on this Island, it was resolved at a meet-"ing held this day, that from and after the 25th day of December next, "being the anniversary of the birth of our Blessed Saviour Jesus Christ, all "children born of slaves shall be free, ... this is to give notice that the "above is to be considered as a Law of the Island, and that from and after "the 25th of December next, being the anniversary of our Blessed Lord and "Saviour, all children born of slaves on the Island are consequently to be "held free . . . ."

This was done by the Hon. E. I. C. fifteen years before the abolition of slavery in the Crown Colonies [1833]; and it was a very beautiful idea, giving freedom to the new-born slaves as a gift in honour of the anniversary of the birth of Christ, and it is startling to stumble on it among the sordid entries of these sere and dusty quartos. *See* also *The Athenæum* of 23rd July 1881, pp. 113, 114.

II.

SUPPLEMENTARY NOTE.

THE MODERN QUEST AND INVENTION OF THE INDIES.

"Elizabeth, that glorious Star, was glorious beyond any of her predecessors. The Great Council of the Parliament was the nurse of all Her actions; and such an emulation of love was between that Senate and the Queen, as it is questionable which had more affection, the Parliament in observance unto Her, or She in indulgence to the Parliament. And what were the Effects? Her Story told them. Peace and Prosperity at Home, Honour and Reputation Abroad; a Love and Observation in Her Friends, Consternation in Her Enemies, Admiration even in All. The ambitious Pride of Spain was broken by Her Power; the distracted French were united by Her Arts; the distressed Hollanders were supported by Her Succours. Violence and Injury were repelled; Usurpation and Oppression counterwrought; the Weak assisted; the Necessitous relieved; and Men and Money in Divers Parts sent out, as if England had been the magazine of them all. She was most Just and Pious to Her Subjects, insomuch that they, by a free possession of their Liberties, increased in Wealth and Plenty."

Speech of Sir John Eliot, M.P. for St. Germains, 1614, and 1625, 1626, and 1628.

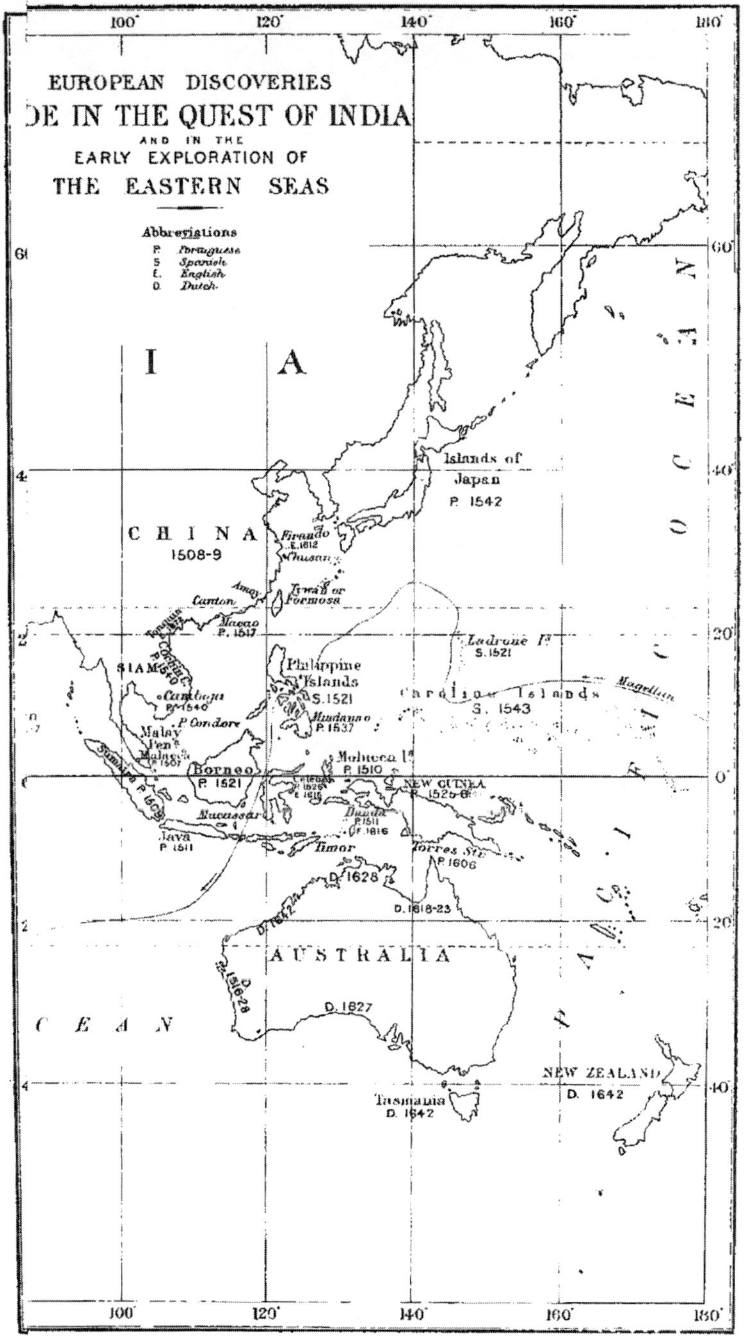

EUROPEAN DISCOVERIES
IN THE QUEST OF INDIA
AND IN THE
EARLY EXPLORATION OF
THE EASTERN SEAS
Abbreviations
P. Portuguese
S. Spanish
E. English
D. Dutch
CHINA
1508-9
Islands of
Japan
P. 1542
Firando
E. 1612
Chusan
Amoy
Canton
Taiwan or
Formosa
Macao
P. 1517
SIAM
Cambogia
P. 1540
P. Condore
Malay
Pen.
Malacca
P. 1507
Philippine
Islands
S. 1521
Mindanao
P. 1537
Ladrone I.
S. 1521
Caroline Islands
S. 1543
Magellan
Molucca I.
P. 1510
Borneo
P. 1521
NEW GUINEA
Macassar
Banda
P. 1511
E. 1616
Java
P. 1511
Timor
Torres Str.
P. 1606
D. 1628
D. 1618-23
AUSTRALIA
D. 1827
Tasmania
D. 1642
NEW ZEALAND
D. 1642

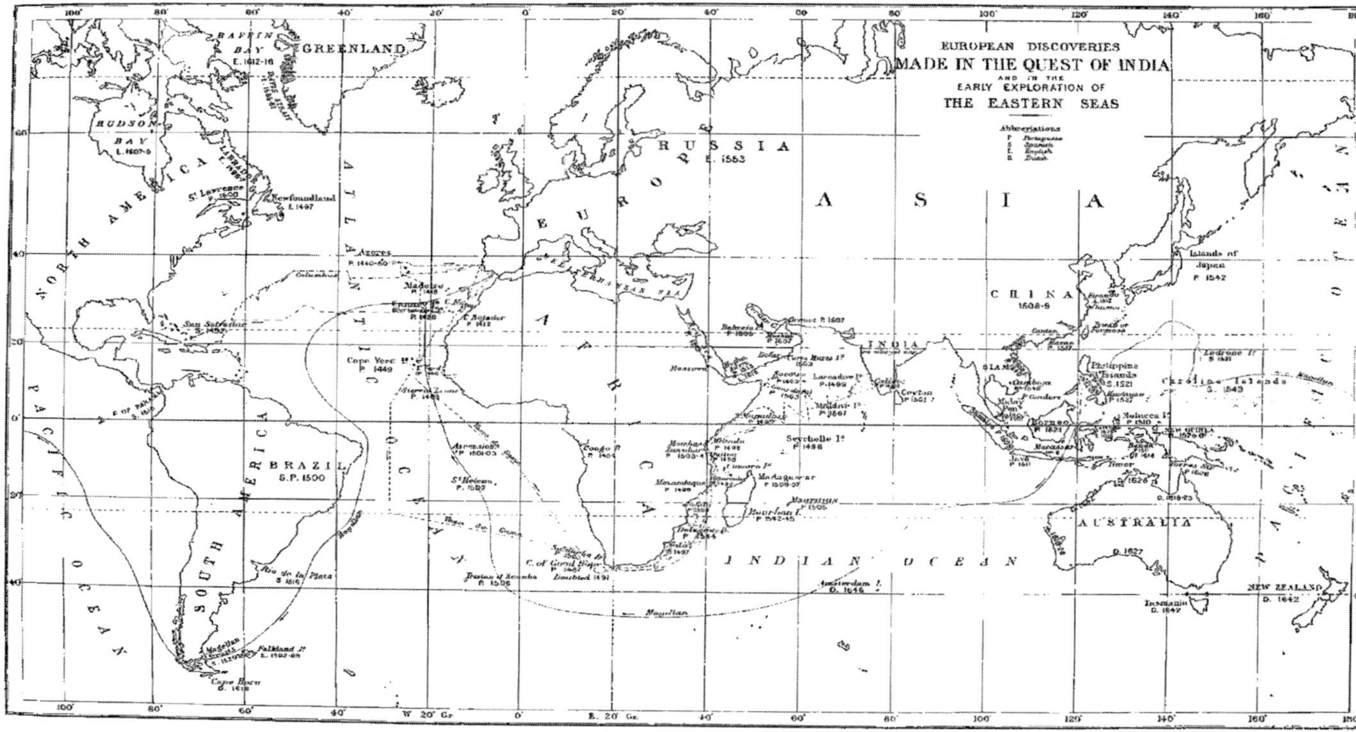

19007 I 253. E & S

Note on the Discovery of India by way of the Cape of Good Hope; and on the early Settlements of the European Nations on the shores and islands of the Indian Seas.

Introduction.

The better to understand the interest and value of the Documents described in the foregoing Report, I found it desirable to examine all the works of travel and history, and of poetry and general literature, of the hundred years—which may be designated the Factory Period—covered by them. The present Note is the result of this special collation.

The title given to it—"The Modern Quest and Invention of the Indies"—indicates the conclusion to which my reading has led me, that the history of modern Europe, and emphatically of England, is the history of the quest of the aromatic gum resins and balsams, and condiments and spices, of India, Further India, and the Indian Archipelago.*

* The following letter from the late Professor W. Stanley Jevons, showing the connection between sun spots, the natural productiveness of "the Indies," and the manufacturing prosperity of Europe, was published in the *Times* of 19th April 1879:—

"Sir,

"Some months since you did me the favour to insert a letter on the subject of commercial crises, in which I endeavoured to answer objections against the notion that the activity of commerce in England ultimately depends upon the solar activity. Public men ask again and again what is the cause of the recent, and it may perhaps still be said the present, depressed state of trade. Yet the only answer which refers this state of things to a definite cause is treated with ridicule. I am repeatedly told that they who venture to connect commercial crises with the spots on the sun are supposed to be jesting.

First I pass in review the "Old Travellers," from after Cosmas Indicopleustes to the date of the discovery of the sea way to India by Vasco Da Gama; and then I treat of the Portuguese Asiatic Empire; and the

---

"So far as I am concerned in the matter, I beg leave to affirm that I never was more in earnest, and that after some further careful inquiry I am perfectly convinced that these decennial crises do depend upon meteorological variations of like period, which again depend, in all probability, upon cosmical variations, of which we have evidence in the frequency of sun spots, auroras, and magnetic perturbations. I believe that I have, in fact, found the missing link required to complete the first outline of the evidence. About ten years ago it was carefully explained by Mr. J. C. Ollerenshaw, in a communication to the Manchester Statistical Society (*Transactions*, 1869–70, p. 109), that the secret of good trade in Lancashire is the low price of rice and other grain in India. Here again some may jest at the folly of those who theorize about such incongruous things as the cotton gins of Manchester and the paddy fields of Hindostan. But to those who look a little below the surface the connection is obvious. Cheapness of food leaves the poor Hindoo ryot a small margin of earnings, which he can spend on new clothes, and a small margin, multiplied by the vast population of British India, not to mention China, produces a marked change in the demand for Lancashire goods. Now, it has been lately argued by Mr. Hunter, the Government statist of India, that the famines of India do recur at intervals of about ten or eleven years. The idea of the periodicity of Indian famines is far from being a new one: it is distinctly discussed in various previous publications, as, for instance, *The Companion to the British Almanack* for 1857, p. 76. The principal scarcities in the North-Western and Upper Provinces of Bengal are here assigned to the years 1782–83, 1792–93, 1802–3, 1812–13, 1819–20, 1826, 1832–33. Here we notice periodicity up to 1812–13, which, after being broken for a time, seems to recur in 1832–33.

"Partly through the kind assistance of Mr. Garnett, of the British Museum, I have now succeeded in finding the data so much wanted to confirm these views, namely, a long series of prices of grain in Bengal (Delhi).

"These data are found in a publication so accessible as the *Journal of the London Statistical Society* for 1843, Vol. 6, pp. 246–48, where is printed a very brief but important paper by the Rev. Robert Everest, Chaplain to the East India Company, 'On the Famines that have devastated India, and on the probability of their being periodical.' Here we have a list of prices of wheat at Delhi for 73 years, ending with 1835, stating in terms of the numbers of seers of wheat—a seer is equal to about 2 lb. avoirdupois—to be purchased with one rupee. As this mode of quotation is confusing, I have calculated

Dutch Indies; and finally of the English in the East, under the two heads of their widespread mercantile

---

the prices in rupees per 1,000 seers of wheat, and have thus obtained the following remarkable table :—

"*Price of Wheat at Delhi.*

Year	Price	Year	Price
"1763	50 M. C.	1800	22
1764	35	1801	23
1765	27	1802	25
1766	23	1803	65 M.
1767	23	1804	48 C.
1768	21	1805	33
1769	24	1806	31
1770	28	1807	28
1771	33	1808	36
1772	38 C.	1809	40
1773	100 M. C.	1810	25 C.
1774	53	1811	28
1775	40	1812	44
1776	25	1813	43
1777	17	1814	30
1778	25	1815	24
1779	33	1816	28
1780	45	1817	41
1781	55	1818	38
1782	91	1819	42
1783	167 M. C.	1820	46
1784	40	1821	38
1785	25	1822	35
1786	23	1823	33
1787	22	1824	39
1788	23	1825	39 C.
1789	24	1826	48 M. C.
1790	26	1827	30
1791	33	1828	22
1792	81 M.	1829	21
1793	54 C.	1830	21
1794	32	1831	26
1795	14	1832	22
1796	14	1833	33
1797	15	1834	40 M.
1798	8	1835	25
1799	17	1836	— C.

"The letter M indicates the maxima attained by the price, and we see that up to 1803, at least, the maxima occur with great regularity at intervals

settlements or Factories, and the British Conquest of India.

---

of ten years. Referring to Mr. Macleod's *Dictionary of Political Economy*, pp. 627, 628, we learn that commercial crises occurred in the years 1763, 1772–73, 1783, and 1793, in almost perfect coincidence with scarcity at Delhi. M. Clément Juglar, in his *History of Commercial Crises*, also assigns one to the year 1804. After this date the variation of prices becomes for a time much less marked and regular, and there also occurs a serious crisis about the year 1810, which appears to be exceptional; but in 1825 and 1836 the decennial periodicity again manifests itself, both in the prices of wheat at Delhi and in the state of English trade. The years of crisis are marked with the letter C.

"Taking this table in connection with a mass of considerations, of which I have given a mere outline at the last meeting of the British Association (see *Journal of the Statistical and Social Inquiry Society of Ireland*, August 1878, pp. 334–342; *Nature*, 14th November 1878, Vol. XIX., pp. 33–37), I hold it to be established with a high degree of probability that the recurrence of manias and crises among the principal trading nations depends upon commerce with the East. This conclusion is confirmed by the fact that these fluctuations are but slightly felt by the non-trading nations, and that what these nations do feel is easily accounted for as an indirect effect.

"It has been objected by the *Economist* that this explanation cannot be applied to the earlier crises in the years 1711, 1721, and 1732, because trade with India was then of insignificant dimensions. But the reading of many old books and tracts of the 17th and 18th centuries has convinced me that trade with India was always looked upon as of the highest importance. A large part of the political literature of the time was devoted to the subject, and under the Mercantile Theory the financial system of the country was framed mainly with an eye to Indian trade. The published returns of exports and imports probably give us little idea of the real amount of trade, as smuggling was very common in those days, and much of the Indian trade went on secretly in private ships, or indirectly through Holland.

"Dr. George Birdwood has lately been studying the records of the India Office, and he gives as the result of his extensive reading 'that the history 'of modern Europe, and emphatically of England, has been the quest 'of the aromatic gum resins and balsams, and condiments and spices, of India 'and the Indian Archipelago.' (*Journal of the Society of Arts*, 7th February 1879, Vol. XXVII., p. 192.) This closely corresponds with the view which I have been gradually led to adopt of the cause of decennial crises.

"Let it be remembered, too, that, because the impulse comes from India, it does not follow that the extent of the commercial mania or crisis here is bounded by the variation of the Indian trade. The impulse from abroad is like the match which fires the inflammable spirits of the speculative classes. The

I give all the "Old Travellers'" routes: and identify the places, and Eastern products, they name; in this, as regards the former, nearly always following the late Sir Henry Yule: and I have added any remarks made by them on the routes of mediæval commerce, and its emporia, in the Indian Seas.

The "Old Travellers."

The earliest trade between Europe and Asia was the overland trade carried on by the Phœnicians along the caravan road by which they are supposed to have originally emigrated, between B.C. 3000 and 2500, from the shores of the Persian Gulf to the narrow Mediterranean coast of Syria. By it also the Eastern arts of pottery, ivory turning, glass making, enamelling, and wood carving were at last carried into the remotest recesses of Germany and Scandinavia, and profoundly influenced the primitive civilizations of those countries. The appearance among the prehistoric remains of Switzerland and Denmark of arms and implements of bronze, in succession to spear and arrow heads of flint, generally affirmed to be due to the displacement of the primeval savage tribes of the West by the immigration of new races of a higher civilization from the East, probably rather marks the age of the earliest Phœnician

---

history of many bubbles shows that there is no proportion between the stimulating cause and the height of folly to which the inflation of credit and prices may be carried. A mania is, in short, a kind of explosion of commercial folly, followed by the natural collapse. The difficulty is to explain why this collapse so often comes at intervals of ten or eleven years, and I feel sure the explanation will be found in the cessation of demand from India and China, occasioned by the failure of harvests there, ultimately due to changes of solar activity. Certainly, the events of the last few years, as too well known to many sufferers, entirely coincide with this view, which is, nevertheless, made the subject of inconsiderate ridicule.

"I am, &c.,

"W. Stanley Jevons."

intercourse with Europe; and when gradually the trade between the East and West took to the routes by the Persian Gulf and the Red Sea, it still remained in the hands of the Phœnicians; and it continued in their hands,* and those of their natural successors, the Arabs, who had shared it with them in the Eastern seas from the first dawn of history, to the discovery, by the Portuguese, A.D. 1487–98, of the open passage to India, round the Cape of Good Hope. The adoption by nearly every civilised nation of the ancient world of the alphabet invented by the Phœnicians is the simplest, most striking, and surest proof of the wide extent and deep abiding influence of their vast and marvellous commerce.

It was not, however, until the date of the Macedonian invasion, B.C. 327, that the people of the West acquired any real knowledge of India. Alexander's expedition and the embassies of Seleucus and the Ptolemies carried our knowledge of that country from Afghanistan and Baluchistan to the delta of the Indus and the lower plains of the Ganges. The *Periplus of the Erythrean Sea* [*circa* A.D. 200; A.D. 80–90 according to C. Müller] extended it to all the ports of Guzerat and Malabar, and beyond them to Masulipatam on the Coromandel coast, and to "the Gangetic Mart" [? Chittagong] at the head of "the great bay" of Bengal. Ptolemy's *Tables* [*circa* A.D. 150] show an acquaintance, derived apparently from the journals of trading vessels, with the whole series of ports on both sides of the Bay of Bengal; though on the East side, and onward to the country of the Sinæ, representing probably a port in Tonquin then subject to China,

* The sea fight off Actium, B.C. 31, may be arbitrarily fixed as the term of Phœnician commerce in the Mediterranean; but it really went on in other hands, until it was again taken up by the Saracens, even as it had survived in full vigour the alleged destruction of Tyre, B.C. 586 and 332, and of Carthage, B.C. 146.

the knowledge is looser, and perplexed by false theories of the Indian Ocean as a closed basin. [*See* Sir Henry Yule, in Dr. William Smith's *Ancient Atlas*, p. 24.] Cosmas Indicopleustes,* who traded in the Red Sea *circa* A.D. 535–50, gives a very clear account of the commerce between India and Egypt in his day. He says that the produce of Kalliana [Callian, represented in mediæval times by Tannah, and in modern by Bombay] was brass [vessels], "sesamine" [*sisoo*, Dalbergia *sps.*] logs, and cotton stuffs; of Sindus, castorin or musk, and spikenard; of Male [Malabar] pepper; and that from Tzinitza [China], and the other countries beyond 'Sielediba,' or 'Taprobane' [Ceylon], came silk, lign-aloes, cloves, nutmegs, and sandal-wood.

The next notices of India are by THE ARABS. The voyages of SINDBAD THE SAILOR, in the "*Thousand and one Nights*," belong to the ninth century, when the commerce of the Arabs under the Caliphs of Baghdad was at its highest activity. In his first voyage Sindbad reaches "the country of the Maharajah," a title given so far back as the second century to a Hindu king whose vast monarchy is said to have comprised the greater part of India, Further India, and Sumatra and Java in the Indian Archipelago; and whose title continued to be borne afterwards by one of the sovereigns of the disintegrated empire, who reigned over the Kingdom of Bijanagar or Vijanagar, known later as "the Kingdom of Narsinga." In Sindbad's second voyage mention is made of the kingdom of 'Riha' [the Malay Peninsula according to some], and the manner of the preparation of camphor, produced in the mountain forests there, is accurately described. In the third voyage the island of 'Selaheth' [Malacca] is mentioned. In the fourth he was carried to a country [Malabar], where he found men gathering pepper; and

* Orosius [*circa* A.D. 400], in what he says of India, but vaguely follows Ptolemy.

from it he went to the island of 'Nacous' [the Nicobars], and on to 'Kela' [Quedah or Keddah]. In the fifth voyage he is shipwrecked on the "island" [*i.e.* country] of the "Old Man of the Sea," probably somewhere on the Concan coast. Thence he crossed the sea to the Maldives, and back again to the pepper country of Malabar, passing on to the peninsula of Comorin, where he found the "aloes wood" called *santy* [? Sanfi, (*i.e.*, of "Sanf" or Maha Champa, S.E. Cochin China,) sandal-wood]; and afterwards to the pearl fisheries of the Gulf of Manaar, whence he travelled back to Baghdad. In the sixth voyage he visited an "island" [*i.e.* country], where were superb "aloes" trees, of the kinds named *santy* [? sandal-wood] and *comary* [? Kumari, *i.e.* of 'Kumar' or Camboja]; and the island of 'Serendib' [Ceylon], the limit also of his seventh and last voyage.

The Abbé Renaudot in his "*Anciennes Rélations des Indes et de la Chine*" [Paris, 1718] gives the notes of travel of two Arab merchants, who apparently visited India and China in the ninth and tenth centuries, and are the first among Western writers to make mention of tea [*tcha*] and porcelain. They also mention arrack and rice. Suleiman, the author of the first part of the "*Rélations*," was a merchant of Bussorah [founded by the Caliph Omar, A.D. 635, purposely to encourage the Indian trade by the Persian Gulf], about A.D. 851. Sir Henry Yule, in the preliminary essay to his "*Cathay, and the Way Thither*," published by the Hakluyt Society in 1866, says that he gives a tolerably coherent account of the seas and places between Oman and China; the 'Sea of Persia,' the 'Sea of Lar' [which washes Guzerat and Malabar], the 'Sea of Harkand' [from the 'Dibajat' or Maldives, and 'Serendib' or Ceylon, to 'Al Ramni' or Sumatra]; the Lankhabalus or Nicobar Islands, and the 'two [Andaman] Islands' in the 'Sea of Andaman,' and of 'Kalahbar,' a dependency of 'Zabaj' [Java], 'Tayumah' [Tiyomen Island]; 'Kadranj' [Siam]; Sanf [Champa and Camboja]; and 'Sandar Fulat' [Pulo Condore]. The port in China frequented by the Arabs was 'Khanfu' [the port of 'Kinsay' or Hangcheu]. ABU ZAID, of Siraf, on the Persian Gulf, the author of the second part of the "*Rélations*," wrote in 916, and he begins by remarking the great change in the commerce of the East that had taken place in the interval since Suleiman wrote. A rebellion had broken out in 'Khanfu,' which had utterly stopped the Arab trade with China, and carried ruin to many families in distant Siraf and Oman. He gives also an account of a visit an acquaintance of his had made to "Khumdan" [Changgan or Singanfu], the capital of China.

IBN-KHURDADBAH, who flourished about A.D. 869–885, is the first who makes mention of galangal and kamala [*Rottlera tinctoria*], and he also mentions porcelain, sugar-cane, pepper, aloes-wood, cassia, silk, and musk.

MASUDI of Baghdad [A.D. 890–956], who visited India and China about A.D. 916, mentions nutmegs, cloves, cubebs, camphor, areca nuts, sandal wood, and aloes wood, as productions of the Indian Archipelago.

EDRISI of Sicily [A.D. 1099–1186] also mentions porcelain, and the fine cotton fabrics of Coromandel, the pepper and cardamoms of Malabar, the camphor of Sumatra, nutmegs, the lemons of 'Mansura' [near the old course of the Indus, N.E. of Hyderabad] on the 'Mehran' [Indus], the assafœtida of Afghanistan, and cubebs as an import of Aden. He names the Concans as the country of 'Saj," *i.e.*, of the *sag* or teak tree.

The Jewish traveller, the Rabbi BENJAMIN of Tudela, who travelled in the East between 1159 and 1173, when already the Empire of the Abbaside Caliphs was rapidly declining, and the Turks were gaining the ascendancy at Baghdad, would appear not to have proceeded beyond the island of Kish [not to be confounded with Kishm], which for a long time was the real terminus of Indian trade through the Persian Gulf. All he relates of India and China is, according to Sir Henry Yule, mere hearsay. Kish he describes as the great emporium "to which "Indian merchants bring their commodities, and the "traders of Mesopotamia, Yemen, and Persia all sorts "of silk and purple cloths, flax, cotton, hemp, *mash* "[*Phascolus radiatus*], wheat, barley, millet, rye, and "all sorts of comestibles and pulse, which articles form "objects of exchange. Those from India export great "quantities of spices." He refers to the pearls of the Bahrein Islands, and to the pepper, cinnamon, ginger, "and many other kinds of spices" produced in Southern India. The island of 'Khandy,' by which he is supposed to mean Ceylon, he places at 22 days distance from Kish, and China 40 days beyond 'Khandy.'

IBN BATUTA of Tangiers [*b.* 1304, *d.* 1377–78,] was the greatest traveller of all the Arab nation. He spent 24 years [from 1325 to 1349] in travelling throughout the East, from Tangiers across Africa to Alexandria, and in Palestine, Syria, and Arabia; down the east coast of Africa to Quiloa; across the Indian Ocean to Muscat, Ormuz, Kish, Bahrein, and El Catif; through Central Arabia to Mecca and Jiddah; and again in Egypt and Asia Minor, and across the Black Sea to Caffa or Theodosia, and by Azov or Tana, "on past the hills of the Russians," to Bolghar on the Volga; but not daring to penetrate further northwards into "the Land of Darkness." Returning south to Haj-Tarkan [Astrakhan], he proceeded, in the suite of the wife of the Khan of Kipchak, the daughter of the Greek Emperor Andronicus, westward to Soldaia [in the Crimea] and 'Costantiniah' [Constantinople — he mentions '*Istambul*' as a *part* of the city —]; whence, returning to Bolghar, he travelled on eastward to Bokhara, and through Khorassan, to Cabul, Multan, and Delhi, where he remained eight years, 1334–42. Being sent by the Sultan Mahommed Tughlak on an embassy to China, he embarked from 'Kinbaiat' [Cambay], and after many adventures at Calicut [where he was honourably received by the '*Samari*,' or Zamorin], and 'Hunawar' [Onore], and in the Maldive islands, and Ceylon, and Bengal, he at last took his passage toward China in a junk bound for 'Java,' as he calls it, but in fact Sumatra. Returning from China, he sailed direct from the Coast of Malabar to Muscat and Ormuz; and travelling by Shiraz, Ispahan, Bussorah, Baghdad, Tadmor, Damascus, Aleppo, Jerusalem, and [for the fourth time] Mecca, Egypt, and Tunis, at last reached Fez again, after an absence from Marocco of half his lifetime. Subsequently he spent six years in visiting Spain and Central Africa, where he was the guest of the brother of a countryman of his own from Ceuta whose guest he had been in China. "What an enormous distance lay between these two!" he exclaims. Such a fact well illustrates the extended ramifications of the Arabian commerce between the East and the West before it was subverted by the rise of the dominion of the Ottoman Turks, and the maritime discoveries of the Portuguese. Notwithstanding the great interest and importance of the travels of Ibn Batuta, they failed altogether in attracting attention and influencing the desire, that soon afterwards began to agitate the Genoese, to trade direct with India. The first detailed account of them was only published in Europe in 1808. He says that in his time Cairo was the greatest city in the world 'out of China,' and that the finest trading ports he had seen were Alexandria in Egypt, Soldaia or 'Sudak' in the Crimea, 'Koulam' [Quilon] and Calicut in India, and 'Zaitun' [Chincheu] in China. He also describes Aden as a place of great trade, to which merchant-ships of large burden resorted from Cambay, Tannah, and all the ports of Guzerat and Malabar. Among the productions of the Indian Archipelago he describes gum benjamin, aloes wood, cloves, camphor, and sandal wood, and enumerates also cocoa-nut palms, areca-nut palms, jack trees, orange trees, mangos, and *jamums* [Eugenia Jambolana]. Porcelain, he says, is made in China nowhere except in the cities of 'Zaitun' and 'Sinkalan' [Canton]. It is exported to India, and elsewhere, passing from country to country until it reaches Marocco.

ABULFEDA of Damascus [1273–1331], the celebrated Arabian geographer, also makes mention of the abundance of pepper grown in Malabar, and the fine cotton manufactures of Coromandel. He divides Hindustan into *al Sind*, the country of the Indus, and *al Hind*, the country of the Ganges. North of India, beyond the Himalaya, the Arab geographers knew, under the name of Mawaralnahar [*i.e.*, *mawar-al-nahar*, "beyond the river"], the vast plains extending westward from the Pamir Steppe, watered by the Oxus and Jaxartes, shown on maps of ancient classical geography as *Scythia intra Imaum*, and designated by modern geographers Transoxiana. Abulfeda describes the plain of Samarcand "as the most delightful of all places which God has made." Beyond this region, Asia [*Scythia extra Imaum*] was occupied by his so-called Turks, a name used by Arab geographers in as diffuse a sense as that of Scythians by the ancients, and of Tartars by ourselves, and applied by them to the same Turanian hordes, included in the Hebrew Scriptures under the names of Gog and Magog, whose secular irruptions into the south lands of Asia, and sometimes into Egypt, constantly, from the earliest ages, interrupted the westward extension of Aryan civilization. In the national legends of Persia, the Oxus is fixed as the everlasting boundary between the Aryan and Turanian races; but, in fact, the result of their immemorial struggle for the possession of the maritime table land of Iran has been to leave the Turanian race predominant over all the wide regions between the Indus and Oxus, and from the steppes of the Caspian Sea to the shores of the Mediterranean and Persian Gulf; while, under the Mo(n)gol Emperors of Delhi, their political supremacy was extended south-eastward beyond the

Nerbudda and the Kistna. The fancy of the Arabian writers transformed the Gog and Magog of Ezekiel into two enormous giants, *Yajuj* and *Majuj*, who are said to have been shut up by Alexander within a stupendous castle at the extremity of Asia. Its walls, formed of iron and brass, and towering to the sky, are evidently the Altai Mountains, out of which hordes of barbarians had so often issued to devastate the world. Other traditions of these destructive irruptions were probably the origin also of the mediæval legends of the unclean "Shut-up Nations."

PARENTHESIS ON THE COMMERCE OF THE SARACENS, AND OF GENOA, VENICE, AND FLORENCE WITH THE EAST. — After the overthrow of the Western Empire by Odoacer, A.D. 476, and during the struggles between the Eastern Empire and the Persians and Saracens, the overland trade with the East languished until the consolidation of the Saracenic power at Damascus, Cairo, and Baghdad. But the trade by the Persian Gulf was again thrown into disorder from the time, A.D. 866, of the ascendency of the Turkish Guard at Baghdad. The Seljukian Turks under Togrel Beg conquered Persia A.D. 1042. The Tartars under Hulaku Khan, a grandson of the famous Chingiz Khan [*b.* A.D. 1163, *d.* A.D. 1227], took Baghdad, and overthrew the Eastern Caliphate A.D. 1258. Palestine was conquered by the Fatimite Caliphs of Egypt A.D. 969; and in consequence of the persecution of the Christians by Hakem between A.D. 996 and A.D. 1021, Peter the Hermit began preaching the first Crusade against the Saracens in 1094. The eighth and last Crusade of St. Louis was concluded in 1272. It was during these times that *VENICE*, which was founded, about A.D. 452, by the last fugitives from the vengeance of Attila the Hun, established commercial relations with Alexandria and Constantinople. So early as A.D. 555, Venice had imported silks from the East, and from A.D. 802 dates her great trade in Eastern spices, drugs, and silks. *GENOA* had entered into the trade of the Levant even before Venice; and having, in the contests between the Greeks and Latins at Constantinople, contrary to Venice, sided with the Greek Emperors, obtained from them Pera and Smyrna, and Theodosia or Kaffa in the Crimea, and Tana or Azov [the ancient Tanais] at the mouth of the Don, as the emporia of its trade with India and the East by Persia and the ports of the Black Sea. About A.D. 1306–15 Genoa established a regular trade with Trebizond, and at one time possessed also Marseilles, Corsica, and Elba; but was always successfully kept by Venice from establishing commercial relations with Alexandria for the Indian trade by Aden. It was during the suicidal competition between Venice and Genoa that *FLORENCE*, under the wise administration of Cosmo de Medicis, obtained so splendid a participation in the Mediterranean traffic with the East. The list of goods sold at Pera, given in the "*Libro di Divisamenti di Paesi*" [known also under the name of "*Pratica della Mercatura*"], written about 1340 by Francesco Pegolotti, a factor in the service of the Bardi of Florence, is the most detailed account we possess of the Oriental trade of Constantinople in the fourteenth century. Both Genoa and Venice derived great wealth and power from their co-operation in the Crusades, and both suffered immensely from the capture of Constantinople by the Ottoman Turks A.D. 1453, and Venice yet further in consequence of the annexation of Syria and Egypt to the Ottoman Empire by Selim, A.D. 1516–17. It was in the interval between the fall of Constantinople and the Turkish conquest of Egypt that, in consequence of the ports of the Black Sea being closed to the Genoese, the Indian trade by the Red Sea, centred in Alexandria, which had been encouraged by every means under the strong government of Saladin [1173–1193] and his successors, now reached in the hands of the Venetians its greatest development in mediæval times. When

Venice, A.D. 1475–87, acquired possession of Cyprus, Famagusta, in succession to Alexandria, became the emporium of its overland trade with the East, both through Egypt and Syria, and continued to be the first commercial city of the Levant until taken by the Turks A.D. 1570–71.

*PARENTHESIS ON THE HANSEATIC LEAGUE.**—The Hanseatic League is generally dated from A.D. 1240–41, when Hamburg joined it; but an earlier confederacy existed among the once pagan cities of East Germany, Bardewic, Julin, Staden, Winet, and others, whose very names have now almost disappeared from history, and continued down to Christian times the yet more ancient Phœnician trade, by which the yellow amber of the Baltic shores was carried by caravans across Europe to the mouths of the Po, and articles of Asiatic, and later of Etruscan and Greek art, were distributed throughout Germany and Scandinavia to "utmost Thule." In the time of the Goths and Vandals, Winet [cf. Venice] became the universal mart of Eastern Europe, and of the Asiatic trade through Russia; and when finally destroyed, with Julin, by the Danes, about A.D. 1169, its pagan merchants withdrew to the new Christian cities founded on or near the shores of the Baltic during the twelfth century; and thus began that commercial association of these cities, under the headship of Lubeck, afterward developed into the Hanseatic League; the first object of which was to protect the confederated cities from the pirates of the Baltic Sea. The word "Hansa"

* Miss Helen Zimmern, the accomplished authoress of *Heroic Tales from Ferdousi*, has recently [1889] published in Mr. Fisher Unwin's "Stories of the Nations" series, a careful and interesting volume on *The Hansa Towns*, and I only regret that it was not in existence when, in 1879, I wrote the above paragraph on the League; but I leave it as then written, contenting myself with directing any readers who may be interested in the subject to Miss Zimmern's admirable monograph.

simply means a "Society," "Company," "Association," or "Corporation." Copenhagen* [*i.e.*, copeman's or chapman's, commercial, cheaping, chipping, or chaffering haven (cf. Copemanthorpe, Chippenham, Chipping Norton, Chipping Camden)] was founded A.D. 1157, and always proved a powerful competitor with the Hanse towns 'of the opposite Pomeranian coast' for the commerce of the Baltic; and when Winet was destroyed, the Swedes of the island of Gothland are said to have carried away any of its ruins, in iron, brass, and marble, that were curiously carved and wrought, and its great bronze gates, and to have used them in the architectural decoration of the town of Wisby, which also in the twelfth and thirteenth centuries became a great entrepôt of the commerce, through Russia, between the East and West. Consul Perry, in his highly interesting "*Report on the Trade and Commerce of the Island of Gothland,*" dated December 10, 1873, writes: "As far back as the eleventh century, "Gothland's commerce with the East by way of Nov-"gorod was already of much importance, and in 1158 "Wisby was declared a free city by the Emperor Lothair. "England, France, Holland, Russia, Lubeck, and Rostock "had warehouses here; and King Henry III. of England, "by a letter dated 1237, granted the merchants of Goth-"land liberty to trade all over England free from duty. "Whilst a member of the famous Hanseatic League, her "wealth grew almost fabulously, and the maritime code "[*Water-recht*, "Water-right"] of Wisby, framed in the "twelfth century, has served as the model of all the navi-"gation laws of Europe. The valuable and yearly "recurring finds of Oriental coins" [chiefly Cufic,—so named from the Arabic inscriptions on them of the period of the greatness of the city of Cufa, where the coins of the early Abbaside Caliphate were struck] "and orna-"ments, as well as of Anglo-Saxon and German coins.

* In Danish *kiobe* is "to buy," *kioband*, "a merchant," and *kiobenhaven*, "commercial harbour."

"bear witness to the former commercial intercourse "between the East, England, Denmark, Germany, and "this island." In Sweden, and especially in the island of Gothland, such an immense number of these Cufic coins has been found, that in the Stockholm Museum alone, Mr. C. R. Markham tells me, 20,000 have been preserved, minted in about 70 different towns within the former dominions of the Abbaside Caliphs. Five-sixths of them were coined by sovereigns of the Samanian dynasty who reigned in Khiva, North Persia, and Transoxiana, from about A.D. 900 to 990. [There was a discovery of these Cufic coins in the Orkneys also, Sir Henry Yule once told me.] A great mass of Eastern ornaments has also been found. There are numerous hints in the Sagas of this Eastern trade, along the obscure line from Khiva [Khwarazm, *i.e.* Chorasmia], round the north of the Caspian, and up the Volga, to Novgorod, and thence across Russia to the Baltic: and it would seem that silver first came into Scandinavia by this route. There was an early distinction between the Easterling or Vandalic Hanse towns [*civitates Sclavicæ*], with Lubeck for their chief, and the Westerling or Teutonic Hanse towns, of which the capital was Cologne. As the trade with Venice and Genoa increased the Hanse merchants began to resort to the harbour of Sluys, the port of Bruges, for the purpose of exchanging the iron, copper, flax, hemp, and timber of the Baltic countries for the spices, drugs, and silks of the East, and the dried fruits and wines of Southern Europe. Thither also the English took their tin, lead, hides, rabbit skins, and wool; and thus Bruges became, in the thirteenth century, the store city for the trade between England and the Baltic and Mediterranean Seas, and the universal mart of Europe, and so remained for nearly 300 years. Bruges was, indeed, the first of the four great comptoirs established by the Hanseatic League; the second being London, and the other two Bergen and Novgorod. In London, the office of the League, "*Guildhala Teutonicorum*," commonly called the "Steel Yard," *i.e.*

Staplehoff* or Warehouse, was in Thames Street; and it had other "Steel Yards" at Boston and Lynn. With the fall of Constantinople and the extension of the Ottoman dominion in Syria and Egypt, the commerce of Bruges suffered proportionally with that of Genoa and Venice; and it suffered further also from the war, begun in 1482, between the Flemings and the Archduke Maximilian, which gradually drove its merchants to Antwerp. The merchandise of India and the East also reached Southern Germany through Milan, the common depôt of the Venetians and Genoese, whence it was transported over the Alps to Augsburg and Nuremberg; and during the hostile rivalry of Genoa and Venice many of the German towns opened direct communications with Constantinople, through which city the whole of Central Europe was supplied with Indian produce at Belgrade, Vienna, Ratisbon, Nuremberg, Ulm, Augsburg, and other cities along the Danube. This trade was carried on until the subjugation of Servia by the Turks A.D. 1459. The myth of the Argonautic expedition probably points to the existence, from the remotest prehistoric times, of this line of overland trade between the East and West.

The "Old Travellers" (continued).

The destructive conquests of the Ottoman Turks made the nations of Christendom aware of the precarious tenure by which their overland trade with India was held, while at the same time they felt that its freedom from interruption was essential to the progress of civilization in Europe: and these considerations now began to turn their thoughts towards the circumnavigation of Africa, and even led them, for a time, to hope, from the victorious career of Chingiz Khan [*b.* A.D. 1163 *d.* A.D. 1227] and Tamer-

* The derivation usually given is from the mediæval *Statera Romana*: the adjective "Romana" here being a corruption of *riman* [*cf.* Rimmon] the name of the "pomegranate" shaped sliding weight or counterpoise [σταθμός, æquipondium] of the steelyard [ζυγόν, scapus] used by the Arabs, in succession to the Phœnicians, and the Greeks and Romans.

lane [*b.* A.D. 1335 *d.* 1405], that an understanding with the Tartars might further their aims of a settled commerce with the East. The first European missions into 'Grand Tartary' ["India Major"] were indeed sent out with a view to staying the further advance of the Tartars. After the successive irruptions of the Goths, Vandals, Huns, Avars, Sclavs, and Turks into the West, it might well have been supposed that the surplus population of the East was exhausted, and that Europe would at last enjoy a prolonged period of peace and prosperity. But this expectation was cruelly dispelled by the overwhelming inundation of the Tartars in the thirteenth century under Chingiz Khan, whose son, Octai or Okkodai, pushed his ravages so far as Poland and the confines of Germany. Batou, a grandson of Chingiz, overran and made conquest of all south-eastern Russia. Also, while Octai was attacking the Eastern frontiers of Europe, the Tartars were, by their advances through Persia and on Baghdad, threatening the sacred possessions the Crusaders had wrested from the Saracens in the Holy Land. Pope Clement IV., as the Spiritual Father of Christendom, felt, therefore, called upon to make an effort to deliver it from the abomination of desolation now imminently threatening it; and accordingly the Franciscan friar, NICOLAS ASCELINUS, was sent, A.D. 1245, to the Tartar camp in Persia, by way of the Holy Land, and JOHANNES CARPINI, another Franciscan, to the Tartar camp on the Volga, A.D. 1247. Carpini travelled through Bohemia, Silesia, and Poland, and on through the vast regions, then known under the name of Comania and now as the country of the Don Cossacks, watered by the Dnieper, the Don, the Volga, and the Yaik, until he at last came to the standing camp of 'Duke Bathy' [Batou], afterward known as the city of Sarai or Sara, on the Volga. Batou sent him on to the Imperial Court, where he arrived, by way of Lake Balkash, at the moment when Kuyuk was being elected to the Grand Khanship of the Tartars, in succession to his father Octai or Okkodai Khan. On his return journey, passing rapidly through the camps of 'Duke Bathy' and 'Duke Corrensa,' who guarded the Tartar frontier in Europe from the nations of the West, he reached Kiev in Russia, within eight months of leaving the imperial Court of Kuyuk Khan. He is the first traveller into Mongolia whose narrative we possess.

While St. Louis was engaged in the seventh Crusade, A.D. 1248–50, and the lieutenants of Octai or Okkodai Khan were simultaneously attacking the Saracens from the side of Persia, the Tartars and the French became united in a common cause. To consolidate their casual concurrence, the general who commanded the Tartar forces in Persia sent an embassy to the French King, expressing the respect he felt for Christianity, and recommending that they should take combined action against their Saracen enemies. A French embassy was at once sent into Persia; and at the same time the pious St. Louis, anxious to lose no opportunity for securing the alliance of the Tartars, sent the Minorite friar WILLIAM DE RUBRUQUIS on his celebrated mission, A.D. 1253–56, to the Tartar chief Sartakh, whose territories bordered on the Black Sea. From Constantinople Rubruquis sailed to Soldaia in the Crimea, one of the entrepôts at that time of the Black Sea trade in Russian furs, and Indian spices, drugs, and silks, through Constantinople, with the rest of Europe; and thence he journeyed northward through the before-mentioned region of Comania, until he came to the camp of Sartakh, by whom he was sent on to the court of his father Batou at Sara or Sarai. Here he was furnished with a guide to the Court of Mangu, who had succeeded his cousin Kuyuk as Khakan or Great Khan at Kara-Korum, on the verge of the great Mongolian desert. From the Mongol capital he returned to the Court of Batou on the Volga, and thence to Europe, not by the Crimea, but over the Caucasus, and through the country of the 'Lesgi' [Lesghis] and 'Gurgi' [Georgians], and Armenia, and by Iconium, where he had an interview with the Ottoman Sultan, and the Cilician port of Ayas, and Cyprus, where, at Nicosia, he found his Provincial. Sir Henry Yule, in his introduction to "*The Book of Ser Marco Polo,*" observes of the Cilician ports at this period [*circa* A.D. 1260]: "Alex-"andria was still largely frequented in the intervals "of war as the great emporium of Indian wares; but "the facilities afforded by the Mongol conquerors, who "now held the whole tract from the Persian Gulf to "the shores of the Caspian and of the Black Sea, or "nearly so, were beginning to give a great advantage "to the caravan routes which debouched at the ports "of Cilician Armenia in the Mediterranean, and at "Trebizond on the Euxine." Rubruquis described Turkey [*i.e.* the kingdom of Iconium] at this time as having "no treasure, few warriors, and many enemies." He also strongly deprecated the system of sending poor friars like himself as ambassadors to the Great Khan, without office, presents, or any of the things that command the favour and respect of the profane.

After these friars come the merchants of the Polo family. In the year 1266, Nicolo and Maffeo Polo, the father and uncle of MARCO POLO, were at Constantinople, whither they had gone from Venice with their wares. Taking counsel together, and having laid in a store of jewels, they resolved to cross "the Greater Sea" [Black Sea], on a venture of trade, to Soldaia; where having stayed a while they thought it well to extend their journey further, "and travelled "until they came to the Court of a certain Tartar "Prince, Barca Kaan [Barka, a brother of Batou "Khan], whose residences were at Sara and Bol-"gara." While here, a great war broke out between "Barca and Alau [Barka's cousin Hulaku Khan], the "Lord of the Tartars of the Levant," and in the end

"Barca, the Lord of the Ponent," was defeated, and so the two brothers, Maffeo and Nicolo, could not get back to Venice by the way they had come, nor until they had gone "across the whole longitude of Asia." Leaving Bolghar they went on to 'Ucaca' [Ukak], and thence departing "and passing the great river Tigris" [Volga], traversed a desert country for 17 days until they came to 'Bocara' [Bokhara]. "Whilst they were sojourning "in that city there came from Alau, Lord of the Levant, "envoys on their way to the Court of the Great Kaan [Mangu Khan, brother of Hulaku], Lord of all the "Tartars in the world." At their request the two brothers joined their party, and journeyed a whole year until they reached the Court of Kublai Khan, who had now succeeded his brother Mangu as Khakan of the Tartars. Before the death of Mangu Khan, A.D. 1259, it had been intended to remove the seat of the Tartar capital from Kara-Korum into Cathay or Northern China; but this step, which in the end converted the Tartar Khan into a Chinese Emperor, was left to be carried out by Kublai Khan. The two brothers were received with great honour and hospitality by Kublai Khan, and when the time came for them to go back to Europe, he charged them with a letter to the Pope, begging that 100 persons of the Christian faith might be sent to him, acquainted with "the Seven Arts," and able clearly to prove that "the Law of Christ" was best; and declaring that, if this was done, he and all under him would become Christians. Kublai Khan also delivered into their hands a golden tablet as a passport throughout the Tartar Empire whithersoever they went. So the two brothers travelled back, on and on, and ever westward, until, after three long, adventurous years, they came at last to 'Layas in Hermenia' [L'Ayas or Ayas], a port on the Gulf of Scanderoon, then "one of the chief places for "the shipment of Asiatic wares arriving through "Tabriz, and much frequented by vessels of the

"Italian Republics." [Yule, "*Marco Polo,*" note to Chap VIII. of Prol.] In April 1269 they reached Acre, where, hearing of the death of Clement IV., they returned to Venice, there to await the end of the long papal interregnum that followed. When Gregory X. was at last elected Pope, they forthwith [about November 1271] started on their second journey to the Court of Kublai Khan, this time taking young MARCO POLO with them. From Acre they proceeded by Ayas and Sivas, and then by Mardin, Mosul, and Baghdad, to Ormuz, at the mouth of the Persian Gulf, hoping to go on to China by sea. This they were not able to do, and so, turning their faces landward, they traversed successively Kerman and Khorassan, Balk, and Badakshan, and ascended the upper Oxus to the Pamir plateau; "a route not known "to have been since followed by any European traveller "except Benedict Goes [1602–1607], until the spirited "expedition of Captain John Wood, of the Indian Navy, "in 1838." [Yule, "*Marco Polo,*" Introduction.] Crossing "the steppe of high Pamere," the travellers proceeded by Kashgar, Yarkand, and Khoten, and the vicinage of Lake Lob, and through the Gobi desert, and on through Tangut, until at length, some time during the midsummer of 1275, they arrived at the "stately pleasure dome" of Kublai Khan "in Xanadu" [Shangtu]. And some time afterwards they proceeded with the Khakan to his capital, 'Cambalu' [Cambala], now Peking. They rose rapidly in the Great Khan's favour. Young Marco was entrusted with several missions to different parts of the Empire, and to Chiampa or Southern Cochin China, and Southern India; while to all the hints of the Venetian merchants to be allowed to return home with their gathered wealth, "the aged Emperor growled refusal;" and, adds Sir Henry Yule, "but for a "happy chance we should have lost our mediæval "Herodotus." Hulaku Khan ["Lord of the Levant"], the founder of the Mongol dynasty of Persia, was succeeded by his son Abaka, who married a daughter of the Greek Emperor Michael Palæologus. His brother Nicolas, who succeeded him, became a Mahomedan, but his son Arghun Khan, who succeeded Nicolas, was hostile to the Mahomedans. He sent embassies [conducted by a Genoese] to the Pope, and to the Kings of France and England, proposing an alliance against the Saracens and Turks; and in 1290 Edward I. sent Geoffrey de Langley on a return mission to him. Now Arghun Khan, having lost his favourite wife in 1286, had sent to Kublai Khan to select another for him; and about the very time that Geoffrey de Langley's mission was setting out for England, the Polos were commissioned by Kublai Khan to escort the new bride he had chosen for his great nephew from "far Cathay," by sea, to the Persian court. The bridal party sailed from the port of 'Zayton' [Chincheu] in the spring of 1292. In the April following they would be in Sumatra, where they probably remained until September; when, passing through the Straits of Malacca, they successively touched at Ceylon, at an Indian port on the Coromandel Coast, at Kayal, a port of Tinnevelly, and at other ports on the Malabar and Concan Coasts of Western India; and at one of these, probably Tannah, they passed the monsoon of 1293. Marco Polo notices the fine cottons of Coromandel, and the abundance of pepper and ginger of Malabar, the incense of Tannah, and the pepper, ginger, indigo, and cotton of Guzerat. Sailing on the close of the monsoon from India, the party reached Ormuz about November 1293, and the Persian camp two months later. Here the fair princess wept as she took leave of the three Polos, who went on to Tabriz, and, after a long halt there, proceeded towards Venice, where they arrived some time in 1295, having been absent from home nearly 24 years. The publication of "*The Book of Ser Marco Polo*" was as the revelation of a new world to his countrymen, and although the slow circulation of that age retarded its effect, in the end it became one of the influences which inspired the mighty emprise of Columbus. Ptolemy had enormously exaggerated the eastern extension of Asia, and as the wonderful lands visited by Marco Polo lay still further eastward, it was thought that no great breadth of ocean rolled between western Europe and eastern Asia; and full of this idea, Columbus launched boldly on the Atlantic, convinced that the first shores reached by him would be those of 'Chipangu' [Japan], Cathay, 'Chamba' [Cochin China], and India. From the time of the Saracen conquest of Egypt, Syria, and Persia, Christians had been forbidden to pass through those countries to the East, and the direct overland trade of Europe with India had entirely ceased. MARCO POLO, therefore, was the first Christian, after Cosmas Indicopleustes [*circa* A.D. 535–550] to give a written account of India; and the people of Europe, as they gradually came to know of his travels, were astonished at the survey of the immense kingdoms, far beyond the limits of what they had thought to be the uttermost bounds of Asia he for the first time laid open to their view, and, as was hoped, to their commercial enterprise. His book is also a perfect Encyclopædia of the mediæval trade and arts of India and the East; in brief, one of those like the Bible, the Iliad and Odyssey, the History of Herodotus, and Pliny's Natural History, "that shew, contain, and nourish all the world;"* books we never tire of, for they are always fresh: and yet we owe its existence to the accident of his having late in life been taken in a sea fight by the Genoese, and thrown into prison; where he was persuaded by a fellow prisoner to dictate his narrative to relieve the tedium of their captivity. As it has been newly translated into English, and edited by Sir Henry Yule, with notes, and maps and illustrations, it leaves, writes Sir Rutherford Alcock in the "*Fortnightly Review*" for July 1875, scarcely

* *Love's Labour Lost*, A. iv., s. 3.

anything to be desired or hoped for as the fruit of further research, and is the most comprehensive and fascinating work we possess on the mediæval geography and history of the East.

The following are the principal ports of the Eastern Seas described by Marco Polo:—

'Kinsay' [Hang-chau-fu] "the capital of the whole country of Manzi [Southern China]." It was said to be 100 miles in circumference, and to have in it 12,000 bridges of stone. There were in the city 12 guilds of different crafts, and each guild had 12,000 houses in the occupation of its workmen. It was a wise ordinance of the King "that every man should follow his father's "business and no other, no matter if he possessed "100,000 bezants." Inside the city there was a lake 30 miles in compass, and all round it were beautiful palaces and gardens. The port of the city was 'Ganfu' [Kanpu], 25 miles distant, "with a vast amount of "shipping which is engaged in the traffic to and from "India, and other foreign ports;" and "a great river "flows from the city of Kinsay to that sea haven, by "which vessels can come up to the city itself." Below 'Ganfu' were 'Zayton' [Thsiuancheu or Chincheu], and 'Fuju' [Fucheu], "a seat of great trade and "great manufactures. . . . Enormous quantities of "sugar are made there, and there is a great traffic "in pearls and precious stones, for many ships of India "come to these parts bringing many merchants who "traffic about the Isles of the Indies. For this city is, "you see, in the vicinity of the Ocean Port of Zayton, "which is greatly frequented by the ships of India with "their cargoes of various merchandise; and from Zayton "the vessels pass on to the city of Fuju. . . . and "'tis in this way that the precious wares of India come "hither."

The 'Haven of Zayton' [Chincheu] was "frequented "by all the ships of India, which bring hither spicery

" and all kinds of costly wares. It is the port also that " is frequented by all the merchants of Manzi [Southern " China], for hither is imported the most astonishing " quantity of goods, and of precious stones and pearls, " and from this they are distributed all over Manzi. And " I assure you that for one shipload of pepper that goes to " Alexandria or elsewhere, destined for Christendom, " there come a hundred such, aye, and more too, to this " haven of Zayton; for it is one of the two greatest " havens in the world for commerce."

Passing southwards to the Indian Archipelago, he describes 'the great country called Chamba' ['Champa,' 'Zampa,' 'Chiampa,' 'Tsiampa,' or Southern Cochin China], and 'the isles of Sondur and Condur' [Pulo Condore], 'the great island of Java,' 'the island of Pentam' [Bintang], and 'the island and city of Malaiur,' which may be Palembang, or Singapore, or Malacca. Sir Henry Yule considers the evidence conclusive against the existence of Malacca in Marco Polo's time. 'Malaiur,' Marco Polo says, was a fine and noble city, and a great trade was carried on there in all kinds of spicery and all other necessaries of life. Marco Polo then describes 'Java the Less' [Sumatra], and the islands of 'Necuveran' [the Nicobars], 'Angamanain' [the Andamans], and 'Seilan' [Ceylon], whence he passes to 'the great province of Maabar' [the Coromandel Coast], to which 'the merchants of Kis and Hormes, Dofar, and Soer [Suhar], and Aden,' bring great numbers of 'destriers and other horses' to sell to the king. After mentioning the town of St. Thomas, he next describes 'the kingdom of Mutfili,' corresponding with Telingana, and taking its name probably from 'Motapalle,' in the Guntur district of the Madras Presidency. "It is in this kingdom that " diamonds are got. . . . No other country but " this kingdom of Mutfili produces them. . . . In " this kingdom are also produced the best and most " delicate buckrams, and those of the highest price; in "sooth, they look like tissue of spiders' web!" The city of Cail [Kayal in the Tinnevelly district] he describes as "a great and noble city. It is at this city "that all the ships touch that come from the West, as "from Hormos, from Kis, and from Aden, and all "Arabia, laden with horses and with other things for "sale." Of 'Coilum' [Quilon] he says "a great deal "of brazil is got here. . . . Good ginger also grows "here. . . . Pepper too grows in great abundance. ". . They have also abundance of very fine indigo. ". . The merchants from Manzi, and from Arabia, and "from the Levant [Persia], come hither with their ships "and their merchandise, and make great profits both by "what they import and by what they export."

After describing 'Melibar' [Malabar] and 'Gozurat' [Guzerat], he says of the kingdom of 'Tana' [Tannah], "no pepper grows there, nor other spices, but "plenty of incense. . . . There is much traffic "here, and many ships and merchants frequent the "place; for there is a great export of leather of various "excellent kinds, and also of good buckram and cotton. "The merchants in their ships also import various "articles, such as gold, silver, copper, and other things "in demand."

Of the kingdom of 'Cambaet' [Cambay], he says, "There is a great trade in this country. It produces "indigo in great abundance, and much fine buckram. "There is also a quantity of cotton which is exported "hence, . . . and a great trade in hides, which are "very well dressed; with many other kinds of mer-"chandise too tedious to mention. Merchants come here "with many ships and cargoes, but what they chiefly "bring is gold, silver, copper, and tutia."

In 'Zanghibar' [Zanzibar], he says, "there is a great "deal of trade, and many merchant vessels go thither; "but the staple trade of the Island is elephants' teeth, "which are very abundant, and they have also much "ambergris, as whales are plentiful."

Of 'Hormos,' 'Hormes' or 'Curmosa,' Marco Polo says, "merchants come thither from India with ships "loaded with spicery and precious stones, pearls, "cloths of silk and gold, elephants' teeth, and many "other wares, which they sell to the merchants of "Hormos, and they in turn carry all over the world "to dispose of again. In fact 'tis a city of immense "trade."

The other emporium of the Indian trade in the Persian Gulf was the island of Kisi [Kishi, Kish, or Kais]. "Baudas [Baghdad] is a great city, which used "to be the seat of the Calif of all the Saracens in the "world, just as Rome is the seat of the Pope of all the "Christians. A very great river flows through the city, "and by this you can descend to the Sea of India. "There is a great traffic of merchants with their "goods this way: they descend some 18 days from "Baudas, and then come to a certain city called Kisi, "where they enter the Sea of India. There is also on "the river, as you go from Baudas to Kisi, a great city "called Bastra [Bussorah], surrounded by woods, in which "grow the best dates in the world."

Aden "is a port to which many of the ships of India "come with their cargoes; and from this haven the "merchants carry the goods a distance of seven days "further in small vessels. At the end of these seven "days they land the goods, and load them on camels, "and so carry them a land journey of 30 days. This "brings them to the river of Alexandria [the Nile], and "by it they descend to the latter city. It is by this "way through Aden that the Saracens of Alexandria "receive all their stores of pepper and other spicery; "and there is no other route equally good and con-"venient by which their goods could reach that "place."

'Babylon' is the name by which Cairo was known to Marco Polo.

In Marco Polo's old age, and the years following his

death, a remarkable land trade, Sir Henry Yule has shown, sprang up between China and the trading cities of Italy, of which curious details are given in the book of Pegolotti already mentioned. The chief imports from the East were the rich satins and damasks of China. European linens were carried for sale on the way; but to China itself, in general, only silver, to purchase goods there. Factories of Genoese merchants were established at Fokien, perhaps at Hangcheu and other cities. This trade probably came to an end about the middle of the 14th century, after lasting 30 or at most 40 years. It was apparently carried on entirely by Italian merchants travelling to make their own purchases. Whether they undertook the trade by sea also is doubtful.

MARINO SANUTO, a Venetian nobleman, who travelled in the East about 1300–1306, in his book entitled "*Liber secretorum fidelium Crucis, super Terræ Sanctæ recuperatione*," presented to Pope John XII. at Avignon, initiates us into all the details of the course of the Venetian commerce with India at this period. Formerly, and even down to his time, it used to take the route by the Persian Gulf. The merchandise of Malabar and Cambay was first conveyed to Ormuz and Kish in the Persian Gulf, and was thence transported to Bussorah on the Euphrates, whence it passed up the Tigris to 'Baldac' [Baghdad] and across the Syrian desert to Antioch and Cilicia, where it was embarked for Europe on board the ships of Genoa and Venice. Latterly, however, the merchants of Southern Arabia had gradually recovered their old commerce, and part of the merchandise of India and the East now came into Europe by way of 'Ahaden' [Aden] and 'Chus' [Coptos] on the Nile, and Alexandria. The rarer commodities, such as cloves, nutmegs, mace, gems, and pearls, were still conveyed up the Persian Gulf to Bussorah, and on to Baghdad, whence they were carried to some port on the Syrian or Arabian Coast of the Mediterranean; but all the more bulky goods, such as pepper, ginger, cinnamon, together with a portion of the more valuable articles, were now reconveyed by the ancient route to the Red Sea, and across the Libyan desert, and down the Nile to Alexandria.

There is very little information directly bearing on the subject of this paper to be derived from the letters and reports of the Missionary Friars of the fourteenth century, published by Sir Henry Yule in his "*Cathay, and the Way Thither*," viz., the letters of the Franciscan Friar, John of Montecorvino [*b.* 1247, *d.* 1328], dated from 'Cambalec' [Peking], the 8th January 1305 and February 1306; of Andrew of Perugia of the order of Minorite Friars, 'Bishop of Zayton' in Manzi [Southern China], dated 'Zayton,' January 1326; of the Dominican Friar Jordanus, dated from 'Caga' [Gogo] the 12th October 1321, and from 'Thana' [Tannah], near Bombay, January 1323; and of the Franciscan Friar, Pascal of Vittoria, whose letter is dated from 'Armalec' [Almalik, not far from the modern Kulja] 'in the Empire of the Medes,' on the feast of St. Lawrence, 1338; and "the Book of the estate of the Great Caan, set forth by the Archbishop of Soltania" [the Dominican Friar John de Cora] *circa* 1330. In the letter from the Dominican Friar Menentillus, forwarding the copy of a letter from Friar John of Montecorvino, among the products of "Upper India" he enumerates aromatic spices, pepper, ginger, brazil-wood, and cinnamon, and he refers to palm sugar and toddy.

The famous Minorite Friar ODORICO DI PORDENONE [*b.* 1281, *d.* 1331], a Beatus of the Roman Catholic church, travelled in the East and in India between 1316 and 1330. He proceeded by way of Constantinople and Trebizond, 'Arziron' [Erzeroum], Tauris, 'Soldania' [Sultanieh], and 'the sea of Bacuc' [*i.e.*, of Baku, the Caspian], 'Cassan' [Kashan], 'Iest' [Yezd], and the 'Sea of Sand,' the ruins of 'Comerum'

[Persepolis], and the kingdom of 'Chaldæa' [Baghdad], to 'Ormes' [Ormuz], whence he took ship to 'Tana' in Salsette, near Bombay. Here, or at Surat, in one of which places Friar Jordanus had deposited them, he gathered the bones of the four missionaries who had suffered martyrdom at Tana in 1321, and took ship again to 'Polumbum' [Quilon]. He notices the immense quantity of pepper cultivated in 'Minibar' [Malabar], where he also visited the coast towns of 'Flandrina' ['Pandarani'] and 'Cyngilin' ['Cynkali,' 'Shinkala,' 'Gingala,' 'Jangli,' or Cranganore]. He then went on to 'Mobar' [the Coromandel Coast], "where lieth the body of St. Thomas," and thence in fifty days sailed to 'Lamori' ['al Ramni'] and to the kingdom of 'Sumoltra' [Sumatra]. From Sumatra he went on to Java, and to another island called 'Thalamasyn' or 'Panten,' which has been thought to be Borneo, and thence to 'Zampa' [Cochin China]. He next notices the island of 'Nicoveran' [Nicobars], and of 'Sillan' [Ceylon], whence his narrative carries us at once to 'Upper India' [China] and the Province of 'Manzi' [Southern China], and the cities of 'Censcalan' [Canton], 'Zayton' [Chincheu], 'Fuzo' [Fucheu], 'Cansay' [Hangcheu], 'Chilenfu' [Nanking], and 'Cambalech' [Peking], and to 'Sandu' ['Xanadu,' Shangtu], the summer residence of the Great Khan. He describes 'the lands of Prester John,' and 'the realm of Thibet,' and the Grand Lama, as Pope of the latter country. He also gives an account of his own dealings with the 'Devils of Tartary,' and of the 'Old Man of the Mountain.'

JOHN DE' MARIGNOLLI, a Minorite Friar of the Franciscan monastery of Santa Croce at Florence, was sent by Pope Benedict on a mission to 'Cathay' in 1338. He sailed from Avignon to Naples, and thence to Constantinople, and on to 'Caffa' [Theodosia] in the Crimea, whence he proceeded to the court of the Khan of Kipchak at Sarai, on the Volga, who forwarded him on to 'Armalec' [Almalik], the capital of the Chagatai

Khans of the 'Middle Tartar Empire.' He arrived at 'Cambalec' [Peking] in May or June 1342, and after remaining there three or four years sailed from Zayton for India, the 26th December 1347, and arrived at 'Columbum' [Quilon], the following Easter. In 1349 he made a pilgrimage to the shrine of St. Thomas on the Coromandel coast, and thence sailed to 'Saba,' piously identified by him with the Sheba of the Bible, but which was probably some country of Further India. Returning to India, he was driven to Ceylon, whence he sailed to Ormuz, and afterwards travelled by the ruins of Babylon to Baghdad, Mosul, Edessa, and Aleppo, and thence to Damascus, Galilee, and Jerusalem, making his way back to Italy by Cyprus.

SIR JOHN MANDEVILLE, the author of, it is said, the first English book that appeared in print* [London, 1499], would appear from his narrative to have traversed the whole East between 1327 and 1372, the date of his death. He speaks of "the marvyles of Inde," but it is certain he was never there. He may be described as the father of English sensation writers, and is not to be trusted even when he may be telling the truth.

During the latter half of the fourteenth century, Tamerlane, taking advantage of the dissensions among the descendants of Chingiz Khan, succeeded in once again uniting the nomad hordes of Central Asia in a career of universal devastation. He was proclaimed Khan of the Chagatai, and made Samarcand his capital in 1369. He overran Persia in 1386–87, and Kipchak several times between 1387 and 1389, in the latter year reaching so far as Moscow. He took Baghdad in 1395, invaded India and stormed Delhi in 1398, invaded Asia Minor and Syria in 1400–1401, and defeated and captured the Emperor Bajazet at the great battle of Angora, July 20, 1404. Tamerlane's triumphant campaign against the Ottoman Turks quickly drew the princes of Christendom

* This is incorrect, as the distinction of being the first printed English book is due to the *Recuyell of the Historyes of Troye*, 1474.

into relations with him. In 1393, Henry III. of Castile sent two noble knights, named Pelayo de Sotomayor and Fernando de Palazuelos on an embassy to his camp. They were received with distinction, and were present at the battle of Angora, and, on their return to Spain, Tamerlane sent an envoy of his own with them with rich presents to the King of Castile, of jewels and women, among them being two lovely Christian damsels, named Angelina and Maria, whom he had rescued from the seraglio of the brutal Bajazet. King Henry thereupon determined to send another embassy to Tamerlane, at the head of which was DON RUY GONZALES DE CLAVIJO, whose narrative of it is of the highest interest, not only for the account it gives of Tamerlane, but for the light it throws on the caravan trade of the period through Persia. Yet it was not until 1869 that an English translation of it was made and edited by Mr. Clements R. Markham, C.B., for the Hakluyt Society. Accompanied by the returning Tartar envoy, Clavijo embarked at the port of St. Mary near Cadiz, in May 1403, and sailed through the Strait of Bonifacio to Gaeta, continuing his course through the Strait of Messina to Rhodes. Here he hired a ship to Chios, and there engaged another to Constantinople. Sailing through the "Strait of Roumania" [the Dardanelles], he saw on one side "the land of Turkey," and on the other "the land of Græcia." He left Constantinople on the 14th of November, passing in the Bosphorus between two castles, one being named "*el Guirol de la Græcia*," and the other "*el Guirol de la Turquia*." Disembarking at Trebizond he proceeded by 'Arsinga' [Erzingan] and 'Aseron' [Erzeroum] through Armenia, and across the 'Corras' [Cyrus] to Tauris or Tabriz and Sultanieh in Azerbijan. The latter city, now a mere mass of squalid ruins, he represents as then very populous, but not so large as Tabriz, although it had more trade. Every year in the months of June, July, and August, large caravans came there from India with spices, "such as "cloves, nutmegs, cinnamon, manna, mace, and other "precious articles which do not go to Alexandria;" and from Ghilan with wrought silk, to be sent to Damascus, Syria, and Turkey; and merchants came there for silks from all countries "even Venetians and Genoese." Silken stuffs, cottons, and taffetas also came to Sultanieh from Shiraz and 'Yesen' [Yezd], and cotton threads and cotton cloths from Khorassan. "From Cathay vessels came within 60 days journey of "this city, having navigated the western sea . . . "and they came to a river which is 10 days journey "from the city of Ormuz." . . . These ships brought pearls and rubies from Ceylon [not from Cathay as Clavijo was told], and spices from India. "All the "merchants who come from the land of the Christians, "from Caffa [Theodosia] and Trebizond, and the mer-"chants of Turkey and Syria, come every year at this "time [June 1404] to the city of Sultanieh to make "their purchases." From Sultanieh the embassy proceeded, by Teheran, to Damghan in Khorassan, and by Nishapore, where Clavijo notices the "torquoises," to 'Ojajan,' where they received a message from Shah Rukh, Tamerlane's celebrated youngest son, inviting them to Herat. From 'Ojajan' they went on to 'Maxaque' [Meshed] and 'Buelo,' after which they had to cross a desert of 50 leagues, at the end of which they found themselves in "the land of Tartary." They now crossed the 'Morghan' [Murghab], and, after passing through 'Vaeq' [Balk], "the great river Viadme" [the Oxus], "another of the rivers of Paradise ". . . which descends from the mountains, and flows "through the plains of the territory of Samarcand ". . . and falls into the sea of Bakou" [the Caspian]. Then, after travelling for several days, they came to the formidable pass of the "Iron Gates," in the mountain chain that guards Tartary "in the direction of India," and going on to Quex [Kesh], the birth-place of Tamerlane, entered his beautiful capital of Samarcand, September 8, 1404. But Clavijo never saw the mighty destroyer, who was already dying. After being most hospitably entertained by his ministers the embassy departed on its return journey on the 21st of November, and, on reaching Tabriz, received the intelligence of Tamerlane's death, which took place at Otrar on the Jaxartes, February 19, 1405. From Trebizond, Clavijo took ship for Pera, where he found two Genoese carracks which had come from Caffa, and were going to Genoa. He embarked on one of them, and, after stopping at Gallipoli to take in a cargo of cotton, and at Chios, and Gaeta, and at Corsica "to spend Christmas Day," reached Genoa, January 3, 1406. He himself reached Seville the following March.

In 1419 Shah Rukh sent Sadi Khoja on an embassy into China, and in 1442 he sent ABD-UR-RAZZAK on an embassy to India. Abd-ur-Razzak set out from Herat in January 1442, and proceeded by way of Kohistan and Kerman to Ormuz. He thus describes this port: "The "merchants of the seven climates, from Egypt, Syria, the "country of Roum [Anatolia], Azerbijan, Irak-Arabi, "and Irak-Adjemi, the provinces of Fars, Khorassan, "Mawaranahar [Turkistan], the kingdom of Deschti-"Kaptchack [Kipchak], the whole of the kingdoms of "Tchin [Northern China or Cathay], and Matchin [Manzi "or Southern China], and the city of Khanbalik [Peking], "all make their way to this port, which has not its equal "on the surface of the globe. The inhabitants of the "sea coasts arrive here from the countries of Tchin, "Java, Bengal, the cities of Zirbad [*India extra Gangem*], "Tenasserim, Sokotora [Socotra], Schahrinou [*shahr-i-*"*nao*, "New City," *i.e.*, Siam], the islands of Diwah-"Mahal [Maldives], the countries of Malabar, Abyssinia, "Zanguebar, the ports of Bidjanager, Kalbergah, Gu-"jarat, Kanbait [Cambay], the coasts of Arabia "which extend so far as Aden, Jeddah, and Yembo.

"They bring hither those rare and beautiful articles "which the sun, the moon, and the rains have combined to bring to perfection. . . . Travellers "from all countries resort hither, and in exchange for "the commodities which they bring, they can without "trouble or difficulty obtain all that they desire. ". . . For all objects, with the exception of gold "and silver, a tenth of their value is paid by way of "duty. Persons of all religions and even idolaters are "found in this city, and no injustice is permitted "towards any person whatever." From Ormuz, after two months' sojourn, Abd-ur-Razzak sailed for Calicut, but, being too late for the S.W. monsoon, was compelled to pass several months at Muscat. He landed at Calicut at the beginning of November 1442, and remained there until the middle of April 1443. He describes it as "a perfectly secure harbour, which, like "that of Ormuz, brings together merchants from every "city and from every country. In it are to be found "abundance of precious articles brought thither from "maritime countries, and especially from Abyssinia, "Zirbad, and Zanguebar. From time to time ships "arrive there from the shores of the House of God "[Mecca] and other parts of the Hedjaz, and abide at "will for a greater or longer space in the harbour. "The town is inhabited by infidels, and situated on a "hostile shore. . . . . The sovereign of the city "bears the title of *Sameri*. . . . . The coast, "which includes Calicut and some neighbouring ports, "and which extends as far as Kayal, a place situated "opposite the island of Serendib, otherwise called "Ceylon, bears the general name of Malibar [Malabar]. "From Calicut are vessels continually sailing for Mecca, "which are for the most part laden with pepper. The "inhabitants of Calicut are adventurous sailors; they "are known by the name of *Chini-batchagan* [sons of "the Chinese], and pirates do not dare to attack the "vessels of Calicut. In this harbour one may find "everything that can be desired. One thing only is "forbidden, namely, to kill a cow or to eat its flesh." From Calicut he went on by sea to Mangalore, "which "forms the frontier of the kingdom of Bijanagar," from which port he continued his route by land to the city of Bijanagar, which he reached by the end of April. He gives a graphic account of the magnificence of this ancient Hindu city, where he was entertained in the most princely state by the King until the following November, when he returned to Mangalore. Going on to 'Honawer' [Onore] he there took his passage to Ormuz, which port he reached April 22, 1444,—the voyage from Onore to Ormuz having lasted 65 days.

NICOLO CONTI, a noble Venetian, travelled in India and the East for 25 years, between 1419 and 1444; and seeking in 1449 absolution from Eugene IV. for the sin of having once denied Christ on the borders of Egypt, in order to save from death his wife and children, who had accompanied him in all his peregrinations, that Pope imposed on him the happy penance of relating his adventures to his famous secretary, Poggio Bracciolini, the immortal author of the "*Facetiæ*." Conti started from Damascus, where he had resided for some years and had learned the Arabic language, and, travelling in company with a caravan of 600 other merchants, passed over the deserts of Arabia Petræa, and through Chaldæa to 'Baldochia' [Baghdad]. Sailing thence down the river Euphrates for 20 days he arrived at 'Balsera' [Bussorah], and four days after at the head of the Persian Gulf, and in five days more at the port of 'Colcus,' and afterwards at Ormuz. Sailing thence towards India he arrived after 100 miles at 'Calacatia' ['Calaite,' 'Calatu,' Kalhat in Arabia], a very noble emporium of the Persians. Here he stayed some time and learned the Persian language, when he and some Persian merchants freighted a ship to India, "having first taken a solemn "oath to be faithful and loyal companions one to "another." At the end of a month at sea he arrived at Cambay, where, he observes, are "those precious "stones, sardonixes." Proceeding southward along the coast of Western India, after 20 days sailing he arrived at two cities on the seashore, "one named Pacamuria, "and the other Helly." In these districts, he says, "grows "ginger, called in the language of the country *beledi*, "*gebeli*, and *neli*." Departing thence, and travelling for about 300 miles inland, he next arrived at "the great city "of Bizenegalia" [Bijanagar]. Eight days' journey from it he came to "the very noble city of Pelagonda" [? Paliconda, now Ongule], and in twenty days more to the seaport 'Peudifetania' [? Pudipatana, on the Malabar coast], "on the road to which he passed two cities, viz., "Odeschiria and Cenderghiria [? Chandgerry in the "Carnatic], where the red sandal-wood grows." He next arrived at 'Malepur' [Maliapur, *i.e.*, the city of Peacocks, or St. Thomé], "where the body of "St. Thomas lies honourably buried; beyond which," he says, "is another city, called Cahila ['Cail,' Kayal], "where pearls are found." He then crossed over to a "very noble island, called Zeilam [Ceylon], ... "in which they find, by digging, rubies, saffares, "garnets, and those stones which are called cats'-eyes. "Here also cinnamon grows in great abundance." He "afterwards went on to the island of Taprobana, which "island is called by the natives Sciamuthera" [Sumatra, which is also called Taprobana, the ancient name of Ceylon, by others besides Conti], where he remained a year, and where he notices the pepper, long pepper, camphor, gold and *duriano* [Durio Zebethinus]. Leaving Sumatra, he arrived, after a stormy passage of 16 days, at 'Ternassari' [Tenasserim], and afterwards sailed to the mouth of the Ganges, and up the river for 15 days until he came to 'Cernove.' He notices the charming villas on both banks of the river, and plantations and gardens, "wherein grow vast varieties "of fruits, and above all those called *musa* [plantains],

" . . . . and also the nuts which we call nuts of "India" [' *nuces Indicæ* ' or cocoa-nuts]. From 'Cernove' he went on to 'Maarazia,' and thence returned to Cernove, whence he went on to 'Buffetania' [not to be confounded with 'Peudifetania'], and thence returning by the Ganges after a month's voyage he arrived at 'Racha' [Aracan], whence he crossed inland to the river Dava [*i.e.*, d'Ava, the Irrawaddy], up which he sailed to the city of Ava. Here in his narrative Conti alludes to 'Macinus' [*i.e.*, 'Mahachin,' 'Machin,' Burma], and 'Cathay' [Northern China], and its capital, "called Cambaleschia" [Peking], and the great city, called 'Nemptai' ['Kinsay,' Hangcheu]. Leaving Ava, he arrived at "the mouth of a moderate "sized river, where there is a port called Xeythona "[? Sittoung], and having entered the river at the end "of ten days arrived at a very populous city called "Panconia [? Pegu]," where he remained four months. Here, he says, they have "the pinus, oranges, chesnuts, "melons, . . . white sandal-wood, and camphor." [It is a mistake to translate "pinus," here, as "pine apples," for they are a product exclusively of America, which had not then been discovered.] He now crossed to Java. He says that "in Further India are two "islands towards the extreme confines of the world, "both of which are called Java . . . distinguished "from each other by the names of the Greater and "Less"—the Java Major and Java Minor of other travellers, usually identified with Java and Baliy, but by which Conti would seem to describe Java and Sumbawa. He remained in Java nine months. At 15 days' sail beyond these islands, eastward, two others, he says, are found, "the one called Sandai [Ceram], in "which nutmegs and maces grow; the other is named "Bandan [Banda]; this is the only island in which "cloves grow, which are exported hence to the Java "islands." Ceram and Bouro are the two largest of the Banda or Bandan islands. He also mentions the *nori* [or *lori*, *i.e.*, "Excellent"] and the *cachi* [cockatoo] as birds of Bandan. Having quitted Java, he bent his course westward for a month to "a maritime city, called "Ciampa [southern Cochin-China], abounding in aloes-"wood, camphor, and gold." In another month he came to 'Coloen' [Quilon] in 'Melibaria' [Malabar], where he again notices "ginger, called by the natives *colobi* [*i.e.*, *colombi*, or of 'Kaulam' or Quilon], pepper, brazil-wood, "and the cinnamon which is called [*i.e.*, by Western travellers] *crassa* [*i.e.*, 'canella grossa,' coarse cinnamon or cassia];" and describes the jack, *amba* [mango], and a tree he names *cachi*. After a further journey of three days he came to 'Cocym' [Cochin], and still going northward visited in succession 'Colanguria,' 'Paliuria,' 'Meliancota,' and then Calicut, "a noble emporium for all India, "abounding in pepper, lac, ginger, a coarser kind of "cinnamon, myrobolam, and zedoary." He then went on to Cambay, which he reached in 15 days, and returning to Calicut took ship to "Sechutera" [Socotra], where he spent two months. Departing thence in five days he reached Aden, "an opulent city remarkable "for its buildings;" and thence he sailed "over to "Æthiopia," and after seven days anchored in the port of 'Barbora' [Berbera]. Sailing thence after a month he arrived at 'Gidda' [Jiddah], and subsequently at a port near Mount Sinai, whence he crossed the desert to 'Carrae' [Cairo], where he lost his dear wife and two of his children of the plague. From Egypt he reached Venice safely with his two surviving children.

The account of the journey into India of ATHANASIUS NIKITIN, a Russian, was first published by Mr. Major, in his volume of the Hakluyt Society's publications entitled "*India in the Fifteenth Century*," which includes also the separate narratives of Abd-ur-Razzak, Conti, and Santo Stefano. Nikitin started from Twer in 1468, and descended the Volga through Kazan, and the several Tartar "*orda*" [whence our word "horde" and the Hindustani word "*Ordu,*" meaning "camp"-language] or cantonments, and Sarai, to Astrakhan. Thence he went on to Derbend and Baku, where he crossed the 'Doria Khvalitskaia' [Caspian Sea, or Sea of Khiva,] to 'Chebokhara' [Bokhara]. He then recrossed the Caspian, and lived for six months at Sareh in Mazanderan, whence he went on by successive stages to Kashan, Yezd, and Bender [Bander-Abbas as it was afterwards called], to 'Hormyz' [Ormuz], where he crossed the 'Doria Hondustankaia' [Indian Ocean] to 'Moshkat' [Muscat], and thence to 'Kuzrat' [Guzerat] and 'Kanbat' [Cambay], where indigo grows, and 'Chivil' [Chaul]. From Chaul he proceeded inland to 'Jooneer,' and on to 'Beurek' [Beder], where he lived for four years, visiting, during his stay there, 'Kalongher,' 'Kelberg' [Kulburga] and 'Pervota' [Pervottum], "the Jerusalem of the Hindus." On his return home he embarked from 'Dabyl' [Dabul]; and after being at sea a whole month, was driven somewhere on the coast of, as he says, 'Æthiopea,' whence he reached Muscat in 12 days, and in nine more Ormuz. He then proceeded by land through Shiraz, Ispahan, Kashan, Sultanieh, and Tabriz, to Trebizond, where he crossed the 'Doria Stembolskaia' [Black Sea] to Caffa or Theodosia in the Crimea, where he safely landed, after a stormy passage of a month's duration, in 1474. His description of the several ports of the Eastern Seas which were the chief resorts of commerce in his time is most interesting and instructive, as will be seen from the following extracts :—

"Hormuz is a vast emporium of the world. You "find there people and goods of every description, and "whatever thing is produced on earth you find in "Hormuz. But the duties are high,—one tenth of "everything."

"Cambayat is a port of the whole Indian sea, and a "manufacturing place for every sort of goods, as "*talach* [a sort of robe]. damask, *khan* [satin], *kiola* "[blankets], and there they prepare the blue stone "colour [indigo]. There also grows *lek daakhyk dalon*." Elsewhere, he says "Cambat produces the agate."

"Dabyl [Dabul in the Concan] is also a very extensive "seaport, where many horses are brought from Mysore, "Rabast [Arabia], Khorassan, Turkestan, Neghostan "[? Abyssinia]. It takes a month to walk from this "place to Beder and to Kulburgha."

"Calecot [Calicut] is a port for the whole Indian sea, "which God forbid any craft to cross. . . . . The "country produces pepper, ginger, colour plants [dyes], "muscat, cloves, cinnamon, aromatic roots, *adrach* "[ginger], and every description of spices, and every-"thing cheap."

"Ceylon is another not inconsiderable port [country] "of the Indian sea. There, on a hill, is the tomb of "Adam, and in the vicinity are found precious stones, "*fasstises* [? emeralds], agate, *cinchai* [? diamonds], crys-"tal, *sumbada*. Elephants and ostriches live there."

The two principal inland cities of India described by him are Beder and Bijanagar. "In Beder there is "trade in horses, goods, stuffs, silks, and all sorts of "other merchandise, and also in black people. . . . "the rulers and nobles in the land of India are all "Khorassanians."

Elsewhere he describes Beder as the chief city of the whole of Mahomedan India.

Of Bijanagar [Hampi] he writes: "The Hindu Sultan "Kadam is a very powerful prince. He possesses a nume-"rous army, and resides in a mountain at Bichenegher. "This vast city is surrounded by three forts, intersected "by a river, bordering on one side on a dreadful *jungel*, "and on the other a dale. A wonderful place, and to "any purpose convenient. . . . . The town is "impregnable."

He mentions the following countries beyond India:

'Shabait,' *i.e.*, *India trans Gangem*, which produces

silk, musk, sandal, gems, beads, elephants; 'Pewqu' [Pegu], the products of which are *manik* [ruby], *iakhut* [hyacinth], *kyrpuk* [? topaz]; and 'Cheen' and 'Machin' [China], where porcelain is made.

He mentions that diamonds are found in 'Rachoor.'

He gives the following distances between the different ports and countries of the Eastern seas:

Ten days from Ormuz to 'Golat' [Kalhat]; from Kalhat to Degh, 6 days; from Degh to Muscat, 6 days; from Muscat to Guzerat, 10 days; from Guzerat to Cambay, 4 days; from Cambay to Chaul, 12 days; from Chaul to Dabul, the last seaport in Hindostan belonging to the Mussulmans, 6 days; from Dabul to Calicut, 25 days; and from Calicut to Ceylon, 15 days; from Ceylon to 'Shabait,' one month; from 'Shabait' to Pegu, 12 days; and from Pegu to China, one month;—"all this by sea," he adds.

HIERONIMO DI SANTO STEFANO was a Genoese, who visited India about 1494–99, as a merchant adventurer. From Cairo, where he laid in a stock of coral beads and other wares, he passed down the Nile to 'Cane' [Keneh], whence he travelled by land through the Egyptian desert for seven days to 'Cosir' [Cosseir] on the Red Sea, where he embarked on board a ship which in 25 days carried him to 'Mazua' [Massonah] "off the country of Prester "John;" and in 25 days more, during which he saw plenty of boats fishing for pearls, to 'Adem' [Aden]; and in 35 days more to Calicut. "We found that "pepper and ginger grew here . . . and the nut "of India" [cocoa-nut]. From Calicut he sailed in another ship, and in 26 days reached Ceylon, "in which "grow cinnamon trees, . . . many precious stones, "such as garnets, jacinths, cats'-eyes, and other gems " . . . and trees of the sort which bears the nut "of India." Departing thence after twelve days he arrived at a port on the coast of Coromandel, "where "the red sandal-wood grows;" and, after a long stay, departing thence in another ship, after 27 days reached Pegu in 'Lower India.' "This country [Pegu] is "distant 15 days' journey by land from another, called "Ava, in which grow rubies and many other precious "stones." From Pegu, where he suffered many and great troubles, he set sail to go to Malacca, and, after being at sea 25 days, one morning found himself in a port of Sumatra, "where grows pepper in considerable "quantities, silk, long pepper, benzoin, white sandal-"wood, and many other articles." After further and greater troubles suffered here, he took ship to Cambay, where, after six months' detention among the Maldives, and subsequent shipwreck, he at length arrived, but stripped of all his goods. He notices that Cambay produced lac and indigo. In his destitution, he was assisted by a Moorish merchant of Alexandria and Damascus, and after a time proceeded, in the ship of the Sheriff of Damascus, as supercargo, to Ormuz; in sailing to which place from Cambay he was 60 days at sea. From Ormuz, "in company with some Armenian and Azami [Irak-Adjemi] merchants," he travelled by land to Shiraz, Ispahan, Kazan, Sultanieh, and Tauris; whence he went on with a caravan to Aleppo, and finally to Tripoli in Syria.

LUDOVICO DI VARTHEMA, a Bologuese, whose travels have been so admirably edited for the Hakluyt Society by the Rev. Dr. George Percy Badger, travelled in India and the Eastern seas from A.D. 1503 to 1508. First he sailed to Alexandria, and entering "the Nile arrived at Cairo." Then, returning to Alexandria, he took ship to 'Baruti' [Beyrut], and travelled by Tripoli to Aleppo, "which is eight days' journey inland [from "Tripoli], which said Aleppo is a very beautiful city, "and is under the grand Sultan of Cairo, and is the "mart [scala] of Turkey and Syria, and they are all "Mahommedans. It is a country of very great traffic "in merchandise, and particularly with the Persians "and Azamini [Adjemi], who come so far as there.

"This is the route which is taken to go into Turkey "and Syria by those who come from Azemia [Irak-"Adjemi]." From Aleppo he went southward by 'Aman' [Hamath] and Menin [near Helbon] to Damascus, "which is extremely populous and very "rich. It is impossible to imagine the richness and "elegance of the workmanship there. Here you have "a great abundance of grain and of meat, and the most "prolific country for fruits that was ever seen, and "especially for fresh grapes during all seasons . . . "pomegranates and quinces . . . almonds and "large olives . . . the most beautiful white and "red roses that were ever seen . . . also good "apples and pears and peaches. . . . A stream "runs through the city, and the greater number of "houses have very beautiful fountains of mosaic work. "The houses are dirty externally, but within are very "beautiful, adorned with many works of marble and "porphyry." On the 8th of April 1503, Varthema set out from Damascus with the Haj caravan to Medina and Mecca, and he is the only European to this day who ever succeeded in reaching these Holy places by this route. Speaking of the merchandise of Mecca, he says: "From India Major there comes a great many "jewels and all sorts of spices, and part comes from "Ethiopia; and there comes from India Major, from a "city called Bangchella [? Gaur in Bengal], a very large "quantity of stuffs of cotton and of silk." It was there that he first heard of the arrival of the Portuguese, by the Cape of Good Hope, in the East, from a Moor who traded with Venice and Genoa, and who complained bitterly to him that articles of merchandise were not arriving at Mecca as usual, and of the King of Portugal as the cause, "he being Lord of the *Mare Oceano* [Atlantic] "and of the Persian and Arabian Gulfs." From 'Zida' [Jiddah], the port of Mecca, he took ship and went on to 'Chameram' [Camaran, an island off the coast of Yemen] and Gazan [Jazan, a city of Yemen] and Aden, "the strongest city that was ever seen on "the level ground. It has walls on two sides, and on "the other sides there are very large mountains. On "these mountains there are five castles, and the land "is level, and contains about 5,000 or 6,000 families. ". . . . This city is extremely beautiful. . . . "It is the rendezvous of all the ships which come from "India Major and Minor, from Ethiopia, and from "Persia. All the ships that are bound for Mecca "put in here." Here Varthema again heard of the Portuguese. The year before his arrival at Aden some Portuguese ships had made their appearance in the sea between India and Ormuz, and seized seven Arab ships, and murdered most of the crews; and while Varthema was at Aden "there ran to the palace "forty or sixty Moors belonging to two or three ships "which had been captured by the Portuguese, and who "had escaped by swimming," and they denounced Varthema as a Portuguese spy. On this the city rose in a tumult, and demanded to slay him. But the Sultan's officers interposed, and sent him to the Sultan at Radaa, by whom he was thrown into prison. Being liberated at the suit of the Sultana, and having at length freed himself from her blandishments, he obtained at Aden a passage on board a ship going to India. On the seventh day of the voyage his ship was driven into the African port of Zeila, "together with 25 ships laden with madder "to dye cloths; for every year they lade as many "as 25 ships in Aden with it. This madder grows "in Arabia Felix [Yemen]." The city of Zeila he describes as a "place of immense traffic, especially "in gold and elephants' teeth. Here also are sold a "great number of slaves . . . . and from this "place they are carried into Persia, Arabia Felix, and "to Mecca, Cairo, and into India. . . . . Much "grain grows here, and much animal food, and oil in "great quantity, made not from olives, but from

" *zerzalino* [ingeniously and rightly identified by " Badger with *juljulan* or *jinjili*, i.e., '*gingelly*,' of " the Indian bazaars, Sesamum orientale], honey and " wax in great abundance." As soon as the weather became favourable, he set sail and arrived at 'Barbara' [Berbera], and in 12 days more [being apparently unable to make the Persian Gulf] arrived at 'Diuobandierrumi' [*i.e.*, Diu Bander-er-Rumi, "Diu, the port of the Turks"]. "There is an immense " trade in this city. Four hundred Turks reside there " continually." From Diu he went to 'Goa' [Gogo, 'Kukah'], whence he crossed the Indian Ocean to 'Guilfar' [Julfar] in the Persian Gulf, whence he visited 'Meschet' [Muscat], and, crossing to the opposite shore of the Persian Gulf, "the noble city of " Ormus, which is extremely beautiful . . . . and " is the chief, that is, as a maritime place, and for " merchandize." From Ormuz he proceeded by land to "a city called Eri [Herat], and the country is called " Corazani [Khorassan], which would be the same as " to say 'The Romagna.' The King of Corazani " dwells in this city, where there is a great plenty and " an abundance of stuffs, and especially of silk, so that " in one day you can purchase here 3,000 or 4,000 " camel loads of silk. The district is most abundant " in articles of food, and there is a great market for " rhubarb. . . . I quitted this place, and travelled " twenty days on the mainland, finding cities and " castles very well peopled." He returned to Ormuz by way of 'Schirazo' [Shiraz], where he notes the " great abundance of jewels, that is, of turquoises, and " an infinite quantity of Balass rubies . . . from a " city which is called Balachsam [Badakshan]. And " in the said city there is a large quantity of ultra- " marine, and *tucia* [*tutiya*, an impure oxide of zinc], " and musk." From Shiraz he made with a Persian merchant an abortive attempt to reach 'Sambragante' [Samarcand], failing in which he went back to Ormuz, and there embarked on board a ship, and in eight days arrived at the port of 'Cheo' [Kow] in the Indies; whence he sailed on to 'Combeia' [Cambay], "a most "excellent city, abounding in grain and very good "fruits. In this district there are eight or nine kinds "of small spices, that is to say, *turbidi* [turpeth], "*gallanga* [galangal], *spiconarda* [spikenard], *saphe-* "*tica* [assafœtida], and *lacra*, and other spices, the "names of which I do not remember. An immense "quantity of cotton is produced here, so that every "year 40 or 50 vessels are laden with silk stuffs, which "stuffs are carried into different countries. In this "kingdom of Combeia also, about six days' journey, "there is a mountain whence cornelians are extracted, "and the mountains of chalcedonies. Nine days' "journey from Combeia there is another mountain, in "which diamonds [probably a vague reference to the "mines of Golconda] are found. . . . . It is im- "possible to describe the commerce of the country. "About 300 ships of different countries come and go "here. This city, and another of which I will speak "in the proper season, supply all Persia, Tartary, "Turkey, Syria, Barbary, that is Africa, Arabia Felix, "Æthiopia, India, and a multitude of inhabited islands, "with silk and cotton stuffs."

Departing from Cambay, Varthema, after 12 days' voyage, arrived at 'Cevul' [Chaul]. "It possesses an "extremely beautiful river, by which a very great "number of foreign vessels go and return, because the "country abounds in everything, excepting grapes, "nuts, and chestnuts. They collect here an immense "quantity of grain, of barley [impossible], and of "vegetables of every description; and cotton stuffs are "manufactured here in great abundance. . . . . "There are in this city a very great number of "Moorish merchants." In two days' voyage from Chaul he came to 'Dabuli' [Dabul], where, he notices, were Moorish merchants "in very great "numbers;" and thence he sailed on to 'Goga' [Goa, 'Sindabur'], from which place he proceeded inland, and after seven days arrived at "a city which is called "Decan" [Bijapur, the metropolis of the Mahomedan Kingdom of the Deccan]. Returning to the coast, in five days he reached the port of 'Bathacala' [Beitkul, Sadaseoghur, or Karwar]. He observes "there are "many Moorish merchants here, for it is a place of "great traffic." He also visited the island of 'Anzediva' [Anjediva], "distant from the mainland half a "mile," and "travelling for one day from the aforesaid "island," arrived at 'Centacola' [Ancola], and in two days more at 'Onor,' and afterwards at 'Mangolor' and 'Canonor.' "Here we begin to find a few spices, such "as pepper, ginger, cardamums, mirabolans, and a "little cassea." Having spent some days at Cananore, Varthema started on another journey up country "towards the Kingdom of Narsinga, and travelled on "the mainland for 15 days towards the East [N.E. by "N.], and came to a city called Bisinegar [Bijanagar] ". . . a place of great merchandize, and is endowed "with all possible kinds of delicacies." Returning to Cananore he went on, by way of 'Tormapatani' [Dormapatam], and 'Pandarini' [a famous port of the Middle Ages, 20 miles above Calicut], and 'Capogatto' [close above Calicut], "to the very noble city of Calicut ". . . the head of India, that is to say . . . "the place in which the greatest dignity of India is "centred." Wherefore it appears fitting to Varthema at this point of his narrative "to bring the First Book "to an end, and commence the Second, which opens "with a graphic description of Calicut and of its King, "called Samory, which in the Pagan language means "God on Earth." This is the Zamorin of the Portuguese discoverers of India, a name really signifying Lord of the Sea, a most appropriate title for the King of Calicut. Calicut he describes as situated on the open beach, and "the sea beats against the walls of the "houses." Varthema found there merchants from all parts of the East, "very many Moorish merchants, "many from Mecca, and part from Banghella [Bengal], "some from Ternasseri [Tenasserim], some from Pego "[Pegu], very many from Cioromandel [Coromandel], "in great abundance from Zailani [Ceylon], not a few "from Colon [Quilon], and Caicolon [Kayan Kulam], "a very great number from Bathacala [Beitkul], from "Dabuli [Dabul], from Chievuli [Chaul], from "Combeia [Cambay], from Guzerati, and from Ormus. "There were also some from Persia and from Arabia "Felix, part from Syria, from Turkey, and some from "Ethiopia and Narsinga [Bijanagar, 'the Kingdom "of Narsinga']. There were merchants from all these "realms in my time. It must be known that the "Pagans do not navigate much, but it is the Moors "who carry the merchandise, for in Calicut there are "at least 15,000 Moors, who are for the most part "natives of the country. . . . . The time of their "navigation is this: from Persia to the Cape of "Cumerin, which is distant from Calicut eight days' "journey by sea towards the south,* you can navigate "through eight months in the year; that is to say, "September to all April; then from the first of May "to the middle of August it is necessary to avoid this "coast because the sea is very stormy and tempestuous. ". . . . At the end of April they depart from the "coast of Calicut, and pass the Cape of Cumerin, and "enter into another course of navigation which is safe "there four months, and go for small spices;" that is, go and trade in the Indian Archipelago. He describes the pepper and ginger plants of Calicut at length, and among the fruit trees of the country mentions the *ciccara* [jack], *amba* or *manga* [mango], *carcopal*

---

* The original has a full stop here, but I have ventured to change it to a comma, which makes the meaning of the paragraph perfectly clear.

[Garcinia Cambogia], *comolanga* [*Kamuranga*, Averrhoa Carambola], *malapolanda* [plantain], and *tenga* [cocoa-nut]. He also mentions that a great quantity of sesamum seed [" *zerzalino* "] is produced in the country. Varthema's Persian companion, whom he had picked up at Shiraz, not being able to dispose of his merchandise at Calicut by reason of the confusion caused by the quarrels of the Zamorin with the Portuguese, the two proceeded by river to 'Cacolon' [Kayan Kulam], where, he notices, were many "Christians of St. Thomas," and then to 'Colon' [Quilon] and 'Chayl' [Kayal], where "we saw those pearls fished for in the sea, in the "same manner as I have already described to you in "Ormus." "We then," says Varthema, "passed "further onwards, and arrived at a city which is called "Cioromandel [Coromandel], which is a marine dis-"trict, and distant from Colon seven days' journey by "sea. . . . I found some Christians in this place, "who told me that the body of St. Thomas was "12 miles distant from this place" [at Maliapur or St. Thomé]. "They told me that Christians could not "live in that country after the King of Portugal had "come there, because the said King had put to death "many Moors of that country, which trembled through-"out for fear of the Portuguese." He then crossed a gulf of "12 or 15 leagues to 'Zailon'" [Ceylon], where he notices the elephants, rubies, garnets, sapphires, jacinths, and topazes, and two fruits named *melangoli* [oranges] and *carzofoli*, and the *canella* or cinnamon tree. From Ceylon he returned to the Coromandel Coast, and at 'Paleachet' [Pulicat], a "place . . . . of immense traffic . . . . and "especially in jewels" from Ceylon and from Pegu, he took ship to 'Tarnassari' [Tenasserim], a thousand miles across the sea, and arrived there in 14 days. "Silk is made there in large quantities, ... and "cats which produce the civet." Thence he took "the route towards the city of Banghella"* [? Gaur the capital of Bengal]. "The Sultan of this place is a Moor ". . . . and he [like the Bijapur Sultan] is always "at war with the King of Narsingha. This country "abounds more in grain, flesh of every kind, in great "quantity of sugar, also of ginger, and of great abundance "of cotton, than any country in the world. And here are "the richest merchants I ever met with. Fifty ships are "laden every year with cotton and silk stuffs, ... "that is to say, *bairam*, *namone*, *lizati*, *cioutar*, *doazar*, and "*sinabaffs* [identified by Badger with *sina-bafta*, 'China-"woven' cloths]. These same stuffs go through all Tur-"key, through Syria, through Persia, through Arabia "Felix, through Ethiopia, and through all India. There "are also here very great merchants in jewels, which come "from other countries." Next he sailed "about a thousand miles to 'Pego' [Pegu], and thence to 'Melacha' [Malacca], opposite to which is "a very large island "which is called Sumatra." "Melacha pays tribute to "the King of Cini [Siam], who caused this place to be "built about 80 years ago, ... and truly I "believe that more ships arrive here than in any other "place in the world, and especially there come here all "sorts of spices, and an immense quantity of other mer-"chandise. . . . A great quantity of sandal-wood "and tin is found here." From Malacca he paid a visit to 'Pider' on the island of Sumatra, where "grows a very "great quantity of pepper and of long pepper, which is "called *molaga*. . . . And you must know that in "this port there are laden with it every year 18 or 20 "ships, all of which go to Cathai [China]. . . . An "immense quantity of silk is produced in this country" [see "*Encyclopædia Britannica*," article on Achin, by Sir Henry Yule]. . . . "A great quantity of benzoin "is also produced here." He mentions also aloes-wood of three sorts, *calampat* [*kalambak*, Alœxylon

* It is doubtful whether Varthema ever got beyond the Malabar Coast.

Agallochum of Cochin China], *loban* ["frankincense"], and *bochor* ["incense"], as if products of Sumatra, but the true aloes-wood is produced in Cochin China; and '*lacca*,' [the dye-wood of 'Tanarius major' of Rumphius, not *lac*, the source of sealing-wax and lake]. Next Varthema accompanied the Persian on a long voyage to the 'island of Bandan' [Banda island], "where "nutmegs and mace grow;" and from it visited the island of 'Monoch' [the Moluccas], "where the cloves "grow;" and the island of 'Bornei' [Borneo]; whence they crossed over to 'Giava' [Java], and then returned to Malacca. Here his companion bought "5,000 "*pardai* worth of small spices, and silk stuffs, and "odoriferous things," and with them they sailed away together westward, and arrived again on the Coromandel Coast, probably at Negapatam, in 15 days. There he met 22 Portuguese, the first, it would seem, he had himself fallen in with in India. From Negapatam he went round to Quilon and to Calicut, where he met two Milanese who had come in the Portuguese ships round the Cape of Good Hope to purchase jewels on behalf of the King of Portugal. They had landed at 'Cocin' [Cochin], from which place they had deserted from the Portuguese to Calicut, to make cannon for the Zamorin. Making his way to Cananore, Varthema was employed for some time in the Portuguese service. He was present in the great fight between the Portuguese and the Zamorin's fleet, A.D. 1506, and was employed for a year and a half as factor at Cochin. Finally, on the 6th of December 1507, he left Cananore in the homeward-bound ship '*San Vicenzo*.' After a course of about 3,000 miles he reached Mozambique, having passed Melinda, Mombasa, Kilwah, Sofala, Pate, and Brava on the way. Then the Cape was rounded, and the '*San Vicenzo*' passed northward under St Helena and Ascension, and finally anchored in the Tagus off Lisbon, where he was warmly welcomed by the King, Don Emanuel, of Portugal.

The high interest of Varthema's travels is that they were undertaken at the very time of the Portuguese discovery of the Cape route to India, and give us a detailed and accurate survey of the commerce of the Eastern seas as it existed just before it was to be completely revolutionized by this great event. The account published by Roscoe of the rare and costly articles of the Indian trade presented by the Sultan of Egypt in 1487 to Lorenzo de Medici, affords a vivid idea of its general character between the fall of Constantinople, which ruined the Genoese trade with the East by the Black Sea, and the discovery of the passage to India by the Cape of Good Hope, which gradually undermined the Venetian trade by Alexandria and Famagusta, and at last completely subverted the through overland trade between Europe and Southern Asia. The consequences of this revolution were of course greatly exaggerated by the Turkish conquest of Syria and Egypt, A.D. 1516–17. In Vansleb's "*Present State of Egypt*," published in 1678, we have the evidence of an eyewitness of the completeness of the ruin of that part of the ancient overland trade between the East and West which, previously to Da Gama's successful enterprise, had gone by way of Aden and the Red Sea.

The "*Description of the Coasts of East Africa and Malabar*" [Lisbon, 1516; London (Hakluyt Society), 1866] left us by the Portuguese geographical discoverer Duarte Barbosa, born 1480, and assassinated at Zebu, one of the Philippine Islands, 21 May 1521, will be more fitly noticed farther on, in the list of works relating to India during the period of the supremacy of the Portuguese in Southern Asia.

The Portuguese Asia.

The Portuguese were the first who, after the Phœnicians, explored the South Atlantic coasts of Africa, and doubled the Cape of Good Hope, and they were the first to discover India by this navigation, and to open up to the nations of Europe the sea way through the Indian Archipelago, and on to China and Japan. The gradual advance in Western civilisation began, during the fifteenth and sixteenth centuries, to force on the sovereigns of Europe a more scientific organisation of their administrative and executive powers, and at a pecuniary expenditure out of all proportion to the resources derived from the royal demesnes and feudal tenures, that had hitherto sufficed for their maintenance. Hence the encouragement of trade, as the first necessity of national existence, by the enlightened statesmen of the period. The great wealth of Genoa and Venice attracted their particular attention to the commerce of India, and the accounts which Marco Polo brought home of the rich Eastern countries through which he had travelled excited the spirit of mercantile discovery and enterprise throughout Europe. As the Turks, succeeding to the Saracens, gained ground in Western Asia, the uncertain and dependent character of the overland trade with India became more clearly recognized; and when Constantinople was taken by Mahomet II., and Genoa in consequence lost Pera and Caffa, the whole thought of the people of Southern Europe, and more especially of the ruined Genoese, became anxiously set on the discovery of the presumptive passage round the southward extension of Africa to the Indies, and the establishment of direct commercial communications with countries where Nature seemed prodigal in the production of everything that could administer to the want and luxury of mankind. It was first attempted, as has been shown, to enter into relations with the Tartars, and much was at one time hoped for from an alliance with 'Prester John,' if haply his half-mythical kingdom might be found; and at a later period, subsequent to Da Gama's voyage, the Genoese, in the hope of recovering their rapidly failing prosperity, proposed to the Grand Duke of Muscovy a plan for bringing the merchandise of India into Europe once more overland through Russia. But it was in vain. The social and political condition of the age required a broader, securer, and more permanent basis for its commerce than the world had yet seen; a universal basis, such as the ocean, free to all, as the common right of Nature, alone could give. Naturally it fell to the Atlantic States of Europe to discover the ocean highway to India, the exploration of which was first systematically undertaken by the Portuguese; a people whose national character had been developed to the highest pitch of courage, energy, and contemporary culture, in their long struggle for independence with the Moors, and who in Prince Henry "the Navigator" [*b.* 1394, *d.* 1460] found a leader worthy to direct them in the adventurous quest. He was the fourth son of King John the Great of Portugal by Queen Philippa his wife, the eldest daughter of John of Gaunt, and was therefore a great-grandson of Edward III. of England. He gained so wide a reputation throughout Europe by the capture from the Moors in 1415 of Ceuta, then the centre of the commerce of Alexandria and Damascus with Africa and Europe, that he was asked by the Greek Emperor Manuel Palæologus to take the command of his armies against the Turks. But his mind had early been attracted "by the treasures of the Arabs, and of "rich India;" and, establishing himself at Cape Sagrez [*i.e.* Sacrum Promontorium], the extreme south-western corner of Europe, overlooking the mysterious waste of the yet unexplored Atlantic, he there devoted himself to the study of astronomy and navigation, and the elaboration of those plans of maritime discovery which at length laid open to Europe the whole of southern Africa, the southern coasts of Asia, and Australasia in the Old World, and the New World of the Americas. The revenues of the Order of Christ, of which Prince

Henry was the Grand Master, provided him with the means for carrying out his unbounded projects, in which, it must never be forgotten, his aim was as much the conversion of the heathen as the extension of the dominion and commerce of Portugal. He had already in 1412, before the reduction of Ceuta, sent a ship to make discoveries on the coast of Barbary. Cape Nun or Non, *i.e.* "No-Further," was the limit of the west coast of Africa as then known in Europe. But the ship sent by Prince Henry passed it, and reached Cape Bojador, so named from its great compass [for it "bulges" out 40 leagues into the Atlantic]; and here were met those strong currents running past it that had been the real barrier to the circumnavigation of Africa by the Phœnicians and Carthaginians from the West; as those that, after the voyage of Da Gama, gave their name to Cape Corrientes, north of Delagoa Bay, had prevented the Arabs from circumnavigating the vast continent from the East. Long before this, however, the Norman navigators of Dieppe are reported to have explored the west coast of Africa to the south of Cape Nun, and to have established factories there, whence they imported many articles of African produce, including ivory, for the manufacture of the carved trinkets and figures for which Dieppe has ever since been known; and in 1402 the Sieur de Bethencourt, a native of Grainville la Teinturière in the Pays de Caux, settled a French colony in the Canaries [so called because they abounded with wild dogs], the discovery of which is also claimed by the Spaniards, who became masters of the islands in 1483.* They were probably originally discovered by the Phœnicians, and have always been identified with the half fabulous *Insulæ Fortunatæ* of classical geography. When also the island of Madeira [so called from its woods] was discovered by the expedition sent out by Prince Henry in 1418–20, it was found to have been previously visited about the year 1344 by a young Englishman named

* The "Canary-bird" was first brought to England about this date.

Robert Machin, who ran away to sea with "fair Anne of "Dorset" [really a Frenchwoman, Anne d'Arfet], and was fortuitously cast with his young wife on this island, where their romantic grave gives its name to the province of Machico. An expedition in 1434–36 succeeded in doubling Cape Bojador, and in 1444 the Portuguese obtained the Papal Bull bestowing upon them the sovereignty over all the lands that they had hitherto discovered, and all that should be discovered as far as the Indies. The several islands of the Azores, so called from the goshawks abounding on them, were discovered at different periods between 1440 and 1450, although the Flemings claim the exclusive discovery of them in 1445. Cape de Verde ["Green"] was reached in 1446, and doubled in 1449; and in 1449 the Cape de Verde islands were discovered. In 1463, three years after Prince Henry's death, the Portuguese had reached the coast of Sierra Leone, so named from the nightly roaring of the lions in the mountains ranging along it; and in 1484 Diego Cam made his great discovery of the Congo River. In 1487 Bartholomew Diaz discovered the Cape of Good Hope, and called it *Cabo Tormentoso*, "Cape of Storms," "No," said the King [John II.] of Portugal, "*Cabo* "*Bona Esperanza* rather," the "Cape of Good Hope"—of finding India.

On the 12th of October 1492, Columbus, seeking India, discovered America. He appears to have formed his theory that the Indies could be reached by sailing to the west about 1474, from a study of the map constructed by Toscanelli of the travels of Marco Polo. After in vain offering his services, first to his native city Genoa, and then in succession to the Kings of Portugal, Spain, and England, he still maintained his faith in the possibility of sailing to India across the Atlantic; and once, when lying sick of fever and hope deferred, he was greatly encouraged by a heavenly voice whispering to him:—"God will cause thy name to "be wonderfully resounded through the earth, and will "give thee the keys of the gates of the ocean, which "are closed with a strong chain." The first American land he sighted was an island, where as soon as he had gained its shore, he set up a crucifix, and, kneeling down before it, thanked the Saviour who had enabled him through so many perils to accomplish the increasing purpose of his life from boyhood. Then, rising from his knees, he proclaimed with a broken voice that henceforth the island should bear the name of San Salvador.* Such was his noble consecration of the quest of India. It was at daybreak on Friday, August the 3rd, 1492, after eighteen years of weary supplication and heart sickness, that Columbus, by the aid chiefly of the old and wealthy seafaring Spanish family of the Pinzons, at last set sail from Palos, carrying with him a letter to the Great Khan of Tartary. On the 2nd of October he was still sailing due west on the parallel of 26° north. On the 7th, Alonzo Pinzon, in the '*Pinta*,' having seen a flight of green parrots going to the south-west, Columbus at once steered after them 'west-south-west'; and at midnight on the 11th, a sailor, Rodrigo de Triana, descried the verdant island, to which, at the break of dawn on the 12th, Columbus rowed in one of the ship's boats, being the first European to set foot on the new tropical world of America. It has been well said that never was an augury more momentous than the apparition of these tropical birds. America was actually first discovered by Bjorn Herjulfson, A.D. 986, and afterwards by Leif Erikson, who reached its shores somewhere between Boston and New York, A.D. 994. But the memory of their discoveries had passed away. Had Columbus known anything of them† he would probably have steered his westward course more

* The name thus given to it by Columbus has disappeared. It is now called Watling Island.

† Others argue, that as Columbus went to Iceland in 1477, and could converse in Latin with the learned there, to whom the voyages of Bjorn, Leif, and others were familiar, he was probably not ignorant of them: and further that Columbus did not seek the northern lands discovered by the Norsemen, but the East Indies.

to the north, and not have followed, into the south, the clamorous streak of green perroquets, whose providential lead thus determined the distribution of the Celtic and Germanic races, and their whole future history, in the New World. By the Bull of May 4, 1493, the Pope confirmed the King of Spain in the sovereignty of America, and strictly prohibited all persons whatsoever, on pain of excommunication, to touch at any port or place within an imaginary line drawn from Pole to Pole, 100 leagues, afterwards extended to 250 leagues, westward of the Azores. The Portuguese were to possess all eastward of this line. The Pope forgot, however, that there were two sides to a globe; a fact which brought the rival sovereignties of Spain and Portugal into collision on the discovery of the Philippine Islands in 1521 by Magellan, then in the service of the King of Spain.

It was on Saturday, the 8th of July 1497, that the expedition commanded by Vasco da Gama sailed from the Tagus for the invention of India. Notwithstanding the passionate popular clamour against the undertaking, King Emanuel, who had succeeded John II. in 1495, was determined to prosecute the project of Prince Henry; and three sloops of war, the *Angel Gabriel*, the *Saint Raphael*, and the *Pilot*, with a store ship, were fitted out, Vasco da Gama being commissioned admiral and general, and his brother Paul, and his friend Nicholas Coello, appointed to commands under him. About four miles from Lisbon, on the sea-shore, stands the sanctuary of Belem [*i.e.*, Bethlehem], built originally by Prince Henry 'the Navigator,' for the resort of sailors. Thither, the night before his departure, Da Gama conducted the companions of his expedition to pray for its success, and there they spent the whole night in the rites of their heart-felt supplication. The following day, when the adventurers marched into their ships, the entire population of Lisbon were on the beach, headed by an unending procession of priests in long robes, bearing banners and singing anthems, the whole crowd singing with them; and when Da Gama gave his sails to the wind, not knowing to what fate they might bear him, the vast multitude remained immovable by the sea until he with his whole fleet had passed away out of their sight. On the 20th of November following, at noon, he doubled the great Cape of Good Hope, and, steering northward, sailed along the beautiful and richly wooded coast so accurately described by Camoëns. On December the 8th, on leaving the wide bay that had been named St. Blaze by Diaz, a violent storm carried the fleet into the southmost sweep of the dreadful current running between the cape, thenceforward called Cape Corrientes, and the southern extremity of Madagascar, which, as above [p. 158] noted, had always prevented the Arabs from extending their southward voyages, along the East Coast of Africa, beyond the Mozambique Channel. On the 15th they sighted the island of Santa Cruz in Algoa Bay, where Diaz had set up a great cross. On the night of the 17th they passed the Rio do Iffante, the extreme point of Diaz's discovery, where Da Gama became extremely alarmed by the increasing force of the Mozambique current. Fortunately the wind was in his favour, and on Christmas Day [" Dies Natalis "] his fleet gained sight of the land he named Terra de Natal. On the 6th of January following [1498], the Festival of the Epiphany, they first saw the river called by them "dos Reyes," or "River of the [three Twelfth Night] Kings;" and on the 22nd, after a short stay for refitting,* left the large river [the Quilimane] to which, from their meeting there two Arab merchants connected with the Indian trade, Da Gama gave the name of Rio dos Bōos Signaes, or "River of Good Signs"; dedicating at its entrance a lofty cross to Saint Raphael. On the 10th of March they anchored off the island of Mozambique, where Da Gama was delighted to hear that "Prester John" had many cities along the opposite African coast. On the 7th of April

* De Barros places the refitting of the ships in the river "dos Bōos Signaes"; but others in the river "dos Reyes," the river "Misericordia" of Correa.

they arrived at Mombas, where a plot for Da Gama's destruction was made between the Moors of the place and the pilots who had brought him from Mozambique. Sailing thence on the 13th of April they fell in with and captured two Arab ships; and on Easter Day, the 15th of April, reached Melinda, where, Da Gama was informed by one of his Arab prisoners, would be found four ships belonging to the Christians of India. He was visited by the King of the place, and by some of the Indian Christians, who warned him against going on shore; and accordingly on Tuesday the 24th of April he left the place, sailing, under the guidance of a Christian Indian pilot named Malemo Canaco, due eastward. On Thursday, the 17th of May [1498], he sighted the Malabar Coast, and on Sunday, the 20th, cast anchor before the city of Calicut [Koli-Kukuga, "Cock-crowing"]. He was warmly welcomed by a Moor there who spoke the Portuguese language, and, with the permission of the Zamorin, at once established a factory, under the superintendence of Diego Diaz, the brother of the first discoverer of the Cape of Good Hope. He also dedicated a cross on the sea-shore before the city of Calicut to St. Gabriel. Visiting Anjediva, and another island near it, where he raised a cross to St. Mary, Da Gama, after having suffered much from the enmity of the Moors towards the Portuguese, set sail on his return voyage westward, from Anjediva, on the 5th of October, carrying a letter with him from the Zamorin to the King of Portugal, to the following effect:—"Vasco da Gama, a "nobleman of your household, has visited my kingdom, "and has given me great pleasure. In my kingdom "there is abundance of cinnamon, cloves, ginger, pepper, "and precious stones in great quantities. What I seek "from thy country is gold, silver, coral, and scarlet." On the 2nd day of January 1499, Da Gama found himself off Magadoxa, and on the 7th again anchored before Melinda, where he consecrated a cross to St. Stephen. On the first of February he reached the island in the Mozambique Channel on which he had landed on his outward voyage, and where he now erected a cross to St. George. On the 3rd of March he touched at the Bay of St. Blaze, and on the 20th again doubled the Cape of Good Hope, and, at the end of August or beginning of September 1499, reached Lisbon, where he was received with great pomp by the King, Emanuel 'the Fortunate,' and with unbounded popular rejoicings. In honour also of Da Gama's splendid achievement, King Emanuel rebuilt the chapel of 'Our Lady of Bethlehem' as a stately church, and placed the statue of Prince Henry the Navigator' over the great door, and his own and his Queen's over the smaller doors flanking it.

But, already, before the arrival of Da Gama at Calicut, the Portuguese had reached India overland. King John II., when he found that the difficulties of the passage to India round the Cape of Good Hope were likely to be surmounted, ordered Pedro de Covilham and Affonso de Payva to travel to India by Egypt, in order to obtain information respecting the trade and navigation of the Indian seas. They set out from Portugal in 1487, and proceeded by Naples, Rhodes, Alexandria, and Cairo to Tor on the Red Sea. There they heard of the great trade with Aden and Calicut. From Aden, Payva went into Abyssinia, and Covilham sailed in an Arab vessel to Cananore, and thence to Calicut and Goa, being the first Portuguese who was ever in India. He returned by Sofala, where he examined the gold mines, and received some information of the island of Madagascar, or "Island of the Moon" as it was called by the Moors; and on arriving in Egypt he was met by the Rabbi Abraham of Beja, and Joseph of Lemago, two messengers who had been sent by King John II. to inquire after his progress, and from whom he learnt of the death of Payva. These men he immediately sent back to King John with the following report:—"That the ships which sailed down "the coast of Guinea might be sure of reaching the ter-"mination of the continent by persisting in a course to "the south, and that when they should arrive in the

" eastern ocean their best direction must be to inquire for " Sofala and the Island of the Moon." Then Covilham, again taking ship to Aden, sailed on to Ormuz, and thence visited Abyssinia. Here he was kept a prisoner until 1526, when he probably returned to Europe with the Embassy of Don Rodriguez de Lima.

When the Portuguese at last, rounding the Cape of Good Hope, burst into the Indian Ocean like a pack of hungry wolves upon a well-stocked sheep-walk, they found a peaceful and prosperous commerce, that had been elaborated during 3,000 years by the Phœnicians and Arabs, being carried on along all its shores. The great store cities of this trade were then at Calicut, Ormuz, Aden, and Malacca. Here were collected the cloves, nutmegs, mace, and ebony of the Moluccas, the sandal-wood of Timor, the costly camphor of Borneo, the benzoin of Sumatra and Java, the aloes-wood of Cochin China, the perfumes, gums, spices, silks, and innumerable curiosities of China, Japan and Siam, the rubies of Pegu, the fine fabrics of Coromandel, the richer stuffs of Bengal, the spikenard of Nepaul and Bhutan, the diamonds of Golconda, the "Damascus steel" of Nirmul, the pearls, sapphires, topazes, and cinnamon of Ceylon, the pepper, ginger, and satin-wood of Malabar, the lac, agates, and sumptuous brocades and jewelry of Cambay, the costus and graven vessels, wrought arms, and broidered shawls of Cashmere, the bdellium of Scinde, the musk of Thibet, the galbanum of Khorassan, the assafœtida of Afghanistan, the sagapenum of Persia, the ambergris, civet, and ivory exported from Zanzibar, and the myrrh, balsam, and frankincense of Zeila, Berbera, and Shehr. From Ormuz these costly commodities were transported in ships up the Persian Gulf and river Euphrates, and by caravans on to Aleppo and Damascus, and Trebizond, whence they were distributed all over Asia Minor, and Southern and Western Europe, and throughout Muscovy. The merchandise collected at Aden was sent on to Tor or to Suez, and thence by caravan to Grand Cairo, and down the Nile to Alexandria, where it was shipped to Venice and Genoa, and other ports of the Mediterranean.

It became a vital object with the Portuguese on entering the Indian Ocean to possess themselves of the great Arab emporia of Calicut, Ormuz, Aden, and Malacca. The difficulties they had experienced in their first voyage at Calicut led them in their second voyage to India to send out a fleet of 13 ships with 1,200 soldiers, which sailed from the Tagus under the command of Cabral, in March 1500. The sum of his instructions was, to begin with preaching, and if that failed to proceed to the sharp determination of the sword. On his way out Cabral was driven by a storm on the coast of Brazil, of which country, notwithstanding the prior claims of Yanez Pinzon, one of the companions of Columbus, and of Martin of Nuremberg, he must be regarded as one of the discoverers. [Its name is derived from that of the well-known brazil-wood or "*sappan*" of the East Indies, a similar fiery coloured dye-wood having also been found in Brazil.] Cabral then proceeded on his voyage, and after visiting Sofala, Mozambique, Quiloa, and Melinda, arrived at Calicut in September. Having quarrelled with the Zamorin, the latter instigated an attack on the Portuguese factory, which was pillaged and burnt, and the 50 people in it massacred. Cabral took ample revenge, and then sailed on to Cochin, where he settled a fresh factory and concluded an advantageous treaty with the Prince. He also visited Cranganore and Cananore. On his homeward voyage he visited the ports of Melinda, Mozambique, and Sofala, and compelled several of the chiefs on the east coast of Africa to become tributary to Portugal. One of his vessels, commanded by Peter Diaz, discovered the port of Magadoxa, south of Cape Guardafui. In March 1501, before Cabral's fleet had returned to Lisbon, four ships were sent out under De Nova, who on Lady Day discovered the island he called Conception. It first received the name of Ascension from Albuquerque, when re-discovered by him, May 20th, 1503. After landing at Cochin and Cananore, De Nova went on to Calicut, where he sank the fleet the Zamorin was preparing against the Portuguese. On his return voyage in 1502, he chanced, on St. Helena's day, to discover the island of St. Helena, which, on account of its excellent supply of water, has ever since proved of such advantage to all engaged in the India trade. In 1500 also, Gaspar Cortereal, who had been sent out by the King of Portugal to prosecute a westward route to India, discovered the Gulf of St. Lawrence, and the southern coast of Labrador. When Cabral arrived in Portugal King Emanuel was convinced by him that it was only possible to secure the splendid fortune that had befallen him in the East by a show of great power, and if necessary by the exercise of overwhelming force ; and accordingly in 1502 he sent out a fleet of 20 ships to India under the command of the great Vasco da Gama, and obtained from Pope Alexander VI. the Bull which conferred on him the title of "Lord of the "Navigation, Conquests, and Trade of Ethiopia, Arabia, "Persia, and India." Da Gama on his outward voyage visited Sofala, and settled a factory there and at Mozambique, and compelled the submission of the Prince of Quiloa. Then proceeding to India he formed an alliance with the Kings of Cananore and Cochin against the Zamorin of Calicut, and having severely cannonaded the town and the Zamorin's palace, and plundered a number of Arab ships in the roads, sailed back to Europe in December 1503. In the same year 9 ships were sent out from Lisbon ; 3 under the great Alfonso de Albuquerque, 3 under Francisco de Albuquerque, and 3 under Antony de Saldanha. Saldanha, who was the first Portuguese to visit Saldanha Bay [1503], was especially commissioned to block the Red Sea against the overland Indian trade through Egypt. One of his lieutenants, Ruy Lorenço, discovered the island of Zanzibar, and, with Mombas and Brava, made it tributary to Portugal in this year. Francisco de Albuquerque, on reaching Cochin, found the King closely besieged by the Zamorin of Calicut, who had made war on him for entering into an alliance with the Portuguese. He was soon compelled to sue for terms, giving the Portuguese permission to build a fort at Calicut; and Francisco de Albuquerque, after settling a factory at Quilon, and another at St. Thomé, and leaving a detachment of his force for the protection of the allies of Portugal in India, set sail for Europe. Neither he nor his ships were ever heard of again. One of the ships commanded by him discovered on the outward voyage the Curia Muria islands, and also the island of Socotra, re-discovered in 1504–5 by Diego Fernandez Pereyra, commander of one of the ships in the small fleet sent out under Lopez Soarez in 1504. The Portuguese discovered the island afterwards known by the name of Mauritius, in 1505. In the same year the King of Portugal sent out another large fleet of 22 sail and 15,000 men, under Francisco de Almeyda, the first Portuguese Governour and Viceroy of India. He reduced Onore, and built a fort at Cananore. His son, in 1507, accidentally discovered the island of Ceylon. In 1506 King Emanuel sent out a fleet of 16 ships under Tristan da Cunha, who discovered the islands of that name, and also the island of Madagascar; and another of 6 ships under Alfonso de Albuquerque, who rapidly extended the power and dominion of the Portuguese in the East. His instructions were to exclude the Indian traders from the Red Sea and the Persian Gulf. In 1507–9 a strong fort was built at Sofala; Malacca was visited for the first time, Muscat rendered tributary and possession taken of Ormuz; the Zamorin also was reduced to complete submission; and the Maldive Islands were surveyed. In 1508 the island of Socotra was taken, and the island of Sumatra first visited; as also was China in 1508–9, the date of the first discovery of that country, from the sea, by Europeans.* It was in this year that the pseudo Caliph of Egypt, secretly abetted

---

* It was not until the expedition of Benedict Goes from Delhi in 1602–7 that they at last learned to identify it with the "Cathay" of the overland travellers of the 13th century. Thus Milton, in *Paradise Lost*, written

both by the Zamorin of Calicut and the Venetians, appeared in the Indian seas to dispute the sovereignty of the Portuguese in the East. The Venetians supplied the timber for building the Sultan's ships, carrying it with great difficulty from Alexandria to Suez; and the fleet when ready sailed for India, and, falling in with a Portuguese squadron at Chaul [some say Diu], defeated it; Lorenzo de Almeyda, the Viceroy's son, being slain in the action. Their defeat raised a spirit of opposition to the Portuguese throughout Western India, but the Viceroy, collecting another fleet, took Dabul, and totally dispersed the Egyptian fleet off Diu in February 1509. Later in this year Albuquerque succeeded as Governour [not Viceroy] to Almeyda, who died on his homeward voyage. In the meanwhile the island of Ormuz had revolted, and forced the Portuguese to retire to Socotra, a disaster so alarming to King Emanuel that he at once ordered out 17 war-ships, with 3,000 troops, under the command of Don Francisco Continho, with orders to co-operate with the Viceroy. This reinforcement was in addition to the 13 ships under De Aguiar, that had sailed a little earlier in the same year 1509. The first demonstration of the united fleets was against Calicut, but they had to withdraw from before it with great loss; and then Albuquerque, in order to recover the prestige of the Portuguese, at once attacked and captured Goa, February 17, 1510. It was soon after retaken by the natives, but on November 22 the Portuguese recovered possession of the place and made it the capital of all their possessions in the East. Albuquerque next set sail for Sumatra, and on July 24, 1511,

---

between 1655 and 1665, still distinguishes between them, Book XI. 387–90:—

> "from the destined walls
> Of Cambalu, seat of Cathaian Can,
> And Samarcand by Oxus, Temir's throne,
> To Paquin [Peking] of Sinæan Kings."

Hakluyt, however, in 1600, wrote of rhubarb, "it cometh from Cathaio or China."

seized Malacca, the key of the navigation, and emporium of the whole trade, of the China Seas and Indian Archipelago. Three of his ships were sent on, in 1511–12, to the Spice Islands, and visited Ternate, Bouro, Amboyna, and Banda. They visited also Palembang in Sumatra, and other ships of the fleet visited Siam. The Portuguese also in this year plundered and destroyed Surat. In 1513 Albuquerque made an unsuccessful attempt upon Aden, whence he proceeded up the perilous Red Sea, then for the first time entered by a Portuguese fleet. He wintered at the island of Camaran. Early in 1514 he recovered possession of Ormuz, and, returning to India, died off the bar at Goa, December 16, 1515, leaving the Portuguese Empire in the East at the height of its glory. In 1516, Soarez, the successor of Albuquerque, reduced Aden to temporary submission, took and burned Zeila, and unsuccessfully attacked Jiddah. In 1517 he personally led an expedition against Colombo, and forced the King to agree to the payment of 1,200 quintals of cinnamon annually to the Portuguese, who also obtained possession of Point de Galle. In this year also they settled a valuable trade at Canton, and took the town of Berbera on the Sumali Coast opposite Aden. In 1518, when Sequeyra succeeded Soarez as Viceroy, the Portuguese first opened their lucrative trade with Bengal.

In 1519 the Spaniards laid claim to the Banda ['United'] or five [really ten*] 'Nutmeg Islands,' and the Moluccas, or five 'Clove Islands,'† as falling within the line of their sovereignty laid down by the Papal Bull of 1493. From 1505 the Court of Spain

* Namely, Pulo Banda, Pulo Nera, 'Lantore' or Lontar, Pulo Ai or 'Pulo Wai,' Pulo Pisang, Pulo Run or 'Pulo Roon,' Pulo Suwanggi, Gunungapi, Pulo Kapal, and 'Rosengyn.'

† The five small islets on the western side of Gilolo, the largest of the Molucca Islands, namely, 'Ternate,' 'Tidore,' Mortir, Makiyan, and Bachian. The name Moluccas is now extended to all the 'Spice Islands' between Celebes and New Guinea.

had earnestly engaged in the project of finding a way to the 'Spice Islands' from the west, and in 1508 Pinzon and De Solis sailed in search of them, and explored the coasts of South America to the 40th degree of south latitude. It was not, however, until 1515 that the Pacific was discovered, when Nunez de Balboa, who in 1510 had been placed in command of the Spanish colony of Santa Maria on the Gulf of Darien, having gone on an expedition into the Sierra de Quarequa, suddenly, from one of its peaks, stared down on the boundless sea outstretched below him. From the narrow isthmus on which he stood, it extended east and west and south until lost in space. This was the true discovery of the Americas, the disclosure that they were not, as Columbus believed to his dying day, the easternmost coast of Asia, or a "West Indies," but a separate twin continent; and as this new world with the vast waste of ocean beyond swam into his eyes, and all its moral significance flashed upon his mind, Balboa, kneeling down upon the scarped summit from which he gazed, raised his hands to heaven in silent wonder and amazement at the immensity of the revelation vouchsafed to him. Then, descending with all his men to the shore of the great unknown sea, and wading out into it, up to his waist, he claimed possession, with his drawn sword, of the infinite expanse, in the proud names of Aragon and Castile. In October 1515 De Solis was again sent out to discover the 'Spice Islands' from the west, and in January 1516 entered tho Rio de la Plata, originally named Rio de Solis; its present name not having been given to the river until 1525, when Diego Garcia found some plates of silver, probably from the mines of Potosi, in the hands of the wild Indians on its banks. De Solis, having anchored in the mouth of the river, went on shore to explore the country inland, when he and eight of his men were set upon and massacred by the natives, and roasted and devoured in sight of his ships; whereupon the disheartened expedition returned to Spain. In 1517 Ferdinand Magellan, who, according to De Barros, had been present at the capture of Malacca in 1511, proceeded to Valladolid, and gave it as his opinion that the 'Spice Islands' fell within the Spanish boundary, and undertook to take a fleet thither by the south of the American continent. Accordingly in 1519 Charles V. gave him five ships for the purpose. Every one of them was accompanied by a Portuguese pilot; and the *Santiago* was commanded by João Serrano, an old Portuguese, on whose knowledge of the East, and especially of the Moluccas, Magellan placed great reliance. On the 21st October 1520, St. Ursula's Day, he reached the Cape, called by him "Cabo de las Virgines" [Virgins' Cape], at the entrance of the Strait we call after Magellan, but named by him, in affectionate honour of his own flagship, *San Vittoria*. From many fires having been seen on the land south of the Strait, he named it Tierra del Fuego. On the 27th of November he emerged from the Strait into the open Pacific Ocean, and the Cape terminating the Strait on his left [on Tierra del Fuego] he named "Cabo Deseado" [the "Desired"], now called Cape Pillar. On the 6th of March 1521, he discovered the beautiful islands to which, from the thievish propensities of their inhabitants, he gave the name of the Ladrones ['Thieves']; and on the 16th, the islands he called the Archipelago de San Lazaro, a name afterwards changed by Villalobos, in honour of Philip II. of Spain, to that of the Philippines. On one of these islands Magellan was slain, 27th April, in a skirmish with the natives, brought on by his proselytising zeal; whereon João Serrano and Duarte [Odoardo] Barbosa were elected joint commanders of the expedition.* On the 8th July 1521 they anchored before the city of Borneo; and on Wednesday, November 6th, 1521,

* Barbosa was killed a month later; and when Serrano also died, Carvalho was elected commander-in-chief.

at last descried the long sought for Molucca Islands, for the discovery of which, by a western route, their daring adventure had been undertaken. On the 8th they anchored at Tidore. In the following December, of the two remaining ships of the expedition, it was resolved to send the *Trinidad* back to Spain by Panama and the Strait of Magellan, and to take the *Vittoria* home, under Sebastian Del Cano, by the Cape of Good Hope. In order to escape the observation of the Portuguese, her course was steered so far south as the 42nd parallel of latitude, but, with all their caution, they approached within five leagues of the Cape on the 6th of May 1522. On the 9th of July, when they reached the Cape de Verde Islands, they were obliged to put in at Santiago, where, to prevent the suspicions of the Portuguese being roused, they said that they had come across from America. It was here they discovered that in sailing round the world they had lost a day, for while by the *Vittoria's* log it was Wednesday, the 9th of July, at Santiago it was Thursday, the 10th. On the 6th of September the *Vittoria* arrived at San Lucar, the only survivor of the noble fleet that had sailed from the same port on the 20th of September 1519. The circumnavigation of the world, originating in the dispute between Spain and Portugal about the possession of the Moluccas, was completed, and the sphericity of the earth demonstrated, against the authority of Cosmas Indicopleustes, which had ruled geographers for nearly a thousand years. Charles V. received Del Cano with the highest distinction, and conferred on him a life pension, and a coat of arms, with branches of clove, cinnamon, and nutmeg for bearings, and a globe for crest, all surmounted by the motto "*Primus circumdedisti me.*" In settlement of the dispute as to the respective rights of Portugal and Spain to the 'Spice Islands,' the King of Spain was confirmed in the sovereignty of the Philippine Islands, and the Moluccas were finally surrendered to the King of Portugal, with the provision that the latter was to lend the King of Spain 350,000 ducats in respect of any claims he might have on the Moluccas, in the possession of which the King of Portugal was not to be disturbed until the money was repaid.

In 1520 the Bahrein Islands in the Persian Gulf were subjugated by the Portuguese, and in 1521 Diu and Acheen were unsuccessfully attacked, and Ternate occupied. In this year also the Venetians, alarmed by the decrease of their overland trade, made a proposal to the King of Portugal to take all the spice annually imported into Lisbon by the Cape of Good Hope, at a certain fixed price; but the offer was rejected. In 1524 Vasco da Gama came out to India for the third time, as the 2nd Viceroy and 6th Governour. In 1525 the Portuguese were besieged by the Zamorin in their citadel at Calicut, and must have surrendered had not Da Gama [who died in 1527] arrived in time to relieve them. In 1525–26 they discovered New Guinea and Celebes, and plundered and destroyed Dofar on the coast of Arabia, and Massouah on the coast of Abyssinia. In 1527 Mangalore, Porca, and Chetwa were burnt by them; and Tidore was taken from the Spaniards, and Borneo discovered. In 1529 the towns of Bassein and Tannah were subjected. In 1530 Damaun was taken, and permission obtained to build a fort at Diu; but the Portuguese were expelled by the natives from the island of Ternate. During 1530, 1531, and 1532, Surat and Gogo, Pate, Mangalore, and most of the other towns on the coast of Guzerat, were destroyed by the Portuguese; in 1532 Aden again became tributary; and in 1534 Bassein was ceded to them in perpetuity. In 1537 they discovered the island of Magindanao or Mindanao; and in this year Malacca was twice attacked by the King of Acheen. In 1538 St. Francis Xavier was sent out to Goa with Don Garcia de Naronha, the 11th Viceroy, his object being the conversion of the natives to Christianity, in the hope that they would thus become better reconciled to the Portuguese rule. In the same year the Turks fitted out a strong fleet at Suez, and made an attempt upon Diu. They failed in this; but on their return to the Red Sea, they succeeded in expelling the Portuguese from Aden. About the year 1540 the Portuguese established their trade with Patania, Camboja, and Cochin China; and in 1542 the coast of Japan was discovered by three Portuguese who were driven thereon in a junk bound for Siam and China. In 1545, the King of Cambay having attempted to drive the Portuguese from Diu, they took and destroyed Gogo. Delagoa Bay was visited by them for the first time this year. In 1547 the King of Acheen made another unsuccessful attempt on Malacca. In 1555 the Portuguese took and plundered Tatta on the Indus, and put 8,000 of the inhabitants to death.

The first half of the 16th century was the period of the greatest renown of the Portuguese in the Indian Seas, although, after the death of Albuquerque, they appear, notwithstanding the large reinforcements sent to them from Europe, to have been rather employed in defending the possessions they had acquired, than in extending, or even consolidating, their power. From Japan and the Indian Archipelago to the Red Sea and Cape of Good Hope, they were sole masters and dispensers of the riches and treasures of the East, and their positions along the Atlantic Coast of Africa and in Brazil completed their ultramarine empire. But from this very period its decay began. It was essentially a commercial empire that had been rapidly raised on an insufficient basis of territorial sovereignty; and the Portuguese never commanded the necessary military and political resources for its maintenance and defence. They were also in another way unprepared for the commerce of which, through their splendid maritime discovery, they had obtained the controul. The national character had been formed in their secular contest with the Moors, and above all things they were knights errant and Crusaders, who looked on every pagan ["blackamoor"] as an enemy at once of Portugal and of Christ. It is impossible for any one who has not read the contemporary narratives of their discoveries and conquests to conceive the grossness of the superstition and cruelty with which the whole history of their exploration and subjugation of the Indies is stained. Albuquerque alone endeavoured to conciliate the goodwill of the natives, and to live in friendship with the Hindu Princes, who were naturally better pleased to have the Portuguese, as governed by him, for their neighbours and allies, than the Mahomedans whom he had expelled or subdued. It was the justice and magnanimity of his rule that did as much to extend and confirm the power of the Portuguese in the East, as the courage and success of his military achievements; and in such veneration was his memory held by the Hindus, and even by the Mahomedans in Goa, that they were accustomed for years after his death to repair to his tomb, and there utter their complaints, as if in the presence of his shade, and call upon God to deliver them from the tyranny of his successors. The cruelties of Soarez, Sequeyra, Menezes, Da Gama, and succeeding viceroys, drove the natives to desperation, and encouraged the Princes of Western India in 1567 to form a league against the Portuguese, in which they were at once joined by the King of Acheen. But their undisciplined armies were not able to stand against the veteran soldiers of Portugal, 200 of whom at Malacca utterly routed and put to flight a force of 15,000 of the enemy, with 200 guns. When, in 1578, Malacca was again besieged by the King of Acheen, the small garrison of Portuguese succeeded in inflicting a loss on him of 10,000 men, and all his cannon and junks. Twice again, in 1615, and for the last time in 1628, it was besieged, and on each occasion the Achinese were repulsed with equal bravery and good fortune. But these incessant attacks on the Portuguese were significant of the decline of their empire, while the necessary increase of the military forces yearly sent out to the East proved an insupportable drain on the revenues and population of so petty a state as Portugal. In 1558, John III., King of Portugal, died, and was succeeded by Sebastian. The credit of the Portuguese in Asia having greatly declined during the preceding reign, Sebastian, in the hope of re-establishing it, appointed Don Constantin de Braganza, one of the royal family, to be the 20th Viceroy with almost sovereign prerogatives. But he was able to effect little more than the construction of a fortress at Damaun, and another at Manaar, and the reduction of the King of Jafnapatam to vassalage; and the rapid sequence of the viceroys appointed after him destroyed all possibility of a revival of the Portuguese power, as the vigorous efforts of a capable governour were over and over again counteracted by the errors of an incompetent successor. Thus Don Luis D'Ataide's energetic rule, as 24th Viceroy, from 1567 to 1571, was followed within the next five years by the weak and disastrous administrations of no less than four different viceroys, Don Antony de Noronha, Antony Monez Barreto, Don Laurence de Tavora, and Don James de Menezes. At this conjuncture, when it seemed as if the Portuguese empire of the Indies might pass away without observation, like the insubstantial pageant of a dream, Don Luis D'Ataide was sent out a second time, in 1579, as 29th Viceroy. Though he lived only one year, he succeeded in restoring something of its old vigour to the government, but it was too late. In 1580, the year in which Don Luis D'Ataide died, the Crown of Portugal, consequent on the death of King Sebastian in 1578, became united with that of Spain, in Philip II.; an event which proved fatal to the maritime and commercial supremacy of Portugal. It proved fatal in many ways, but chiefly because the interests of Portugal in Asia were now subordinated to the interests of Spain in Europe.

In 1640 Portugal again became a separate kingdom,

but in the meanwhile the Dutch and English had appeared in the Indian Ocean, and before their indomitable competition the Asiatic trade and dominion of the Portuguese had withered away as rapidly as it had sprung up. They obtained possession of Macao, as a station for their China trade, in 1586, but from this date the only notable events in their Eastern history are their repeated losses.

The Portuguese would appear to have, at different times, possessed the following places* in the East:—

On the East Coast of Africa: Melinda, Quiloa, Querimba, Zofala, Mosambique, and Mombasa [expelled A.D. 1631].

In Arabia: Aden and Mascate [expelled by the Arabs A.D. 1648].

In Persia: Bazora and Ormuz.

In India: Tatta on the Indus, Bandel, Diu, Damam, Assarim, Danu, St. Gens, Agaciam, Maim, Manora, Trapor, Basaim, Chaul, Morro, Dabul, Salsette, Bombay, Tana, Caranja, Goa, Onor, Barcelor, Mangalor, Cannanor, Calicut, Granganor, Cochim, Angamale, Coulam, Negapatam, "Meliapor, with the city which is a bishoprick of the "late called St. Thomas," Masulapatam, and several other places on the Coromandel Coast, and in Bengal.

In Ceylon: Manar, Point de Galle, Columbo, Jafnapatam, and other places.

In Further India: Malaca, and factories at Pegu, Martaban, Junkceylon, and other places.

In the Indian Archipelago: Mindanao, or Magindanao, the Moluccas, and Banda Islands, a fort on the island of Timor, and other places.

In China: Macao, and the island of Formosa.

All these possessions were held in subordination to the Supreme Government at Goa, where the Viceroy presided

* I adopt, for the most part, the Portuguese spelling of the names of the places cited.

over the civil and military, and an Archbishop over the ecclesiastical, affairs of the whole of Portuguese Asia. Strange to say, they had no possessions in either Java or Sumatra.

The period of the highest development of their commerce was probably from 1590 to 1610, on the eve of the subversion of their power by the Dutch, and when their political administration in India was at its greatest degradation. At this period a single fleet of Portuguese merchantmen sailing from Goa to Cambay or Surat would number as many as 150 or 250 carracks. Now only one ship sails from Lisbon for Goa in the year, and the only remaining Portuguese possessions in India are Goa, Damaun, and Diu; so low have fallen a people who once commanded all the coasts of Africa and Asia from the Cape of Good Hope to China and Japan, and the whole commerce of the Eastern Seas.

*Contemporary writers on the early Portuguese Period.**

The narratives of contemporary travellers throw great light on the early operations of the Portuguese in India; and the most interesting of them all is the description left us of *The Coast of East Africa and Malabar*, by Duarte [Odoardo] Barbosa, which was translated and edited for the Hakluyt Society, by the Honble. Henry G. T. Stanley, in 1866. Barbosa was a cousin [? brother-in-law] of Magellan, and was with him at the capture of Malacca, and accompanied him in his voyage for the circumnavigation of the globe. He fully describes the East African and Malabar Coast, Bijanagar, Bengal, Orissa, Further India, the Indian Archipelago, and China, and

* This reference to the contemporary writers on the Early Portuguese period of the commerce of Europe in the Indian Ocean, includes only those of them I happened to have looked through in the course of the preparation of this Report, and would be quite inadequate as an independent review of them, dissociated from the special purposes of my Report.

the trade of the Eastern Seas as it was found by the Portuguese on their first entering them. He gives a detailed account of the trade in rubies, diamonds, emeralds, and other precious stones, a special account of cloves, ginger, and cinnamon, and a most interesting price list of the drugs and spices then sold at Calicut; namely, "lacca" of Martaban, "lacca" of the country, "atincar" [borax], "canfora grossa," "canfora" for anointing the idols, "Aquila" [eagle-wood], "genuine aloes" [*i.e.*, aloes-wood or eagle-wood of superior quality], "almiscar" [musk], "beijoim" [benjamin], "tamarindos," "calamo aromatico" [sweet flag], "mirrha," "encenso," "ambar," "mirabulanos ["myrobolaneiros" is another Portuguese spelling], eynblicos, bellericos, et quebolos," cassia, "sandalo vermelho" [red-saunders wood], "espicanardo," "sandalo blanco" [sandal-wood], "noz moscada" [nutmegs], "macis," "herba lonbrequera" [wormwood], "turbiti," "anil" [indigo, i.e., *nil*], "erva de vermes" [wild silk], "zer-"umbeth," "zedoaria," "sagapeno," "aloes sacotorino," "cardamomo," "rheubarbo," "atulia" [Lapis Tutia], "china cubela," [cubebs], "opio," and "opio" prepared in Cambay.

Camoens travelled in India and the East, and wrote the greater part of the *Lusiad* there, between A.D. 1553 and 1569.* On his return from Macao he was wrecked on the coast of Camboja, and of all his property succeeded only in saving the MS. of the *Lusiad*, deluged with the waves, through which, clinging to a plank, he forced his way to the shore. It is not simply the national epic of the Portuguese, but the epic of the modern system of universal commerce founded on the discovery of the sea way to India. There can be no doubt of the historical truth which underlies the supernatural machinery and elevated imagery of Camoens'

---

* He went out with the fleet commanded by Fernan Alvarez Cabrol in 1553.

great poem; and indeed his geographical descriptions, more particularly of the new found coasts of southern Africa, often fail through their very explicitness to affect the imagination, as Milton so powerfully does by his vague enumeration of

> "The less maritime kings,
> Mombaza, and Quiloa, and Melind,
> And Sofala, thought Ophir, to the realm
> Of Congo, and Angola farthest south."

The real value of the *Lusiad*, however, is not as a record of authentic discovery, but as evidence of the higher moral and spiritual aims of the Portuguese in their inquisition of the Indies; the history of which, but for the light thrown on it by Camoens, would only preserve the memory, better lost, of deeds of indescribable tyranny, senselessness, and shame. Ferdinand Mendez Pinto has incurred everlasting infamy as a liar, simply on account of the incredible atrocities he describes without any reticence or apparent consciousness of their guilt. It is to him that Congreve refers, in "Love for Love," II., 5: "Ferdinand Mendez Pinto was but a type of thee, thou liar of the first magnitude." Sometimes he is contemptuously nicknamed "Mendax Pinto." But Faria y Sousa, the author of *The Portuguese Asia*, regards him as a truthful writer. He was a promiscuous vagabond, pirate, and cut-throat in the Eastern Seas, from 1537 to 1558; and his *Peregrinations*, published in 1614, affords a harrowing picture of the frightful moral depravity and inhuman bloodthirstiness of the Portuguese adventurers of the period, and of the confusion and misery brought by them on the indigenous populations of the southern shores of Asia, whose peaceful overland commerce with Europe, of 3,000 years' growth, they overthrew within a generation of Da Gama's rounding the Cape of Good Hope.

In 1520 the Portuguese Governour in India sent an embassy by way of Ormuz to the Persian Court, the narrative of which by Antonio Tenreiro [Coimbra, 1560] is one of the earliest accounts we possess of the trade through Persia at the time when it first began to be affected by the competition of the Cape route.

Nearly a century later, in 1611, Fray Gaspar de San Bernardino, of the order of St. Francis, undertook the journey by land from India by way of Mombas and Socotra and the Persian Gulf to Portugal; and his narrative bears witness to the complete revolution that had now taken place in the course of the trade between India and Europe through the Euphrates Valley and Syria.

To Englishmen, one of the most interesting travellers in the East was François Pyrard de Laval. He went out to India in 1601, and about 1609-11 was in Goa, where, he tells us, he met Italians, Germans, Flemings, and Frenchmen, the adventurous spirits, in short, of every country of Europe, as well as of Asia. There too he met three Englishmen, among the first ever seen in India, who probably belonged to Hawkins' expedition, prisoners of the Portuguese: and he observes of them, with a sort of prophetic apprehension, that, even fast bound in irons as they were, they were a proud-looking set, who took every opportunity of showing their contempt for the Frenchmen and other foreigners around them. Before going to Goa, Laval had been detained for several years in the Maldive Islands, on which he is still the best authority. His *Discours du Voyage*, 1619, has recently been translated for the Hakluyt Society by Mr. Albert Gray.

In 1663, Father Manuel Godinho, of the Society of Jesus, returned from Goa to Lisbon overland by way of Gombroon. He begins by deploring the almost total downfall of the Portuguese Asiatic Empire, and describes the rising trade of Surat, which city, under the English, had gradually supplanted Goa as the emporium of Southern India. He describes it as being then perhaps the richest emporium of the world.

The *Peregrinacion de la Mayor Parte del Mondo* of Don Pedro Sebastiano Cubero was published at Saragossa in 1688. He set out about 1650 from Moscow with the Russian Ambassador to the Court of Persia. From Ormuz he sailed to "Damayn," and Surat and Goa, where he found the capital of Portuguese Asia in a state of miserable decay, and its trade almost gone since the "perfidious heretics," the Dutch, English, Swedes, and Danes, had carried it off. From Goa he sailed to Masulipatam, and thence to Malacca, already in the hands of the Dutch, and on to Manilla, where he took ship across the Pacific to Mexico.

Giovanni Francesco Gemelli-Careri of Naples, in his narrative [*Giro del Mondo*], published in 1699, of six years travel round the world, notices that at this date the remnants of the Portuguese conquests in Asia were so inconsiderable as scarcely to defray their own expenses.

The great work of Geronimo Osorio, *De Rebus Emanuelis virtute et auspicio gestis*, 1571, is universally recognized as of the highest authority on the early history of the Portuguese acquisitions in Asia; and, as based on this, may be mentioned the useful compilation of Faria y Sousa, entitled *Asia Portugueza*, published in 1666–75; as also the *Decadas da Asia*, published by De Barros, 1552–63. Major's *Discoveries of Prince Henry the Navigator*, published by the Hakluyt Society, in 1877, is a most excellent monograph on the life of the high-hearted leader of the modern exploitation of the Indies.

The Dutch in the East.

The Dutch were later than the English in trying to get to the East, but, owing to their early established indirect trade with India through Lisbon, they succeeded in getting there before us, and they altogether outstripped us in the great geographical discoveries of the 17th century in the South Sea.

Before Lisbon rose to notice, and while Venice and Genoa were still at the height of their prosperity, the carrying trade of the Netherlands for its own fisheries and manufactures rendered its cities the natural entrepôts for the commerce between northern and southern Europe. The imports of Genoa and Venice from the East were originally distributed over northern Europe by the merchants of Bruges, and through Central Europe by those of Nuremberg and Augsburg. When the trade was diverted to Lisbon, and Venice, and Genoa, Nuremberg, and Augsburg became in consequence deserted [and Bruges also, owing to the interruptions to which the port of Sluys was about this time subjected], the productions of the Indies were in turn distributed to northern Europe through Antwerp; and after the destruction of that city by the Spaniards [1576–1585], through Amsterdam. On the seven northern provinces ["United Provinces"] of the Netherlands declaring their independence in 1580, Philip II., under whom the Crown of Portugal was in the same year [1580–81] united to that of Spain, forbade the merchants of Amsterdam to trade with Lisbon. This interdict, however, served only the more to quicken the native spirit and enterprise of the Dutch, and the eventful period from the sack of Antwerp in 1576 to the treaty of Westphalia or Munster in 1648 was that of the rise of their Eastern commerce and dominion. By that treaty this energetic and indomitable people actually compelled the Spaniards to trade with the East only by Cape Horn;* and thus, by a

---

* Discovered by Cornelius Schouten in 1606 in one of the earliest Dutch voyages by the west to the "Spice Islands." It was named after Hoorn, on the Zuyder Zee, the birthplace of Schouten and also of Tasman. The island near it was called Staten Island, in honour of the States of Holland, and the passage between it and the main shore Strait Lemaire, from the projector of Schouten's voyage.

stroke of the pen as it were, deprived Spain and Portugal of all the advantages of the discoveries of Columbus and Da Gama. Between 1602 and 1620 they seized the principal settlements of the Portuguese in the East, and by 1661 had expelled them from all but the lifeless remnants of their once world-wide empire they hold to the present day. At this time also they scarcely tolerated the English in the Indian Ocean, and the 80 years from 1661 to 1741 was the time of the greatest fortune and power of the Dutch in the East.

When the supremacy of Spain on the high seas was shattered at a blow by the destruction of the "Invincible Armada" in 1588, the merchants of Antwerp, who had emigrated to Amsterdam, at once saw their opportunity for establishing a direct trade with India. At first, to avoid interference with the Portuguese rights under the Papal Bull of 1493, they, following the example of the English, attempted to open communications with the East by sailing round the north coasts of Europe and Asia. William Barents made his first abortive attempt in 1594, and the second in 1595, and the third, in which he perished, in 1596. Then the Dutch resolved to take the direct passage round the Cape of Good Hope, and Cornelius Houtman's fleet was despatched to India. He left the Texel on the 2nd February 1594/5, "crossed the Line" the 14th of June, "doubled the Cape" the 2nd August, landed at Sumatra the 11th July 1596, and entered the harbour of Bantam the 22nd July following. He returned to the Texel in 1597. Before his return another set of merchants had sent out James Van Neck; and Houtman's second expedition, in which he was slain, went out in 1598, and returned in 1600–1601.* Companies were now formed all over the United Provinces,

* It was with this expedition, consisting of the *Lion* [*De Leeuw*] and *Lioness* [*De Leeuwin*] that John Davis sailed [in the *Lion*] as Chief Pilot. Houtman's official title was *General*, but he is always designated the *Baas*, *i.e.*, "Boss."

and in 1602 they were amalgamated by the States General into one Joint Stock Corporation, entitled "The Dutch East India Company." They had in their first voyage to Bantam experienced much opposition from the Portuguese, in consequence of which a war commenced, by which the Portuguese interests in the East suffered considerably. In 1603 the Dutch, with a large force from Europe, made attempts to dislodge the Portuguese from Mozambique and Goa, but failed in both. On the other hand they succeeded, during 1604–5, in settling factories on the Coasts of Malabar and Coromandel, in Ceylon, and in Java, at Jacatra and Bantam. In 1604 the Spaniards at Manilla, being aware of the defencelessness of the islands in the Indian Archipelago under the Dutch, proceeded with an expedition and captured them all. But the Dutch fleet hurrying back from Malacca, the covetous siege of which they at once raised, succeeded in wresting the whole of the islands back again from the Spaniards, and in 1607 also expelled them from Ternate and Tidore. At this period the ever prosperous Hollanders are stated to have had factories at Mocha, in Persia, at Cambay, in Malabar, Ceylon, Coromandel, Bengal, Aracan, Pegu, in Sumatra, at Acheen, Jambi, and Palembang, in Java at Bantam, in Camboja, Siam, Cochin China, Tonquin, China, and Japan, exclusive of the entire possession of the Moluccas and the factories taken from the Portuguese in the Banda Islands. The Mauritius, first discovered by the Portuguese in 1505, had been occupied by the Dutch in 1598, and named after their renowned General and Stadtholder Prince Maurice of Nassau [Orange].

In 1611 they were driven out of Tidore and Banda by the Spaniards. In 1612 the King of Candy called in the Dutch to assist him against the Portuguese, and in return gave them the monopoly of the cinnamon trade of the island; and in this year also they took Timor from the Portuguese. In 1614 they established factories at Masulipatam, and in Siam, and in 1619 acquired the sovereignty of Java, where, on the 12th of August in that year, they laid the foundation of the city of Batavia [Jacatra] as the seat of the Supreme Government of the Dutch Possessions in India, which had previously been at Amboyna. It was about the same time, namely in 1622–23, that they founded the city of New Amsterdam [Manhattan], now New York, in America. On the 17th February 1622/3* they massacred the English in Amboyna; and although the English people, then entering on their troubles with the Stuart dynasty, were forced for a time to submit to the outrage, the lasting animosity of the nation was thereby all the more roused against the rivals of the "London" Company, which thenceforth was always sure of the popular sympathy in its deadly contest with the Dutch for predominance in the East. Yet from the date of the massacre of Amboyna to 1650 was a period of great humiliation for England in the Indian Seas, and everywhere we were vilified and oppressed by the Dutch.

The Dutch were the discoverers of Australasia. The idea which the ancients had of a *Terra Australis* originated simply in the extension by some of their geographers of the African continent eastward to the Malay Peninsula. There is better ground for the presumption that the 'Great Java' of the Portuguese of the 16th century really refers to Australia. It would appear to have been first sighted by a Spanish fleet which sailed from Peru with Quiros as Pilot Major in 1595. In 1605 Quiros, accompanied by Louis Vaez

* The date is frequently given as 1622; as that of the English "glorious Revolution" is invariably given as 1688 ["the Revolution of 1688"] instead of 1689. The explanation is that until the "New Style" Calendar was introduced into Great Britain in 1752, the year did not legally commence in England before the 25th of March; and consequently before that year events that occurred in the months of January, February, and March [to 25th *idem*] usually bear, in official documents, the date of two years. This has been a constant source of perplexity to me, and doubtless often of error.

de Torres, commanded the expedition which discovered Tahiti and the New Hebrides. The latter islands he mistook for the broken coast of a new continent named by him *Australia del Espiritu Santo,* and he designed a capital for it, to be called 'the New Jerusalem.' The following year Torres, who had become separated from Quiros in a storm, sailed from east to west through the strait that now bears his name. But before this Cornelius Wytfliet, in 1598, had distinctly indicated the position of Australia:—"The "*Australis Terra* is the most southern of all lands, "and is separated from New Guinea [first discovered by "the Portuguese in 1526] by a narrow strait." The *Luca Antara,* discovered by Manuel Godinho de Eredia in 1601, has also been identified with Australia. Still its first practical discovery was made by the Dutch. In 1606 one of their ships from Bantam reached Cape York at the top of the eastern main of the great Gulf, named, about 1628, after Pieter Carpentier, then Governor of the Dutch Indies. In 1618 the *Pera* and *Arnhem* from Amboyna explored this Gulf, the latter ship giving its name to 'Arnhem's Land.' In 1623 Jan Carstensz was in the Gulf and named the River Carpenter. In 1616 Dirk Hartogs touched at 'Dirk Hartogs Island' on the coast of Western Australia, which, after it had been further explored by the Dutch in 1628, received the name of 'De Witt's Land.' In 1627–28 the *Guldene Zeepaard,* carrying Pieter Nuyts to the Dutch embassy in Japan, coasted along the whole of the Great Bight of Southern Australia. In 1642–44 Abel Tasman discovered Van Diemen's Land, so named after the daughter of the Dutch Governor at Batavia, and New Zealand, and further explored the coast of North Australia from 'Dirk Hartogs Island' to 'Arnhem's Land.' These great discoveries of the Dutch led to the States General formally naming the new found 'South Land,' New Holland.

In 1635 the Dutch expelled the Portuguese from Formosa, in 1638 from Batecalo, Trincomalee, Negomba, and Point de Galle, and in 1640, when Portugal again became a separate sovereignty, from Malacca. The loss of Malacca was a fatal blow to the Portuguese trade in the Indian Archipelago and with China, while its capture by the Dutch at once set them above all rivals in the East. In the same year the Portuguese, at the instigation of the Dutch, were expelled from Japan. In 1651 the Dutch settled a colony at the Cape of Good Hope, and abandoned St. Helena, which they had occupied since 1645. In 1656 they obtained possession of Calicut from the Portuguese. In 1658 they captured Negapatam [afterward, in subordination to Bantam, the head of all their establishments on the Coromandel Coast], and Jafnapatam, the last stronghold of the Portuguese in Ceylon. In 1661–64 they expelled the latter from Quilon, Cochin, Cananore, Cranganore, and other places on the Malabar Coast, and in 1669 from St. Thomé and Macassar.

The following is a list of their settlements and agencies submitted by the Dutch Company to the States General the 22nd October 1664:—

Amboyna, with its subordinate islands, "which supply "the whole world with spice": the Banda islands, "which "produce nutmeg and mace": Pulo Roon [sometimes spelled Rohun], "ceded to the English by treaty, *but not* "*given over to them*": Ternate, and the other Moluccas: Macassar and Manado in Celebes: Timor: Bima on Sumbawa, "where is a little trade in rice and sappan wood": in Sumatra, Jambi, Palembang, and Indraghiri, "with a "contract for all the pepper procured on the west coast"; [Acheen, *i.e.* "City of Peace," had been given up].

Malacca, with Tenasserim, and Junkceylon, *i.e. Ujung Salang*, "Salang Headland": [the factory in Siam had been withdrawn, likewise the one in Ligor:] Aracan, an agency for the purchase of rice and *slaves*: in Tonquin, a factory: in Pegu, factories at Ava and Sirian.

In Coromandel, Pulicat, Negapatam, and Masulipatam, for the purchase of piece goods: in Bengal, 'Hughley,' Cossimbazaar, Dacca, Patna, "in command of a great "trade in silk, cotton goods, saltpetre, sugar, rice, &c.;" in Orixa, a factory for rice and other provisions supplied for Ceylon: Ceylon, one of the most important possessions of the Company,—with garrisons at Colombo, Point de Galle, Negomba, Manaar, and Jafnapatam: Tuticorin, opposite Ceylon, with a good trade in cotton goods and pearls: in Malabar, Cochin, Cranganore, Quilon, Cananore:—"the Samorin of Calicut, and other princes have "contracted with the Company to sell all their pepper to "them": at Porca, whence "the English had been "ordered to withdraw": in Guzerat, a factory at Surat, in charge of the trade of Hindostan, "which is very con-"siderable," with dependent posts at 'Amedabad' and Agra.

In Persia, Gombroon and Ispahan: in the Persian Gulf, Bassorah: [in Arabia, Mocha had been recently given up].

The island of Mauritius.

The Cape of Good Hope.

Java, "where was their capital Batavia, producing pro-"digious quantities of rice, sugar, fruits, &c."

In Japan the Company traded only and chiefly for gold and silver.

In China no trade had yet been done, but much was hoped from the Emperor in consideration of the Dutch delivering him from the formidable pirate 'Coxenga.' In later documents their possessions also include Banjarmassin, Padang, Landak, and Succadana.

In 1672–73 they took from us St. Helena, which we had occupied from 1651. Before the latter date they had held the island, which was discovered by the Portuguese in 1501, from 1645. We recovered it immediately, and made it over [by Charter of Charles II., dated 16th December 1674] to the English ["London"] East India Company.

In 1677 William of Orange married the Princess Mary of England.

In 1682 the Dutch expelled our factory from Bantam, thereby forcing us to abandon also our factories dependent on it in Siam and Tonquin, and at Amoy, and other places in the uttermost Indies.

In 1688–89 William of Orange became King of England.

In 1693 Pondicherry was surrendered to the Dutch, but was restored to the French by the Treaty of Ryswick, 1697.

In 1759 the Dutch, comprehending the full significance of Clive's great victory at Plassey, made a desperate effort to expel the English from Bengal, but were ignominiously repulsed by Colonel Forde, and sueing for peace pledged themselves never in future to keep more than 125 European soldiers in their Bengal factories.

In the great wars from 1781 to 1811, Holland lost all her colonies to us; but in 1813, when the country was restored to the House of Orange, most of them were given back by us ; and Java in 1816, and Sumatra in 1824 in exchange for Malacca.

The Dutch would have been unable to maintain their independence without the trade of the East, and when they lost it they rapidly sank into their present state of commercial and political stagnation. They lost it entirely through the narrow and exclusive spirit in which they pursued it. Although their enterprise ended in the formation of an empire, their sole object from first to last was to engross the spice trade of the Moluccas and Banda Islands. With this object they made the mistake, and long persisted in it, of establishing the seat of government in the remote island of Amboyna, and it was not until John Pietersoon Koen, on his own authority, transferred it to Java, and in 1619 founded the city of Batavia, that the supremacy of the Dutch in the Indian Archipelago was secured. Still the sordid object of their pursuit, the monopoly of the spice trade, continued to injuriously affect their reputation, and gradually it undermined their power, so inexorably true is it that "Man shall not live by "bread alone." They suffered still more through the egotistical national spirit, characteristic of every Teutonic race, which blinded them to the true European policy of the United Provinces. If the Dutch, instead of doggedly secluding themselves within their own green 'polders,' had opened up their canals to German commerce, and their Indian colonies to German emigration, and had identified German interests with their own, they would have maintained their supremacy on the seas, and probably supplanted us in the Empire of the East. They stood up boldly against us, and were hard to beat down; but they were too few, and their great Eastern commerce, even with the possession of Java, had too straitened a basis of territorial sovereignty to have ever made it possible for their power to survive a protracted struggle with England. It was fortunate indeed for England that their early opposition to us at Bantam and Amboyna led to our transferring the seat of the English ["London"] East India Company's Government from the Indian Archipelago to the continent of India, the inevitable conquest of which gave us in the end the command of the commerce of the East, from Constantinople to Peking, and from Australia and New Zealand to the Cape of Good Hope.

The present possessions of the Dutch in the Indian Archipelago are Bencoolen and Palembang on Sumatra, and the islands of Banca and Billiton off its coasts, the islands of Java, Madura, Bally, Lombok, and Celebes, districts on the west, south, and east coasts of Borneo, the Moluccas or 'Spice Islands,' the Islands of Timor and Sumbawa, and districts on the western side of New Guinea or Papua.

The contemporary works of travel connected with the early settlement of the Dutch in the East will be referred to among the books relating to the Factory Period of the English East India Company.

The English in India.

The first English attempts to reach India were by the north-west passage. In 1496 Henry VII. granted Letters Patent to John Cabot [Giovanni Gavotta] and his three sons to fit out two vessels for the discovery of this passage to India. They failed, but discovered the islands of Newfoundland and St. John, and explored the coast of America from Labrador to Virginia. In 1527 Dr. Robert Thorne, whose father was one of the discoverers of Newfoundland, and who himself had lived for many years at Seville in Spain, addressed a "persuasion to "King Henry VIII. for the discovery north-westward, "being a declaration of the Indies and lands discovered "and subdued unto the Emperor of Germany and King "of Portugal, and also of other parts of the Indies and "rich countries to be discovered." As the Portuguese had obtained a passage to India by a course to the south-east, and pretended a right, which they defended by force, to its exclusive occupation, he supposed that his countrymen might reach the same part of the globe by sailing to the north-west, and thus obtain a passage at once expeditious and undisputed. It is not certain whether Thorne's representations had any direct effect on the mind of Henry VIII., but they contributed to encourage the efforts which were made at the period to find a practical way by the Arctic Ocean to India or 'Cathay.' In 1549 Sebastian Cabot, the son of John Cabot, obtained sanction for a Charter from Edward VI., which was confirmed by Queen Mary, 1554–55, for "the discovery of lands, countries, and isles not before "known to the English," by this passage; and on the 10th of May 1553 Sir Hugh Willoughby, with Richard Chancellor [with whom was Stephen Boroughs] second in command, sailed on their wild errand. Sir Hugh and all his men perished miserably of cold in a river or haven called 'Arzina' [Warsina] in Lapland, but

Chancellor arrived at a port in the White Sea, where Archangel was afterwards [1584] founded; and thus was Russia practically first discovered by the English. Sir Martin Frobisher thrice attempted to pierce a northern passage to the East, in 1576, 1577, and 1578, on behalf of the 'Company of Cathay;' and having in his first voyage discovered an inlet on the Coast of Labrador running westward, he was on his return home "highly "commended of all men for the great hope he brought "of a passage to Cathaia." John Davis conducted three expeditions for its discovery, between 1585 and 1587, under the patronage of the London Company entitled the "Fellowship for the Discovery of the "N.W. Passage." George Waymouth's abortive attempt in 1602, and John Knight's in 1606, were made after the adoption by the English of the route to India by the Cape of Good Hope, which was thought to be too long. Henry Hudson's three voyages were made in 1607–08–09. As the N.W. and N.E. Passages had been found impracticable, he attempted in his first voyage to sail right across the North Pole. In his last voyage he discovered Hudson's Bay, which he thought to be the Pacific Ocean. In 1612 it was explored by Sir Thomas Button, who hoped to reach Japan by crossing it. He was disappointed, and the coast that blocked his further progress was therefore called "Hopes Checked." The designation has disappeared from modern maps, but the Cape off the entrance of Hudson's Strait still bears its quaint old name of "Hopes Advance." The last attempts to find the long desired outlet through North America and the Arctic Regions to the East were made by William Baffin in 1612–13–15–16. It is interesting to find it stated in Ramusio [see Hamel's *Early Voyages to the White Sea,*] that so far back as 1525 a Russian map was shown to a scientific person at Augsburg in order to demonstrate that it might be possible to reach India by way of the Icy Sea. It was not, however, till 1741 that Vitus

Behring, a Captain in the Russian Navy, discovered the broad strait, since known by his name, giving entrance from the Arctic Ocean to the Pacific.

Chancellor travelled from the mouth of the Dwina to the Court of the Grand Duke of Moscow, and laid the foundation of the Russian Company [as the "Company for the Discovery of Lands not before known" was henceforth called] for carrying on the overland trade with India, through Persia, Bokhara, and Moscow. In 1557 Anthony Jenkinson and Richard and Robert Johnson sailed to Russia to explore the route of this trade. From Moscow they went to "Nyse Novogorod," and down the Volga to "Ozan," whence they went on to Astrakan and to "Boghar" [Bokhara], from which place Jenkinson returned to Moscow in 1559. In 1561 he was sent out again to explore the route through Persia, and, travelling by Moscow and Astrakan, he proceeded by way of Derbent so far as Casbin, where he met a number of native merchants from India. Chenier's expedition followed, and after that Richard Johnson's expedition, of which Laurence Chapman is the narrator, was sent out in 1565. Jenkinson was again at Moscow in 1566 and 1571, in the interests of the Russian Company; but although they laid the foundation of the sea-borne trade of Russia, and of the Russian Navy, the Company found it impossible to compete profitably with the Portuguese in the importation of Indian goods into Europe. Not even the most precious articles would now bear the costs of the overland transit. This gradually led to the formation of the Turkey and Levant Company in 1581, in the hope of establishing trading relations with India by way of the Levant and Persian Gulf. Peter the Great was very anxious to develope the trade with India through Russia, and in 1717 sent Beckowitz, the son of a Circassian prince, to explore the Amu Darya: and in 1723 employed Peter Henry Bruce [*Memoirs*, &c., London, 1782] to survey the Caspian. John Elton [see

Jonas Hanway's *Historical Account of British Trade over the Caspian Sea*, 1753,] was also employed to survey the south-eastern frontier of Russia, and sent home so enthusiastic an account of the new opening by this route for English trade with India, that, in spite of the opposition of the Turkey Company and of the East India Company, an Act was passed permitting the importation of silk and other Eastern commodities through Russia. Unfortunately Elton's success with the Persians excited the jealousy of his Russian companions; and Jonas Hanway had to be sent from St. Petersburg in 1743 to arrange the differences between them. It was in vain, and in 1746 the Russian Government formally announced that the English would no longer be allowed to pass through their territories for the purposes of trade with India.

The Turkey and Levant Company [founded in 1581] having in the prosecution of their trade sent merchants from Aleppo to Baghdad, and thence down the Persian Gulf, and purchased Indian articles at Agra, Lahore, and Malacca, greatly stimulated the desire then prevailing in England for participating with Portugal in the direct trade with India by sea. In 1577 Sir Francis Drake fitted out four ships, and sailed through the Straits of Magellan, returning home [his expedition reduced to the *Golden Hind*] by the Cape of Good Hope. In the course of his voyage he touched at Ternate, one of the Moluccas, where the king agreed to supply the English nation with all the cloves the island produced; and Drake was thus the first person to open direct commercial intercourse between England and the East Indies, as well as the first Englishman to circumnavigate the globe. The first Englishman who actually visited India was Thomas Stephens in 1579, unless there be any foundation in fact for the statement of William of Malmesbury that, in the year 883, Sighelmus of Sherborne, being sent by King Alfred to Rome with presents to the Pope, proceeded thence to the East Indies to visit the tomb of St. Thomas [at Maliapur, "Peacock-town"], and brought back with him a quantity of jewels and spices. Stephens was educated at New College, Oxford, and in Goa was Rector of the Jesuits' College in Salsette. His letters to his father are said to have roused great enthusiasm in England to trade directly with India. In 1583 three English merchants, Ralph Fitch, James Newberry, and Leedes, went out to India overland as private mercantile adventurers. The jealous Portuguese threw them into prison at Ormuz, and again at Goa. In the end Newberry settled down as a shopkeeper at Goa [Fitch says he went home through Persia]; Leedes entered the service of the Great Mogul; and Fitch, after a lengthened peregrination in Ceylon, Bengal, Pegu, Siam, Malacca, and other parts of the East Indies, returned to England.

In 1586, Sir Thomas Cavendish, following Drake's example, commenced his circumnavigation of the world, by the Straits of Magellan and the Cape of Good Hope, touching at the Ladrones on the way.

In 1587, the Spaniards being about to invade England, a strong fleet was sent out under Drake to annoy their trade and that of the Portuguese; and among the ships of the latter seized by him was the *St. Philip*, the first Portuguese carrack coming from the East Indies the English had ever taken. The papers of this vessel afforded so much information as to the value of the Indian trade, that they are considered to have at last fixed the determination of the English to establish direct communication with India.

Early in 1588 the Spanish Government complained to Queen Elizabeth of Drake and Cavendish having infringed their divine rights by sailing round the globe. Elizabeth haughtily replied that what it was lawful to Spaniards to do, was lawful also to Englishmen, "since the sea and air "are common to all men." Thereupon the Spaniards sent forth the "Invincible Armada" to conquer these islands. It was met by the English fleet under Lord Howard of

Effingham, Lord Thomas Howard, Sir John Hawkins, Sir Martin Frobisher, and Sir Francis Drake, and scattered to the four winds. Its Providential destruction gave the English great confidence in their navy, and their ability to cope with the Spaniards and Portuguese on the high seas; and from this date the merchants of London, like those of Holland, began earnestly to devise measures for opening direct commerce with the East Indies by the Cape of Good Hope.

In 1591 some merchants of London fitted out three ships, the *Penelope*, *Merchant Royal*, and *Edward Bonadventure*, under the command of George Raymond and James Lancaster, for trading in the East, and harrying the Spaniards and Portuguese. The expedition came to a bad end, and it was only after many grievous adventures that Lancaster at last returned home without his ship.

In 1592 some English privateers captured the great Portuguese carrack the *Madre de Dios*,* and brought her into Dartmouth, when it was found that her principal cargo, after the jewels, consisted of aloes, ambergris, gum benjamin, cloves, cinnamon, cocoa-nuts, camphor, civet, ivory, ebony, frankincense, ginger, galangal, hides, musk, myrobalans, mace, nutmeg, pepper, and porcelain vessels, raw silk and silk stuffs, and other piece goods, taffaties, sarcenets, cloth of gold, calicoes, lawns, quilts, carpets, canopies, and various other rich commodities. There was also found in her "*The Notable Register or Matricola of the* "*whole Government and Trade of the Portuguese in the East* "*Indies*," on which the memorial of the promoters of the London East India Company to Queen Elizabeth in 1599 was principally founded.

In 1596 Sir Robert Dudley fitted out three ships, under the command of Captain Benjamin Wood, for the India and China trade; but the expedition was very un-

* She was one of the fleet of six ships sent out from Lisbon to Goa under Ferdinand de Mendosa in 1591, and was taken on her return voyage.

fortunate, not one of the company ever being heard of again.

In 1599, the Dutch, who had now firmly established their trade in the East, having raised the price of pepper against us from 3*s.* per lb. to 6*s.* and 8*s.*, the merchants of London held a meeting on the 24th September "at Founders' Hall,"* under the Lord Mayor, and agreed to form an association for the purpose of establishing direct trade with India. Queen Elizabeth also sent Sir John Mildenhall by way of Constantinople to the great Mogul to apply for privileges for the English Company, for whom she was then preparing a charter; and on the 31st December 1600 the English East India Company was incorporated by Royal Charter under the title of "*The Governor and Company of Merchants of London trading into the East Indies.*" The early "Voyages" of the Company, "Separate" and "Joint Stock," have already been enumerated in the body of the "Report on the Old Records" [pp. 45–50], and I now at once proceed to trace out the settlement of the Company's Factories in the East Indies.

THE COMPANY'S TRADE.

One of the documents connected with the Company's application for a charter was a memorandum distinguishing the countries in the East Indies with which the Spaniards and Portuguese had trade from those with which trade might be freely opened by the English. Among the latter they name—

"The Isle of Madagascar or San Lorenso, upon the "backeside of Africa."

"The kingdoms of Orixa, Bengala, and Aracan."

"The rich and mightie kingdome of Pegu;" and of "Junçalaon," Siam, "Camboia," and "Canchinchina."

"The most mightie and welthy empire of China."

---

* Now in St. Swithin's Lane, but then at Founders Court, Lothbury. I find no contemporary evidence of this meeting being held at Founders' Hall. It was possibly held in the house of Sir Stephen Evance, Lord Mayor of London. The meeting of the 23rd September 1600 was held in Founders' Hall.

"The rich and goulden island of Sumatra;" and "Java Major," "Java Minor," and Bally; Borneo, Celebes, Gilolo, and "Os Papuas."

"The long tracte of Nova Guinea and the Isles of "Solomon."

"The rich and innumerable islands of Malucos, and the "Spicerie, excepte the two small islands of Tidore and "Amboyno, where the Portugals have only two smal "forts;" Mindanao and Calamines, "and the greate and "smal Lequeos."

"The manifold and populos sylver islands of the "Japones;" and "the countrey of Coray newely dis- "covered to the north-east."

Sir Foulke Grevile, in replying to Sir Francis Walsingham's demand for "the names of such kings as are "absolute, and either have warr or traffique with the "Kinge of Spaigne," begins, "in Barbarie with the "kingdoms of Fess and Morocco," and continues all round the coasts of Africa to "Sues" at the top of the Red Sea ["in the bottom of this Sea"]. Then he goes round the peninsula of Arabia to Ormuz, and on through the countries beyond the Persian Gulf to "the "kingdome of Cambaia, which is the fruitfullest of all "India, and hath exceedinge greate traffique." Then he passes in review "the cuntrie of the Malabars, "who are the best souldiers of India," subdivided into the six kingdoms of Baticola, Cochin, "Chananor," "Choule," "Coulon," and "Caléchut." Beyond the Malabars "is the Kingdome of Narsinga," "then the "Kingdome of Orixen and Bengolen," "as also of "Aracan, Pegu, Siam, Tanassaria, and Queda." "The "island of Sumatra or Taprobuna is possessed by many "kynges, enemies of the Portugals; the chief is the "Kinge of Dachem, who besieged them in Malacca, "and with his gallies stopped the passage of victualls "and trafficke from China, Japan, and Malacca." "The Kynges of Acheyn and Tor are in like sorte "enemies of the Portugalls." "The Philippinas be-

"longed to the crowne of China, but, abandoned by "him, were possessed by the Spaniards, who have "traffique there with the merchants of China." "They "trafficque also with the Chinois at Mackau and "Japan." "And, lastlie, at Goa, there is great resort "of all nations from Arabia, Armenia, Cambaia, Ben- "gola, Pegu, Siam, Malacca, and China, and the "Portugals suffer them all to lyve there, after their "own manners and religions; only for matter of justice "they are ruled by the Portugal law." This letter of Foulke Grevile affords an admirable bird's eye view of the political and commercial relations of the countries along the shores of Africa and Asia at the period of the first appearance of the English Company's ships in the Eastern Seas. A list of the principal imports from the East Indies into Portugal and Holland was also prepared by John Chamberlain for the Company, and proved most useful to them. As it has never before been published, I give it here entire, being indebted for it to Mr. Noel Sainsbury, of the Public Record Office, who has had it extracted from the "East Indies" series, Vol. I., No. 19.

"*The Comodities of the Este Indies.*"

"Sinemonde, pepercase, pepper callycowe [of Calicut], longe pepper, cloves, maces, nutmegges, ginger, mirabolanes in conserve, mirabolanes drye, grene ginger, nutmegges in conserve, synamon water, camfyer, burrassie, gallingale, cardamente, red sandes [red Saunders wood], white sandes [sandalwood], tamoryndes [tamarinds], myrre, balsamum, momya [wax from mummies], masticke, peper in pickell, muske and syvitt, amber greise, amber blacke, Benjamyn fyne, Benjamyn course, lignum alloes, blew Indea [indigo], lacrya to die wethall, hard wax, turbythe, radix china, alloies Sicotrinan, spignard, oyle of maces, rubarbe, goom appopanare, gum Selapin, gum Elemne, castorium, opium, tacamihaca, tutia, boill [?], Indies nuttes [cocoa nuts], silke in clothe, silke rawe, clothe of erva [herba], paynted clothes, callycow clothe, œanazneñas bengallas, lynen clothe of fyner sort than callycow clothe of goulde, pussellanas [porcelain] certain dishes and plates so called, targattes, ffaunes, a stone called bazar [bezoar], diamondes, rubyes, saffiers, esmeraldes, pearles greate, seide of pearle, turkeis [turquoise], callimas armaticus [calamus aromaticus], incense, zedoarya cubebes, quiltes of silke."

Richard Hakluyt also, the Archdeacon of Westminster, and indefatigable collector of narratives of voyages and travels, did very important service to the East India Company during the early years of its existence. As Mr. Winter Jones remarks in his edition [Hakluyt Society, 1850] of the *Divers Voyages*, "Hakluyt saw "clearly the course in which lay the advantage and "glory of his country; he saw that maritime traffic, "and the acquisition of territory by colonisation, were "the means by which England was to improve the "moral condition of her people, and maintain her "position as a great naval power." To promote these objects he actively engaged in schemes for the colonization of Virginia, and liberally gave his time and his great stores of information to the work of establishing trade with India. He supplied the Company with instructions for the guidance of their commanders, and with lists of products and of merchandise likely to be in demand at the various Eastern ports; and he published the narratives of the earliest voyages to India.

The following extracts are from his list of the chief places where "sondry sorte of spices do growe in the "East Indies":—

Pepper in Malabar, and embarked at "Onor, Barzelor, "Mangalor, Cananor, Crangenor, Cochin, and Coulan;" "all which places are in the Portugalas possession." "It groweth also about Calicut; but the Kinge of "Calicut and they are seldom in amity." "Out of

" the Portugales jurisdiction" it was to be obtained in the Isle of "Zeilon," and Sumatra, and "in Queda " on the Maine of Malacca," "also in the Kingdome of " Patane," in Siam, "in the territories neere Malacca," and in the "Isles of Nicubar." "Long peper" was found in Sumatra, Pegu, "Bangala," and in the "Isle of " Baratene."

"The best sinamon groweth in the Isle of Zeilon, the " Kinge whereof is the Portugales mortall enemy; where " nevertheless they have a small fort called Colombo. " Wild sinamon, called by the Portuguese *Canella de* " *Mato*, groweth in Malabar . . . . in the isles of " Nicubar, ... likewise . . . in the islande " of Java, and on the Maine by Malaca."

Cloves "in the isles of Maluco, namely, in Tarenate, " Tidore, Motelo, Machian, Bachian, Alatua; on the " north-west end of the Isles of Ceiran [Ceram], and in " the isles of Ambonio." "Great store of cloves are " to be sold in Bantam, and cloves are also brought " from Siam to Malaca." "In the isles of Tidore and " Ambonio the Portugales have two small fortes, as " appeareth by the greate Italian map, taken in the " *Madre di Dios*, which I have translated and caused to be " drawne for the Company."

"Nutmegges and maces, chiefly in the Isle of Banda, " and the seven isles thereto adjoyninge, ... " likewise . . . in three other greater isles to the " north-west, called Ama, Liazer, and Rucellas, . . . " and in . . . Borneo, . . . Java, and . . . " Sunda," and "in the Isle of Baratave."

" The best camphora groweth in canes in the Isle of " Borneo," and " about Chinchen, in a citty of China," and in Sumatra and Java.

" Anil or Indico" in Cambaya, "but is sold good cheape " in Bantam."

Amber is "found on the coaste of Africa about Gofala, " Mozambique, and Malinde," also near the isles of Maldivar, and on the coast of China.

"Muske cometh from Tartarie and from China. It is "often falsified by the Chinois and Jewes."

"Civet, called by the Portuguese Algalia, is found in "Bengala, the which people falsifie."

"Beniamin groweth much in the kingdome of Siam," and in Sumatra, Java, and the country near Malacca.

"Frankincense . . . groweth in Arabia Felix."

"Myrrhe . . . commeth out of Arabia Felix, and "out of the country of the Abassins."

Manna from Arabia and Persia, "but most out of "the province of Usbeke, lying behind Persia, in Tar-"tarie."

"Rheubarbe groweth about Campion, a province and "city lying north of China. It is most brought by land "through the country of Usbeke . . . and so cometh "to Ormus, and thence to Sumatra and Java. The best "is brought for the most parte over land to Venice. "Rheubarb also groweth abundantly in the country of "Malabar. It also cometh from Cathaio or China to "Malaca by water."

"Sandalo or sanders are of three sorts,—white, yellow, "and red. The white and the yellow [sandalwood] which "is the beste come from the islands of Timor and Solar. ". . . The red sanders grow in Coromandel and "Tenasseri, on the coast of Pegu."

Snakewood, or Palo da Cobra "groweth most in the "Isle of Zeilon."

Lignum aloes or "Palo d'aguilla," called in the Indies "Calamba," is most plentiful in Malacca, Sumatra, Camboya, Siam, "and the countries borderinge on the "same."

"The roote of China" grows in no place but China.

"Of opium, tamarindi, mirabolans, spikenard, aloe "zocotrina, anacardi, calamus aromaticus, costus, cubebes, "galanga, &c., read Linschoten from the 78th to the 83rd "chapter."

Next follows a long table of the prices of "diamantes" or "diamondes," rubies, "pearles," and "saphires;"

and lastly "notes of certayne comodities in good request "in the East Indies, the Maluceos, and China," in which it is interesting to observe the great demand for silken and woollen stuffs and precious stones in the East, *e.g.*, "velvets, damasks, satins, armesine of Portugal, safron, "and skarlets, . . . woollen cloth made at Venice ". . . murrey, violet, redmosine, skarlet, light or "grasse greene," and "emeraulds from Cairo and the "Spanish Indies." Also are noted "opinno or affron," "chekines* of gold," and "counterfeiete stones . . . "brought from Venice, to deceve the rude Indians "withal." In completing his great work, Hakluyt said, with truth, "the honour and benefit of this common-"wealth hath made all difficulties seem easy, and pains "and industry pleasant, and expenses of light value and "moment to me."

THE CHRONICLE OF "THE OLD COMPANY."

The English were everywhere opposed from the first, as the Dutch had been, by the Portuguese; but James Lancaster succeeded in the "First Voyage"† in establishing commercial relations with the King of Acheen in 1602, and at Priaman in the island of Sumatra, and with the Moluccas, and at Bantam in the island of Java, where he settled a Factory or "House of Trade" in 1603 [see 1621, 1629–30, 1634–35, 1677, and 1682].

---

* That is, the Venetian *zecchino*, *cecchino*, or sequin; which again is the Arabic *sikkat*, a stamp for coins. In the mouth of Anglo-Indians of the 17th century the word became *chekine* or *chickeen* and *chick*, in which forms it is still current in India in such phrases as "to spend a *chick*" [4 rupees]; "I bet you a chick": and "chicken stakes." We use the same word direct from the Arabic in the phrase "sicca-rupee."

† These early voyages of the Company inspired Milton with some of the finest imagery in his descriptions of Satan.

Thus in "*Paradise Lost*," Book II., 629–43:—

"Meanwhile . . . . .
Satan . . . .
Puts on swift wings . . . .
. . . .
Up to the fiery concave towering high.

The good fortune of this voyage was so great that it induced a number of private merchants to endeavour to obtain a participation in the new trade; and in 1604

As when far off at sea a fleet descried
Hangs in the clouds, by equinoctial winds
Close sailing from Bengala, or the isles
Of Ternate and Tidore, whence merchants bring
Their spicy drugs; they on the trading flood
Through the wide Ethiopean to the Cape
Ply stemming nightly toward the pole. So seemed
Far off the flying fiend."

And again, Book IV., 131-168:

"So on he fares, and to the border comes
Of Eden, ...
. . . .
A sylvan scene . . .
. . . .
Of stateliest view . . .
. . . . . able to drive
All sadness but despair; now gentle gales
Fanning their odoriferous wings, dispense
Native perfumes, and whisper whence they stole
Those balmy spoils. As when to them who sail
Beyond the Cape of Hope, and now are past
Mozambic, off at sea north-east winds blow
Sabean odours from the spicy shore
Of Araby the Blest: with such delay
Well pleased they slack their course, and many a league,
Cheered with the grateful smell Old Ocean smiles:
So entertained those odorous sweets the fiend
Who came their bane."

Mr. Markham has pointed out, in the volume of *Lancaster's Voyages* edited by him for the Hakluyt Society, that *Hamlet* and *Richard the Second* were performed by the sailors of Keeling's ship the *Dragon*, in the *Third Voyage*; and the Company's sailors were possibly equally well known to Shakespeare. The following are his two most interesting allusions to the new ocean trade with India:—

"I will be cheaters [*i.e.*, escheator—lapse-heir] to them both, and they shall be exchequers tome; they shall be my East and West Indies, and I will trade to them both."—*Merry Wives of Windsor* [1601], Act. I., sc. 3.

"He does smile his face into more lines than are on the new map with the augmentation of the Indies." — *Twelfth Night* [1601], Act III., sc. 2.

The "new map" thus immortalised was, Mr. Markham tells me, the map produced in 1599 by Edward Wright, on the projection called Mercator's, but the true principles of which were first demonstrated by Wright. The map is literally covered with lines, drawn from many centres to guide the eye on various bearings. Hence the allusion to "more lines than are on the new map." "The augmentation of the Indies" refers to the great extension and improvement in delineating the lands of the East, for which this map was long famous. Japan, now, for the first time, assumes its modern

James I. granted a license to Sir Edward Michelborne and others to trade "to Cathay, China, Japan, Corea, "and Cambaya." Michelborne, however, on arriving in the East, instead of exploring new sources of commerce, as the East India Company were doing, followed the pernicious example of the Portuguese in plundering the native traders among the islands of the Indian Archipelago. He in this way secured a considerable booty, but brought great disgrace on the British name, and much hindered the Company's business at Bantam.

In 1604 the Company undertook their "Second Voyage," commanded by Sir Henry Middleton, who, notwithstanding the antipathy created by Michelborne's piratical proceedings, extended their trade to Banda and Amboyna.

In the Company's "Third Voyage," 1606–7, consisting of the *Dragon* under Keelinge, the *Hector* under William Hawkins, and the *Consent* under David Middleton, Hawkins sailed direct to Surat, and thence sending the *Hector* on to Bantam, himself travelled to Agra, with a letter from James I. to the Great Mogul [Jehangir, 1605–27]. Through the machinations of the Portuguese he failed in his mission, and returned to England in 1613. At Bantam, the *Dragon* and *Consent* and *Hector* were loaded with pepper and other spicery, including a small quantity of

---

shape, and there is a marked development in the geography of India, Ceylon, Cochin China, and Corea.

One of the most remarkable of Shakespeare's allusions to India, as illustrating the minute knowledge of the people of that country possessed by Englishmen in his day, is to be found in *Henry VIII.* [brought out as "All is True," 1613], Act V., sc. 3, where the Porter, resisting the angry mob at the door of the Palace Yard, exclaims:—"Or have we some strange Indian with the great tool come to Court, the women so besiege us?"

The allusion is to the Saiva *gosain*, Vaishnava *viragi*, and other wandering devotees of Siva and Vishnu in their phallic aspects, who, on approaching a village, are met by the Hindu women, and pressingly entreated to honour them by accepting the hospitality of their persons. For particulars see Picart's *Ceremonies et Coutumes Religieuses*, Amsterdam, 1728.

cloves from Amboyna, which were sold in London for 36,287*l.*, or over twelve times the price paid for them, viz., 2,948*l.* 13*s.* The net profits on this voyage amounted to 234 per cent. upon the original subscription.

In the "Fourth Voyage," 1607–9, the *Ascension* under Keelinge, after the latter had obtained a grant of free trade to Aden, in April 1609, was wrecked off Diu; and the *Union* under Richard Rowles, after loading with pepper at Priaman, was lost on her way home off the coast of France.

In 1608 Captain D. Middleton, in command of the "Fifth Voyage," was prevented by the Dutch from trading at Banda, but succeeded in obtaining a cargo at Pulo Way.

In 1608 also the Company constructed the Dockyard at Deptford [the "Royal Dockyard" was established there about 1513, and closed 13th March 1869]; and this was the beginning, observes Sir William Monson, "of the "increase of great ships in England." At the date of Queen Elizabeth's death there were not more than four merchant ships in the kingdom of 400 tons each, and the whole number of ships was barely 150, of an average of 150 tons each.

In 1609 the Company received their new charter [dated 31st May] from King James I., by which the exclusive privileges granted them by Queen Elizabeth to 1615 were made perpetual.

In 1611 Sir Henry Middleton, in command of the "Sixth Voyage," after a vain attempt to settle an agency at Mocha, arrived before Cambay, and having resolutely repulsed the Portuguese, who tried to beat him off, obtained some important concessions from the native powers. He then proceeded to Ticcoo, in Sumatra, where, and at Bantam, he loaded the *Peppercorn* and *Darling* with pepper and spices, and sent them home; he remaining behind to repair the damage done to the *Trades Increase*, of 1,100 tons, the largest merchant ship as yet built in England. She capsized, however, while being overhauled, and was then burnt by the natives; and her loss so much affected Sir Henry that he died of grief shortly afterward. But notwithstanding her destruction, the net profits on this voyage were over 120*l*. per cent.

In 1610–11 also, Captain Hippon, commanding the "Seventh Voyage," succeeded in establishing agencies at Pettipollee [? Pedapali] and Metchlipatam [Masulipatam], on the Coromandel Coast, and in Siam, and opened a free trade also at Patania or Patany on the Malay Peninsula; but he was prevented by the Dutch from trading at Pulicat.

In 1612 the Company's fleet, of the "Tenth Voyage," under the brave and discreet Captain Best, was attacked off Swalley, the port of Surat, north of the mouth of the river Taptee, in overwhelming force by the Portuguese, whom after four successive engagements he utterly defeated, to the great astonishment of the natives, for they had hitherto considered them to be invincible. The firstfruits of this decisive victory were the obtaining of the privilege to keep an English Ambassador at Agra, and the settlement of a factory at Surat, with subordinate agencies at Gogo, Ahmedabad, and Cambay. Trade was also opened with the Persian Gulf. But the chief trade of the Company was still with the Indian Archipelago, and though Surat was their greatest emporium in India, it long continued subordinate to Bantam [see 1606–7 and 1617].

In 1612 Captain Newport, commanding the *Expedition*, of the "Twelfth" and last "Separate Voyage," took out Sir Robert Shirley, and Sir Dodmore Cotton, the King's Ambassador to Persia [Shah Abbas], and after having failed to establish an agency at Diu, sailed on to Ticcoo [or Tecoa] and Bantam, and loaded home with pepper.

In 1613, Captain Saris, commanding the "Eighth Voyage" [sailed 1611], established an agency at Firando in Japan.

In 1614 an agency was established by Mr. Edwards of the Surat factory at Ajmere.

It was in this year the Dutch Government proposed to the English Government to put an end to the rivalry between the English and Dutch Companies in the East by amalgamating them, on the basis of their capture of the Moluccas from the Spaniards and the subscription of a joint capital stock of 1,200,000*l.* But the English ["London"] Company rejected the tempting offer, on the ground that war was a State business, and contrary to the course to be pursued in commercial enterprises, and intended to be pursued by them, and that it was opposed to sound commercial principles for two nations to join in monopolising a trade to the exclusion of others, and more-over impracticable.

In 1615 Sir Dudley Digges published his famous pamphlet entitled *A Defence of Commerce*, showing that the re-export of Indian goods from England to the Continent had yearly exceeded the value of the bullion exported from England to India; that the English nation had, from the time of the establishment of the East India Company saved 70,000*l.* a year in the price of pepper and other spices; and had further benefited from the commerce with India by the increase of the customs revenue and the building of great ships, and the employment of large numbers of Englishmen in the Company's business. In the previous year, 1614, the Company had exported to India 14,000*l.* worth of English woollen goods, "bays, kersies, and broadcloths," and 10,000*l.* worth of iron, lead, and foreign merchandise, against 12,000*l.* sent out in bullion; while the shipping employed by them that year had cost 34,000*l.*, and the provisioning of them and other contingent charges had amounted to 30,000*l.* more.

In the same year Sir Thomas Roe was sent out by James I. as Ambassador to the Court of Jehanghir, and, on arriving at Agra in the following year, succeeded in placing the Company's trade in the Mogul dominions on a more favourable footing. Also in this year a temporary agency was opened at Cambello in the island of Amboyna.

In 1616 we established factories at Calicut and Cranganore ; and the Danes established their factories at Serampore and Tranquebar, sold to us in 1845.

In 1617 possession was obtained of the islands of Pulo Roon and Rosengyn, and a factory was established at Macassar; and at this period the Company had, in the Archipelago, factories at Acheen, Jambi, and Ticcoo [or Tecoa] in Sumatra, at Bantam, Jacatra [afterward Batavia], and Japara in Java, in Banda, at Succadana and Banjarmassin in Borneo, at Patania in the Malay Peninsula, at Siam, at Macassar in the island of Celebes, at Firando in Japan, at Masulipatam and Pettipollee on the Coromandel Coast, at "Amedavar," Agra, "Agimere," "Brampore," and Surat in "the Moguls Dominions," and at Cranganore and Calicut on the Malabar Coast; the whole of these factories being subordinate to Bantam. The factory at Surat was the chief seat of the Company's Government in Western India [as it was of all their possessions in the East Indies between 1629 and 1635], until the Presidency was transferred to Bombay in 1685–87. In the year 1617 also the Dutch established factories at Surat and Broach.

In 1618 the English established a factory at Mocha; but the Dutch compelled us to resign all pretensions to the 'Spice Islands.' In this year also the Company failed in its trade with Dabul, Baticola, and Calicut, through a want of sincerity on the part of the Zamorin.

In 1619 the Company was permitted to settle a factory and build a fort at Jasques, in the Persian Gulf.

It was in 1619 also that the "Treaty of Defence" with the Dutch, to prevent the harassing and disastrous disputes that were always going on between them and ourselves in the East, was ratified, but it came to nothing. When proclaimed at Bantam, hostilities were solemnly suspended for the space of an hour, while the Dutch and English fleets, dressed out in all their flags, and with yards manned, saluted each other with great cordiality; but the treaty ended in the smoke of that stately salutation, and the perpetual and fruitless contentions between the Dutch and English Companies continued as before.

Up to this time the English Company had not any portion of territory in sovereign right in the Indies, excepting the island of Lantore or Great Banda. This island was governed by a commercial agent of the Company, who had under him 30 Europeans, as clerks, overseers, and warehousemen; and these, with 250 armed Malays, constituted the only force by which it was protected. In the islands of Banda, Pulo Roon, and Rosengyn, and at Macassar and Acheen, and Bantam, the Company's factories and agents were without any military defence. Such was the precarious situation of the English in the East on the eve of their long struggle for commercial equality with the Dutch, whose ascendancy in the Indian Archipelago was already firmly established on the solid basis of territorial dominion and authority.

In 1620 the Dutch, notwithstanding the Treaty of Defence, concluded the previous year, expelled us from Pulo Roon and Lantore, and in 1621 from Bantam. The fugitive factors attempting to establish themselves first at Pulicat, were effectually opposed there by the Dutch, and afterward found an asylum at Masulipatam [1622].

In 1620 also the Portuguese made an attack upon the English fleet under Captain Shillinge, but were again defeated with great loss; and from this time the estimation in which the Portuguese were held by the natives of India steadily declined, while that of the English was proportionately raised.

In 1620 also the Company established agencies at Agra and Patna; and the "Indico" or "Indian woad" imported from Agra this year amounted to 200,000 lbs., bought at 1*s*. 2*d*. per lb. and sold in London at 5*s*.

In 1621 Sir Thomas Mun, Deputy Governour of the Company, published his *Discourse of Trade from England to the East Indies*. In this he showed that the annual consumption in Europe of the following articles from Southern Asia then was:—

				lbs.
Pepper	-	-	-	6,000,000
Cloves	-	-	-	450,000
Nutmegs	-	-	-	400,000
Indigo	-	-	-	350,000
Mace -	-	-	-	150,000
Raw silk [Persia]		-	-	1,000,000

This, by the old overland route, would have cost 1,465,000*l*., but by the new sea route cost only 511,458*l*. Moreover, the English consumption of these articles being about one tenth of the continental, the original price paid for them by the Company was more than recovered on the portion of them re-exported to the Continent: besides which the entire cost of the ships, wages, provisions, and insurance, was paid out of the gross profits of the Company's trade to the English people. In fact, the only bullion exported by the Company out of England was but a fractional portion of what was imported into the country from the Continent of Europe in payment of their re-exported cargoes of pepper and other Indian spices.

In 1622 the English, joining with the Persians, attacked and took Ormuz from the Portuguese, and obtained from Shah Abbas a grant in perpetuity of half the customs of Gombroon. This was the first time that the English took the offensive against the Portuguese.

On the 17th February 1622/23 occurred the "Massacre of Amboyna:" and from this time the Dutch remained masters of Lantore and the neighbouring islands, and of the whole trade of the Indian Archipelago, until these islands were recaptured by the English in the great naval wars between 1781 and 1793 and 1811.

In 1624 the English, unable any longer to oppose the Dutch in the Indian Archipelago, withdrew nearly all their factories there, and in the Malay Peninsula, Siam, and Japan. Some of the factors and agents retired to the island of Lagundy in the Strait of Sunda, but were forced, by its unhealthiness, to abandon it.

In 1625–26 a factory was established at Armagon on the Coromandel Coast, subordinate to Masulipatam; and in 1628 Masulipatam was, in consequence of the oppressions of the native governor, abandoned for a time in favour of Armagon.

In 1626 the English, with the Dutch, seized the island of Bombay on the Malabar Coast from the Portuguese, but for some unexplained reason immediately abandoned it.*

---

* Among the "SHIPS' JOURNALS" preserved in the Record Department of the India Office are the "Journals" of three Englishmen present on the occasion above referred to; and, as they are the earliest English notices of Bombay, I extract at length the entries relating to this obscure and long forgotten, but, to all "Ducks," deeply interesting event:—

A. *From Andrew Warden's Journal in the William:*—"1626, Oct. 15. In the moringn stood in and ankred and landed of ye Eingles and the Duches sum 400 meane at the leaste and tocke the forte & casell and the towne, and sett fire of it and all the towne, and all the howesem [housen, *i.e.*, houses] theraboutes, the pepell being all run away that night and ded caray away all the best cometeies [commodities] levein nothein butt trashe.

"Oct. 16. In the moringen we sete sayle."

B. *From John Vian's Journal in the Discovery:*—"1626. Oct. 13. This 13th daye we and the whole ffleete both of English & Duch went into Bumbay and came to an anckor in 9 fatham, one pointe beareinge W.N.W. p compasse, the other S. S. W., the one 3 mile of, the other 3 leagus of; this was in the entringe of the harbor.

"Oct. 14. This daie we went with the whole ffleete in further, neare a small towne or village, where there were Portingalls. Wee anckored and rode a mile of, in 6 fadd., one point p comp. beareinge W.S.W. 5 mile of, the other S. @ b. W. soune 5 lea. of. Wee came soe neere the Towne with two of our shipps that wee drone them all awaye with our great ordnance, viz. the Morrice of the English, and ye Mauritius of the Duch. In safetie we landed our men on shore, whoe pilladged the Towne, and set their houses all on fire with their ffort neere the water side. Yea, we staide there the 15th daye doeinge all the spoyle that possiblie we could, but we gott nothinge to speake of but vittuall. Soe when wee had done all the harme we could, the 15th daye in the euening wee gott our men aboord leaueinge the Towne on fire, and

"The letters *B B* is the Bay; *t* is the Town; *Ry* is the three rivers; the *Ro:* (Road) is two rocks, one both sides (? one each side). Where the stem (?) of the anchors (is), we rode before the great house without (outside) the stakes. Where the wood (is), is the island. The higher great pyramid is a castle, as we think, up in the land. The letter *C* by the great tree is a hermitage. The letter *M* is a monastery, and the little town of cittjohn (? citizen) houses betwixt it and the wood. Where the letter *f* (is), there were a dozen frigates riding. The letter *N* over Bassein is a nunnery."

Plate VII. SKETCH MAP OF BOMBAY HARBOUR, 1626.

(from David Davies' Journal).

In 1629 the factory at Bantam was re-established as a subordinate agency to Surat; and in 1630 Armagon, reinforced by 20 soldiers, was placed under the Presidency of Surat.

In 1632 the Company re-established their factory at Masulipatam under a firman, known as the "Golden Firman," from the King of Golconda [Abdallah-Kulb Shah, 1611–72]. Under an extension of this firman, obtained in 1634–35, the Company founded a factory at Verasheroon [Viravasaram]. It was withdrawn in 1662 and re-established in 1677.

In 1633 Azim Khan, Governor of Bengal [1632–37], having received orders from the Great Mogul [Shah Jehan, 1628–58] "to expel the idolaters [Portuguese] from his dominions," the Portuguese fort at Hugli, under Michael Rodrigues, was seized after a brave resistance, and its defenders driven out of Bengal. None of them

---

"The 16 daye in the morneinge when the winde cam of shore, wee wayed anckor, and went of to sea again."

C. *From David Davies' Journal in the Discovery.*—1626. "Oct. 13. The 13th we went into the Baye and Roade w[th]out the stakes, as you maye see in the draft following.

"The 14th the Moris & ij° Dutch shipps went in neere the greate howse to batter agaynst it, in w[ch] batterie ij° of the Moris ordnance splitt; the same daie we landed 300 men Englishe and Dutch and burnt all their kittjonns [citizens'] howses and tooke the greate howse w[t] ij basses ["the smallest kind of cannon used in the 16th and 17th centuries"—see Murray's *New English Dictionary*] of brasse & one sakor [saker, *i.e.*, literally, 'a hawk,' * a denomination of cannon] of iron.

"The 15th all our men embarkqued aboorde the shipps being sonday in the evening, and lefte the greate howse w[ch] was boath a warehowse, a friory, and a forte, all afire burning wth many other good howses together wth two nywe frigates not yett frome the stockes nor fully ended; but they hadd caried awaye all their treasur and all things of any vallue, for all were runde awaye before our men landed."

The sketch map appended to David Davies' *Journal* is reproduced in the plate opposite [No. VII.].

I am indebted for these extracts to Mr. W. Foster, B.A., of the Registry and Records Department under Mr. F. C. Danvers.

---

* Professor Max Müller has pointed out in his *Lectures on Language* [2nd series, 1864, p. 229] how on the decline of falconry the names of the birds used in that sport were transferred to firearms. Thus, the "musket" took its name from the dappled ["muscatus"] sparrow hawk. In Italy this bird [*terzolo*] gave the name of *terzeruolo* to the pistol, and in France to the *sacre*, or, in English, saker, a gun of which there were three denominations, carrying shots weighing respectively 4, 6, and 9 pounds.

were personally ill-treated, but their "idols" were all ruthlessly destroyed.

In 1634, by a firman dated February 2nd, the Company obtained from the Great Mogul the liberty to trade in Bengal, without any other restriction than that their ships were to resort only to Pipley, or Pippli, in Orissa, where they had had a factory from 1624.

In 1634–35 Bantam was again raised to an independent Presidency; and an agency was established at Tatta, or "Scindy."

In 1637 Courten's Association [chartered 1635] settled agencies at Goa, Baticola, Carwar, Acheen, and Rajapore in the dominions of the King of Bijapur [Mahomed, 1626–56]. Their ships had the year before plundered some native vessels at Surat and Diu, a piratical act which disgraced the Company with the Mogul authorities [who could not comprehend the distinction between the Company and the Association], and depressed the English trade with Surat, while that of the "lustick Dutch" was proportionately increased.

In 1638 Armagon was abandoned as unsuited for commerce; and in consequence Fort St. George ["Madraspatam," "Chineepatam"] was founded by Francis Day,* 1639–40; the factors at Armagon being at once removed

* In the first volume of the "*Black Books*" [*see* pp. 30–1], page 32, the following entry is made of a letter from "Surratt," dated "27 Jan: Anno 1641":—

"Frauncis Day blamed to bee the first projector of the forte of St. George. The worke begunne by Frauncis Day and paid for out of the Company's cash."

Again, at page 33, among the charges which Andrew Cogan [Agent for the Coromandel Coast] is to be required to answer, the following head the list:—

"To answeare the building of the ffort St. George, the charge whereof hath cost from ye first of March 1639 to ye 30th June 1643, pagods new 9250.

"To give accompt whether it bee finished or how farre it is proceeded.

"To answeare what the charge of ye souldiers monethly is to mainteyne the ffort; as well for wages, victuall and otherwise."

Mr. Cogan's answer to these interrogations will be found in O. C. 1751.

I am indebted for these instructive extracts to Mr. W. Foster, B.A., of the Registry and Records Department under Mr. F. C. Danvers.

to it. Fort St. George was made subordinate to Bantam, until raised in 1653–54 to the rank of a Presidency. Its site was the first territorial acquisition of the English in India.

In 1640 the Company established an agency at Bussorah, and factories at Hughly and Carwar.

The Company's trade having now become much extended, their yard at Deptford was found too small for their ships, and they therefore purchased some copyhold ground at Blackwall, at that time a waste marsh, without an inhabitant; and there they opened another dockyard, and built the *Royal James*, of 1,200 tons, the largest merchant ship yet seen in England.*

In 1642 the factory at Pipley was transferred to Balasore; and in this year the first regular despatches were received by the Company from Mr. Francis Day from both Fort St. George and Balasore.

In 1645 additional privileges were granted to the Company by Shah Jehan; and in 1646 the Governor of Bengal [Sultan Shujah, 1639–60] made further concessions, placing the factories at Balasore and Hughly on the most favourable footing. At this period, 1645–50, however, the trade of the Company suffered great depression owing to the ascendancy of the Puritan party in England affecting the home demand for silks, figured stuffs, and other denominations of artistic piece goods; and to rumours of the civil war in England having at length reached the East. The Company was seriously injured thereby, particularly in Persia, where the "tragicall storye of the Kinge's beheadinge" [Charles I., 30th January 1649] made a deep and lasting impression.

In 1647 Courten's Association established their colony at Assada, in Madagascar.

---

* The *Henry Grace de Dieu*, commonly called the "Great Harry" of the Royal Navy in 1522 is said, in the Pepysian papers at Cambridge, to have been of 1,500 tons burden; but in all other accounts it is given as 1,000 tons. The largest ship in Queen Elizabeth's Navy, the *Triumph*, commanded by Martin Frobisher against the Spanish Armada, was of 1,100 tons burden.

In 1651 the Dutch founded their colony at the Cape of Good Hope, abandoning St. Helena, which they had held from 1645. Thereon the English Government took possession of the island, which on being wrested from them by the Dutch in 1672–73 was at once re-taken by them, and made over to the East India Company by the charter of Charles II., dated 16th December 1674. Already by the charter granted by Charles II., the 3rd of April 1661, the Company had been authorised to plant and fortify St. Helena.

In 1652 Cromwell, the author of the obsolete "Navigation Laws," "the Palladium of England," wearied out of all patience with the Dutch, on account of their long accumulated cruel injuries against the Company, at last declared war against them, and prosecuted it with such vigour that the Dutch were speedily constrained to entreat for peace on any terms the great Protector might please to prescribe.

Accordingly, by the Treaty of Westminster, 1654, the Dutch agreed to restore Pulo Roon [elsewhere "Rohun"] to the English Company, to pay them an indemnity of 85,000*l.*, and a further sum of 3,615*l.* to the heirs and executors of the victims of the "Massacre of Amboyna." This settlement gave new life and spirit to the Company's trade, that at this time had, from various causes, but chiefly from the unyielding antagonism of the Dutch, become greatly depressed. But the rapacious and wily Dutch took care before ostensibly leaving Pulo Roon to grub up all the spice trees on the island; and then, lest we might lay out new plantations of them, they, in defiance of the Treaty of Westminster, continued in surreptitious possession of the place, doing all the mischief they could to it, until Major Willoughby was appointed English Governour in 1663. But in 1664 the Dutch again seized the island, and held it until it was finally ceded to them by the Treaty of Breda, 1667.

In 1653 the Company's factory at Lucknow was withdrawn. No record has been found of its establishment.

In 1653–54 Fort St. George [Madras] was constituted a Presidency, with Mr. Aaron Baker, at that time Agent under the President at Bantam, as first Governour.

In 1655, in the "Masulipatam Consultations" of December 4th, mention is made of a factory at Daladie, in addition to the factories at Verasheroon and Pettipollee already mentioned. In this year also the Company of "Merchant Adventurers," composed of the rump of Courten's "Association," obtained their charter from Cromwell to trade with India; but in 1657 were united by Cromwell with the "London" Company.

In 1656–57 the Dutch established a factory at Chinsurah. It was taken by us in 1795, given back to the Dutch in 1814–15, and finally ceded to us with Malacca, in exchange for Bencoolen, by treaty in 1824–25.

In 1658 the Company established a factory at Cossimbazaar ["Castle Bazaar"]; and made their establishments in Bengal subordinate to Fort St. George, instead of to Bantam. This arrangement remained in force until 1681.

In 1660–61 they established a mint at Madras.

In 1661 the factory at Biliapatam was founded.

In 1661 also Bombay was ceded, and in 1665 delivered up, to the British Crown; and transferred by Charles II. to the East India Company by the charter of the 27th of March 1669, which specifies that the Port and Island were to be held by the Company, "as of the Manor of East Greenwich," in free and common soccage, at a farm rent of 10*l.*, payable on the 30th of September each year. The seat of the Western Presidency was removed to Bombay from Surat in 1685–87.

At this time the Company's establishments in the East Indies consisted of the Presidency of Bantam, with its dependencies of Jambi, Macassar, and other places in the Indian Archipelago; Fort St. George and its dependent factories on the Coromandel Coast and in the Bay of Bengal; and Surat, with its affiliated dependency of Bombay, and dependent factories at Broach, Ahmedabad, and other places in Western India, and at Gombroon in the Persian Gulf, and Bussorah in the Euphrates Valley.

In 1663 the factories established at Patna, Balasore, and Cossimbazaar were ordered to be discontinued, and purchases made only at Hugly.

In the years 1663 and 1664, the English at Surat and in the Indian Archipelago were much harassed by the Dutch.*

---

* "Great talk of the Dutch proclaiming themselves, in India, Lords of the "Southern Seas, and denying traffick there to all ships but their own, upon "pain of confiscation; which makes our merchants mad."—*Pepys*, 9th Feb. 1663/64.

"This afternoon Sir Thomas Chamberlin" [son of the Judge William Chamberlayne, created a baronet 1642] "came to the office to me, and "shewed me several letters from the East Indys, shewing the height that the "Dutch are come to there, shewing scorn to all the English, even in our own "Factory there at Surat, beating several men, and hanging the English "standard St. George under the Dutch flag in scorn; saying that whatever "their masters do or say at home they will do what they list and be masters "of all the world there; and have so proclaimed themselves Soveraigne of "all the South Seas; which certainly our King cannot endure, if Parliament "will give him money. But I doubt, and yet do hope, they will not yet, "until we are more ready for it."—*Idem*. 15th Feb. 1663/64.

"Mr. Coventry and I did long discourse of the business of the office" [Admiralty], "and the war with the Dutch, and he seemed to argue mightily "for the little reason that there is for all this. For first, as to the wrong we "pretend that they have done us,—that of the East Indies, for their not "delivering Poleron,—it is not yet known whether they have failed or no; "and that of their hindering the *Leopard* cannot amount to above 3,000*l*., if "true."—*Ibid*., May 29, 1664.

The English Company were the more exasperated by the hindrances and oppressions of the Dutch because their trade was at this time becoming prosperous, of which both Evelyn and Pepys give evidence.

"One Tomson, a Jesuit, showed me a collection of rarities sent from the "Jesuits of Japan and China, . . . brought to London in the East India "ships for them, ... rhinoceros horns, and glorious vests [vestments] "wrought and embroidered in cloth of gold, with such lovely colours that for "splendour and vividness we have nothing in Europe that approaches it; a "girdle studded with achats and rubies of great value and size, . . . knives, ". . . fanns with long handles curiously carved, and filled with Chinese cha-"racters; a sort of paper, very broad and thin and fine, like abortive parch-"ment, exquisitely polished, of an amber colour, exceeding glorious and "pretty, and seeming to be like that which my Lord Verulame describes in "his '*Nova Atlantis*'; prints of landskips, idols, saints, pagodas of most "ugly, monstrous, and hideous shapes; pictures of men and countries, "painted on a sort of gum'd calico, transparent as glass; flowers, trees, "beasts, birds, excellently wrought on a kind of sleeve silk, very natural;

In 1664 Surat was pillaged by Sivaji, but Sir George Oxenden bravely defended the English factory; and the Mogul Emperor [Aurungzib, 1658–1707], in admiration of his conduct, granted the Company exemption from customs for one year.

In this year also the Company suffered great loss through the decision against them that calico was to be regarded as linen.*

In 1665, Mr. George Foxcroft, having been sent out as President at Fort St. George in succession to Sir Edward Winter, was [16th September] seized by the latter and, with his little son, and Mr. [afterward Sir] Jeremy Sambrooke, thrown into prison; Sir Edward Winter contumaciously holding on in office for three years more, or until 22nd August 1668.

In 1666, on the Honourable Sir Gervase Lucas becoming Governour of Bombay, he threw his officiating predecessor, Mr. Humfrey Cooke [Secretary to Sir Abraham Shipman], into prison for extortion and peculation. Cooke escaped to Goa, and there, with the assistance of the Jesuits, organized a levy for the capture of Bombay; but was frustrated in his attempt, and proclaimed a traitor in 1668.

In 1666 also tea was first imported for sale into England

"divers drugs, that our druggists and physitians could make nothing of, "especially one called '*Lac Tigridis*'" [see note on Lac, page 39]; "several "book MSS., a grammar, with innumerable other rarities."—*Evelyn's Diary*, 22nd June 1664.

"To Eriffe; . . . and there he [Lord Brouncker] and Sir Edmund Pooly "carried me down into the hold of the India shipp [a Dutch prize] and "there did show me the greatest wealth lie in confusion that a man can see "in this world. Pepper scattered through every chink, you trod upon it: "and in cloves and nutmegs I walked above the knees, whole rooms full. "And silks in bales, and boxes of copper-plate, one of which I saw opened." —*Pepys*, 16th Nov. 1665.

* "Sir Martin Noell told us the dispute between him, as farmer of the "Additional Duty, and the East India Company, whether calico be linen or "no; which he says it is, having been ever esteemed so [!]; they [the Com- "pany] say it is made of cotton woole, and grows upon trees, not like flax "or hemp. But it was carried against the Company, though they stand out "against the verdict."—*Pepys*, 27th Feb. 1663/4.

from Holland. The Company's first importations of tea, direct from Bantam, were received in 1669 [see p. 26, *note*].

In 1667 Pulo Roon was, as above [1654] stated, finally abandoned to the Dutch by the Treaty of Breda.

In 1668 a factory was established at Vizagapatam.

In this year [1668] also the survivors of the King's [Charles II.] soldiers sent out with Sir Abraham Shipman to garrison Bombay, on the transfer of the island to the Company volunteered into their service, and became the cadre of the Honourable Company's "1st European Regiment," or "Bombay Fusileers," afterward the 103rd Foot.

In 1671 the Company ordered the building of two brigantines at Bombay, and this was the beginning of their famous Dockyard there.

In this year also the Bombay Mint was founded; and, by the King's Letters Patent, dated 5th October 1677, was authorized to coin "*Rupees* [*rupya*, silver-'stamped,' "*i.e.*, 'coined,' from *rupa*, 'form'], *Pices* [*i.e.*, *paisa*, "$\frac{1}{4}$th of an *anna*, or $\frac{1}{64}$th of a *rupee*], and *Budgrooks*"* [*badaga-ruka*, "base coin," $\frac{1}{12}$th of an *anna*, and identical, therefore, with the present "pie," *i.e.*, *pai*].

---

* Tavernier, writing in 1676 of "the money which the English and Hol-"landers coin in the Indies," says:—"Formerly the English never coined any "Silver or Copper Money: for . . . they find it more profitable to carry "Gold from England than Silver. . . . . But since the present King of "England married the Princess of Portugal, who had in part of her Portion "the famous Port of *Bombeye*, where the English are very hard at work to "build a strong Fort, they coin both Silver, Copper, and Tinn. But that "Money will not go in Surat, nor in any parts of the Great Mogul's Domi-"nions, nor in any of the Territories of the Indian Kings; only it passes "among the English in their Fort, and for some two or three leagues up the "Country, and in the Villages along the Coast, the Country people that "bring them their wares being glad to take that Money; otherwise they "would see but little stirring, in regard the Country is very poor, and the "people have nothing to sell but *Aqua Vitæ*, made of Coco-Wine ['tody'] and "Rice."

The earliest money struck for the use of the English in India were the "Portcullis" Crowns, half-Crowns, Shillings, and Sixpences of Queen Elizabeth, who would not permit the Company to transport the Spanish dollar into Asia, but insisted on the circulation of coins bearing her own imperious superscription. The earliest coins minted by the English in India were of copper, stamped with the figure of an irradiated *lingam*, the phallic "Roi Soleil." The

In 1672 the Company ordered factories to be established at Tonquin, Tywan, and Siam, and in Japan, and China. They sent a vessel to Japan, but in consequence of the King of England having married a princess of Portugal [Charles II. m: Catherine of Braganza, 1661–1662], were refused permission to trade there. The ship then proceeded to Macao, but here the Company's agents were greatly hindered by the intrigues of the Portuguese, and an attempt to open trade with Formosa proved equally unsuccessful.

In 1673 the Hooblee factory, subordinate to Surat, was for the second time attacked by Sivaji. In this year also the notable fact is recorded of the Company having sent out Englishmen to Bengal to teach the Natives to dye silks the green and black colours in fashion at home.

Between 1672 and 1674 the French settlement at Pondicherry [sometimes spelled 'Pont de Cheree' as if *Pont du Chéri*, and Pordicheri] was founded by Martin.

In 1675 the Company wrote out to their Agents in India

---

mintage of this coin is unknown [? Madras], but without doubt it must have served to ingratiate us with the natives of the country, and may have given origin to their personification of the Company under the potent title of KUMPANI JEHAN, which, in English mouths, became "John Company." The earliest known coins of the Bombay mintage are the four rupees in the British Museum, dated 1675, 1677, 1678, and again 1678, respectively. The first has stamped on the reverse the arms of the "Old" India Company as described at page 21, and the remaining three the Royal Arms of England of the date, viz., quarterly, the three Lions of England, the Lion of Scotland, the Harp of Ireland, and the 3 *fleur-de-lis* of France. The first of the two 1678 rupees is milled on the edge, milling having been introduced into the English Mint in 1662. In a Bombay rupee of 1687 the Company's arms reappear on the reverse. See "The Coinages of the East India Company at Bombay," by the late Edward Thomas, in *The Indian Antiquary*. Fanams were also coined by the Company at Bombay during the reign of Charles II., bearing on the obverse two linked C's [CC], and on the reverse the figure of the Hindu monkey-god Hanu-man ["Long-Jaw"]; and these rare coins are now worth a pound a piece. Among the earlier numismatical types used by the Company was their bale mark. The familiar scales were introduced late in the 18th century, and the Arms of the United Company about 1803. The money circulated by the Company in India never bore the effigy of a British sovereign until 1837, when they ceased to coin in the name of the titular emperors of Delhi, and stamped their rupees with the head of King William IV.

that Lahore Indigo was being undersold in London by West Indian; and that less lac would be required in future, because of "the new practice of using wafers instead of wax" for sealing letters.

In this year, also, the sale of pepper began to fail in Turkey, and Eastern and Northern Europe, on account of the wars in Poland, Austria, and Turkey; and, as the wars continued, its place in the general domestic consumption of the west of Europe was gradually taken by ginger.

About this time [1675] also, Indian piece-goods, or calicoes [*i.e.*, of Calicut] and muslins [*i.e.*, of Mosul,—see foot-note, page 88] of every description, began to largely supplant the use of cambrics, lawns, and other linen fabrics. "Byrampauts," "Beteelles" [Spanish, *beatilla*, "a veil"], Chintzes [*chint*, "figured"], "Dhooties" [*dhoti*, "loin-cloth"], "Guinea Stuffs" [*i.e.*. Gunny (*goni*, "sacking") Stuffs], and Long-cloths [*lungi*, a cloth passed "between the thighs"] made at Baroach, Jamboseer, Ahmedabad, and other places in Guzerat, were received from Surat, and later from Bombay; white cotton cloths from Anjengo; Chintzes of all sorts and Ginghams [the Tamil *kindan*, and, borrowed, Javanese *gingang*] from Masulipatam, and, later, from Madras; and "Baftas" [*bafta*, "woven"], Bandannas [*bandha*, "bound," certain portions of the cloth being "bound" up in knots, to form the patterning, before being dipped in dye], "Herba [*i.e.*, Jute (*juta*, "matted")] Taffaties" [*tafta*, "woven"], "Mulmuls" [*malmal*, "muslin"], *et cætera*, collected from all parts of Hindustan, Allahabad, Mhow, Lucknow, Dacca, Patna, and Malda, and exported from Pippli, Hugli, and [after 1686–9] Calcutta.*

* This profitable trade between India and England promised, all through the last quarter of the 17th and the first half of the 18th centuries, to grow to unbounded proportions, but after 1721 was deliberately and pitilessly destroyed by the prohibitory duties and other penal enactments enforced against it; first, by those interested in bolstering up the woollen, linen, and silk manufactures of this country in their rapidly languishing competition with the cheap, light, and gaily-figured cotton cloths of India; and then, after Sir Richard Arkwright's revolutionary invention [1767–69] had made it im-

In 1677 the Javanese, at the instigation of the Dutch, sacked the Company's factory at Bantam, and assassinated the Agent; in consequence of which the factory books were closed and conveyed to the Court of Directors.

In this year also the Company's factory at Madapolam is first mentioned.

In 1678 permission was obtained for settling a factory at Tonquin: and in 1679 a factory was established at Amoy.

In 1681 Bengal was separated from Madras, and Mr. [afterwards Sir William] Hedges appointed "Agent and Governour" of the Company's affairs "in the Bay of

---

possible to secure a monopoly for our woollen, linen, and silk manufacturers, by those interested in the new English cotton manufactures founded on Hargreaves's "spinning jenny" [1764–67], and Arkwright's "spinning frame." In 1700 it was enacted, "that from and after the 29th day of September "1701 all wrought silks, and stuffs mixed with silk or herba, of the manu- "facture of Persia, China, or the East Indies, *and all calicoes, painted, dyed,* "*printed, or stained there*, which are or shall be imported into this kingdom, "shall not be worn or otherwise used in Great Britain; and all goods im- "ported after that day shall be warehoused and exported again." An Act of 1721 imposed a fine of 5*l.* upon the weaver, and of 20*l.* upon the seller of a piece of calico; and a like penalty for wearing, or using in any bed, chair, &c., such calico "or any stuff made of, or mixed with cotton, printed, dyed, "or stained," except muslins, and "calicoes dyed all blue." In 1736 this Act was so far modified that calicoes manufactured in Great Britain were allowed to be worn provided the warp was of linen. In 1774 a statute was passed, expressly to encourage the English calico manufacturers, allowing goods wholly of cotton to be made and used, and reducing the duty on the same from sixpence to threepence per yard. This started the great piece-goods industry of Lancashire. India still continued to enjoy a monopoly in the production of the fine muslins of Dacca. But when in 1785 the use of the "mule jenny" [invented by Samuel Crompton 1779] was introduced at Nottingham, and two years afterward 500,000 pieces of muslin were woven in the United Kingdom, an end was at once put to the importation of this last immemorially famous denomination of the artistically perfected textile manufactures of the East [see pages 59–60]. It is impossible, however, to suppress for ever the industrial force of 200,000,000 of patient people in possession of so naturally productive a country as India; and since the introduction at Bombay, in 1857, of English cotton mills, notwithstanding that the cost of building and working them there is double what it is at home, they have, for the past 33 years, been turning out yearly increasing quantities of yarns and cloths, until they are now actually supplying, in yearly increasing quantities, the lower counts of twists and coarser denominations of cotton cloths to all the chief Eastern markets, hitherto, that is from 1827, monopolized by Manchester.

"Bengal, and of the factories subordinate to it, or "Cossimbazaar, Patna, Balasore, Malda, and Dacca. "A corporal of approved fidelity, with 20 soldiers, to "be a guard to the Agent's person, and the factory at "Hooghly, and to act against interlopers." [See 1686, 1689, and 1698–99.]

In the same year Mr. [afterwards Sir John] Child, brother of Sir Josia Child, was appointed President at Surat.

In 1682, the Company first ordered opium to be sent from Bengal to England; but up to 1786 the importation amounted only to about 750 lbs. a year, being about one-tenth of the quantity received into England from other countries than India.*

---

* It was not until 1773 that the Company undertook the supervision of the manufacture of opium in Bengal, Behar, and Orissa. In 1797 the cultivation of the poppy for opium was restricted to Behar and Benares, and discontinued in Bengal. An immense trade had been going on between India and the surrounding countries in this drug long before the Company monopolized it. Thus Barbosa [1516] mentions that the Chinese ships on their return voyages loaded at Malacca with "much *anfiam*, which we call opium." Valentijn [1726] writes:—"Java alone consumes monthly 350 packs of opium, each being of 130 *catis*." And Hamilton [1727]:—"The Chiefs of "Calecut for many years had vended between 500 and 1,000 chests of "Bengal opium yearly up in the inland countries, where it is very much "used." The regular exports of the Company from Bengal began in 1796. Opium smoking is known to have prevailed in China at least fifty years before this; while the artistic elaboration of the opium pipe of the remoter parts of that country points backward to very remote centuries as the date of the origination of the habit. This, however, is a mere inference, and the recorded contemporary evidence of the extension of the use of opium from Egypt and Asia Minor renders it probable that its introduction into Persia and India, at least, was due to the Mahomedan traders of the 9th and 10th centuries A.D. If this was actually the case, we owe to them at once the provision of alcohol as the special stimulant of the western and northern nations of the Old World, and of opium as the favourite narcotic of its southern and eastern populations. For the New World there was tobacco; and it is likely, in time, to everywhere supplant both ardent spirits and opium as the popular φάρμακον νηπενθής. In packet 14 of the collections of India Office Records enumerated in the Statistics and Commerce Departmental List No. 2,397, there is a letter, written in 1711, from Vizagapatam to Mr. Thomas Woolley, who was for more than twenty years Secretary to the "United [East India] Company," enlarging on the uses of opium to vegetarians. It will be found reprinted in the *Times*, 27th July 1886. See

In 1682–83 Bantam was taken by the Dutch, and the English, Portuguese, French, and Danes driven out. As a consequence the English Company was obliged to withdraw its factories from Tonquin, Amoy, Siam, and other places subordinate to Bantam. They, however, obtained a settlement at Bencoolen, on the south coast of Sumatra; and there, in 1685–87, built Fort York,* and, in 1714, Fort Marlborough, to protect it against the Dutch.

In 1684 we were expelled from the whole island of Java; but it was not until 1817 that we formally withdrew from Bantam.

In 1683–84 Captain Richard Keigwin's curious mutiny against the authority of the Company at Bombay caused considerable alarm. It would make an interesting subject for an exhaustive monograph by such a writer as Mr. James Douglas. Whatever Keigwin's faults as an official may have been, he was a splendidly brave man, as his escalade of "Keigwin's Rock," St. Helena [15th May 1673], and attack on "Sevagee's Armada" off Henery-Kenery [18th October 1679, *see* page 83] prove; and one's personal sympathies are entirely with him in his quarrel with the Company's officials at Bombay, among whom both Mr. George Bourchier [also spelled Bowcher], and Mr. John Petit appear to have been disposed to extenuate, if not justify, his misconduct.

In 1683 a factory was settled at Tellicherry; and during 1683–84, the one at Cuddalore was definitively established. There had been commercial relations with the latter place, and Thevnapatam or Tegnapatam [afterward Fort St. David], apparently, from 1674.

In 1684 Sir John Child was made "Captain General and Admiral of India," and Sir John Wyborne "Vice-Admiral and Deputy Governor of Bombay."

---

also my letters on the opium question in the *Times* of 6th December 1881 and 20th January 1882.

* William Dampier, the maritime discoverer, served for some time as a gunner at Fort York.

In 1685 a factory was established at Priamau, an island off Sumatra, and fortified; and an island on the Ganges was also fortified; and the factory at Masulipatam temporarily dissolved. Angengo was probably first occupied in this year, but its early history is obscure. [See pp. 86–7.]

In 1685–87 the seat of the Presidency of Western India was finally transferred from Surat to Bombay [see 1617, 1629–30, and 1661].

In 1686 the factory at Hugly was much oppressed by the Mogul Governour of Bengal; and the Company's business in India suffered generally from the wars of the Moguls and Mahrattas. Sir John Child was therefore appointed "Governour General,"* with full

---

* Sir William Hunter, in the "*Imperial Gazetteer of India*," Vol. VI. [India], p. 370, after stating that Sir John Child was appointed "Governour General," with full power in India to make war or peace, observes in a footnote:—"Sir George Birdwood's *Report on the Old Records of the India Office* "quotes this title from the MSS. It is therefore nominally a century older "than is usually supposed; but Hastings was the first real Governour General." On reading this I at once began to inquire into the question thus raised, but failed in being able to trace in the India Office MS. records the original authority for so early a use of the title of "Governour General." But finding that Mr. James Douglas, the author of *A Book of Bombay* [1883], and *Round about Bombay* [1886], two most interesting books of old local history, had also in the former volume, at page 60, applied this title to Sir John Child, I wrote to Mr. Douglas, asking if he could refer me to his authority for it. In reply, he wrote, 4th November 1886, as follows:—

"I received yours of the 15th October yesterday; and, as the mail is late, I am sorry I have not the time to consult books. I do not think that *you*, Mr. James Campbell [see *Bombay Gazetteer*, Surat, p. 98], and I could have, independently, called Sir John Child 'Governour General' without authority for it. It is no doubt in Bruce's *Annals*, which I have not beside me."

"Mr. James Campbell's words, at page 98 of the Surat volume of the *Bombay Gazetteer*, are:—'Bombay was [1687] to be fortified in the strongest 'manner, and to become the capital of the Company's Indian possessions, 'and the residence of the Governour General [Sir John Child].'"

"I don't think we all three could have invented this name, and conclude it is in the second volume of Bruce, or in Anderson's *English in Western India*."

It is clear, however, that Mr. Campbell [like, and probably following, Bruce, *Annals*, II., 568], uses the phrase descriptively, and not officially, and I suppose that in copying it out of his book, or from Bruce's *Annals*, I,

power to make war or peace in India; and ordered to proceed to inspect the Company's possessions in Madras and Bengal, and arrange for their safety. On the 20th of December the Company's agent Job Charnock [" Chanak " of Indian writers], with his council, quitted the open factory at Hugly, and retired to Chuttanuttee.* [See 1698–99.]

Thevnapatam, or Tegnapatam, a suburb of Cuddalore, was first settled in this year [1686]; and Fort St. David was definitively established there in 1690–92.

In 1687–88 Sir John Wyborne and Mr. Zinzan [see page 31] were dismissed† the Company's service at Bombay for disputing the authority of Sir John Child.

---

through heedlessly placing it between inverted commas, gave it a titular look and meaning.

From an admirable little report by Mr. F. C. Danvers, Registrar and Superintendent of Records at the India Office, on the succession list of the Chiefs, Agents, and Governours of Bengal, it appears that Mr. [afterward Sir] William Hedges was the first Agent who was also styled Governour, 1681–83. His successor, Mr. William Gyfford, from Fort St. George, was styled President and Governour, 1683. Then both these titles were dropped until the appointment of Sir William Eyre as President and Governour from 1699; after whom they were borne by all his successors down to Warren Hastings, who was appointed [under Lord North's "Act for the Regulation of India," 1773] "Governour General," and was the first to bear that title in India, 1774–85. Lord [afterward Earl] Canning, the fourteenth Governour General, was the first Viceroy of British India, 1856–61. On Warren Hastings' appointment as "Governour General," the title of "Governour of the Presidency of Fort William in Bengal" remained for a time disused; but was revived in 1833 as a second title of the Governour General, who continued to hold the separate office of "Governour of the Presidency of Fort William in Bengal" to 1853–4, when the offices were separated, and as much of "the Presidency of Fort William" as was not placed under the Lieutenant Governour of the North-West Provinces was made into a Lieutenant Governourship of Bengal, with Mr. [now Sir Frederic] Halliday as first Lieutenant Governour.

* The three villages included in the new English settlement founded by Job Charnock [b. ? , d. 1693] were called Chatanati, Govindpur, and Kalikata. Only the name of the last survives in the present Calcutta.

† The entry, in the second volume of "the Black Books" [*see* above pp. 30–31], from a Bombay Letter of the 6th of January 1687/8, is:—"Sir John Wyborne and Mr. Zinzan quite turned out." From another entry, from a Bombay Letter of the 9th *idem*, it would however appear that Mr. Zinzan

In 1688 the Post Office was established at Bombay.

It was in this year also that the French obtained "Frasdangeh" or Chandernagore [Chandannagar, "Sandal-wood city"] from Aurungzib.

In 1689 the Company retired from their factories in Bengal to Madras [see 1681 and 1698–99].

In the same year their factories at Vizagapatam and Masulipatam were seized by the Moguls, and the factors massacred; and Bombay was pillaged up to the "Castle" walls, by the Sidi [Saed] of Jinjira.

It was in this year [1689] therefore that the Company, in order to acquire the political status of an independent power in their relations with the Moguls and Mahrattas, at last determined to consolidate their position in India on the basis of territorial sovereignty. To this end they formed the following resolution for the guidance of the local governments in India:—"The increase "of our *revenue* is the subject of our care, as much "as our *trade*; 'tis that must maintain our force "when 20 accidents may interrupt our trade; 'TIS "THAT MUST MAKE US A NATION IN INDIA; without "that we are but a great number of interlopers, united "by His Majesty's Royal Charter, fit only to trade "where nobody of power thinks it their interest to "prevent us; and upon this account it is that the wise "Dutch, in all their general advices that we have seen, "write ten paragraphs concerning their Government, their "civil and military policy, warfare, and the increase of "their revenue, for one paragraph they write concerning "trade."*

---

had already died on the 23rd of November previous, *i.e.*, 1687. The charges against both Wyborne and Zinzan were for opening the secret letters to Sir John Child, and for their "carriage" toward the latter, who is said to have "ill resented" the same.

* This resolution was undoubtedly dictated by Sir Josia Child, the ruling spirit of the Company at this critical period. In the second volume of *The Diary of Sir William Hedges*, p. 117, Sir Henry Yule quotes the following

In 1690 Sir John Child died at Bombay.

In 1690–92 the factory at Thevnapatam, or Tegnapatam [Cuddalore], first settled in 1686, was fortified, and called Fort St. David. From 1746 to 1752 it became the chief seat of the Company on the Coromandel Coast.

In 1691–92 the factory at Baroach was dissolved.

In 1693 the Company spent 90,000*l.* in bribing the Privy Council to renew their charter, and prevent the incorporation of the new "English Company."

In 1694 Angengo was fortified from Bombay.

In 1698, in spite of all their bribes, "the old East "India Company lost their business against the new "Company by ten votes in Parliament, so many of "their friends being absent, going to see a tiger baited by "dogs." [Evelyn's *Diary*, March 5th.] The new Company was styled "the English Company trading to the "East Indies," in contradistinction to the old "Governour "and Company of Merchants of London trading into "the East Indies." On this "the Old Company" exerted itself "with a true Roman courage," as one of their official letters to their servants in India states; and at Madras and elsewhere all their old factories and stations were resumed, so as to exclude "the New Company," and Bengal was again made independent of Madras. [See 1681, 1686, and 1689.]

In 1698–99 the "London Company" obtained from Prince Azim Ushan, Governour of Bengal [1697–1704] a grant, confirmed by the Emperor Aurungzib [Prince Azim's father] in 1700, of the towns of Chuttanuttee, Kaleecutta [not yet known as Calcutta] and Govindpore, and pushed on the construction, commenced in 1696, of

---

equally remarkable paragraph, attributed by him to Sir Josia Child, from a Company's letter to *Fort St. George*, dated 12th December 1687:—"That "which we promise ourselves in a most especiall manner from our new Pre- "sident and Council is that they will establish such a Politie of civill and "military power, and create and secure Such a large Revenue to maintain "both at that place, as may bee the foundation of a large, well grounded, "sure English Dominion in India for all time to Come."

Fort William, to this day the only stronghold the English possess in India. From this period Calcutta was virtually a separate Presidency, but was not formally constituted one until 1707. [See 1634, 1681, 1689. See also note on 1686.]

In 1698 the "English Company" established a factory in Borneo.

In 1700, in consequence of the great cheapness of the silks imported by the Company from India, the English manufacturers forced the Government to pass the Act, already quoted [page 225, *note*], in connection with the popular agitation against the Company's importation of Indian cotton fabrics, whereby it was declared that from Michaelmas 1701 no Persian, Indian, or Chinese silks should be sold, worn, or in any way used in England.

In 1708 a factory was established at Anjeram [? Anjier, in Java, on the Strait of Sunda];* and in 1714 Fort Marlborough [Bencoolen] was built in supersession of Fort York, built in 1685 [see under 1682–83].

In 1702–8–9 the "Old" ["London"] and "New" ["English"] Companies were amalgamated under the style of "The United Company of Merchants Trading to the East Indies;" since commonly known and officially described as, "the Honourable East India Company."†

In 1707 Aurungzib died, after a reign of upwards of 50 years; and from the period of his death commenced those internal troubles which gradually broke up the great Mogul Empire, and paved the way for the conquests of the Honourable East India Company.

---

* Where is the tomb of Colonel Cathcart, who died on his voyage out to China, as British Ambassador to the Court of Peking, and was buried here in 1788?

† In 1707 also the legislative union of Scotland with England was effected, and the "*placebo*" administered to the Scots on the occasion was the free return to them, out of English revenues, of the capital they had, in futile rivalry with the "London" Company, subscribed to the "Company of Scotland trading to Africa and the Indies," founded in 1695, with five per cent.

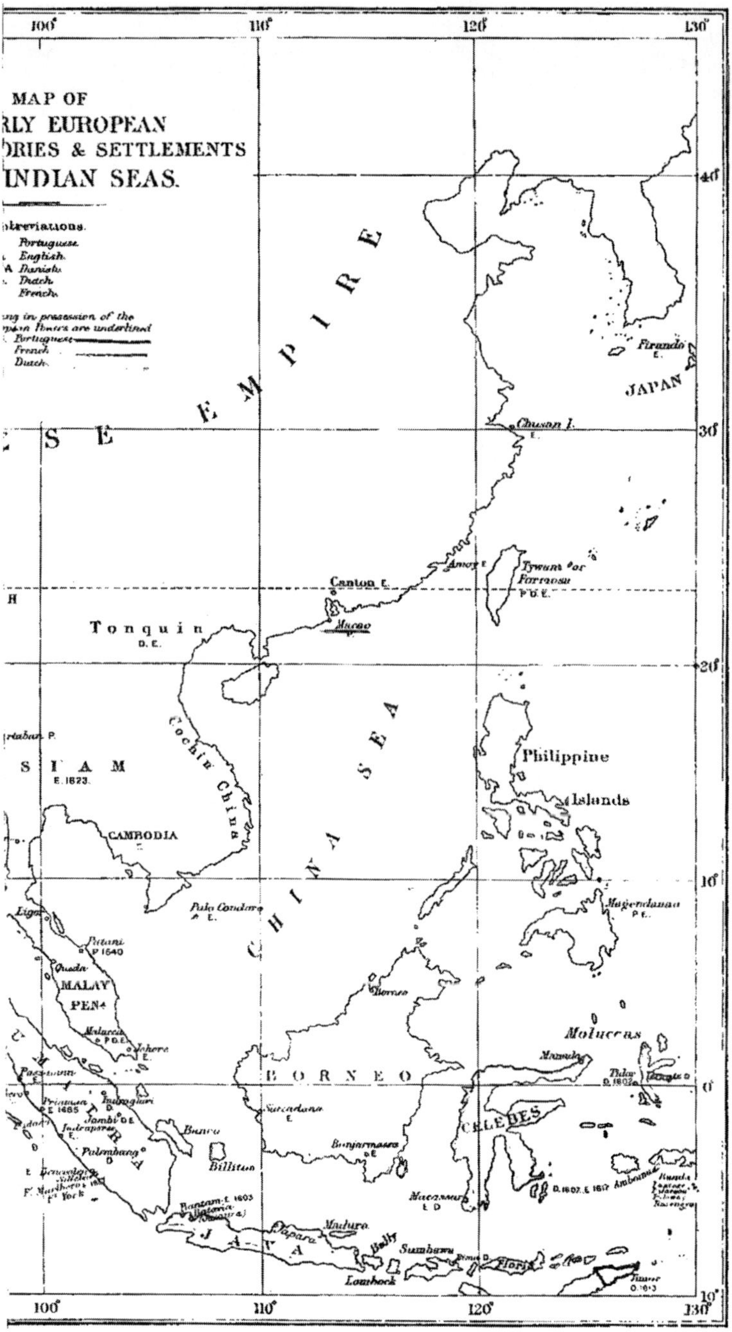
MAP OF
RLY EUROPEAN
ORIES & SETTLEMENTS
INDIAN SEAS.
Portuguese
English
Danish
Dutch
French
EMPIRE
JAPAN
Firando
Chusan I.
Amoy
Canton
Macao
Tonquin
Cochin China
SIAM
CAMBODIA
CHINA SEA
Philippine Islands
Malacca
MALAY PEN.
BORNEO
CELEBES
Moluccas
Banca
Billiton
JAVA
Madura
Sumbawa
Lombock
Timor
Sumatra

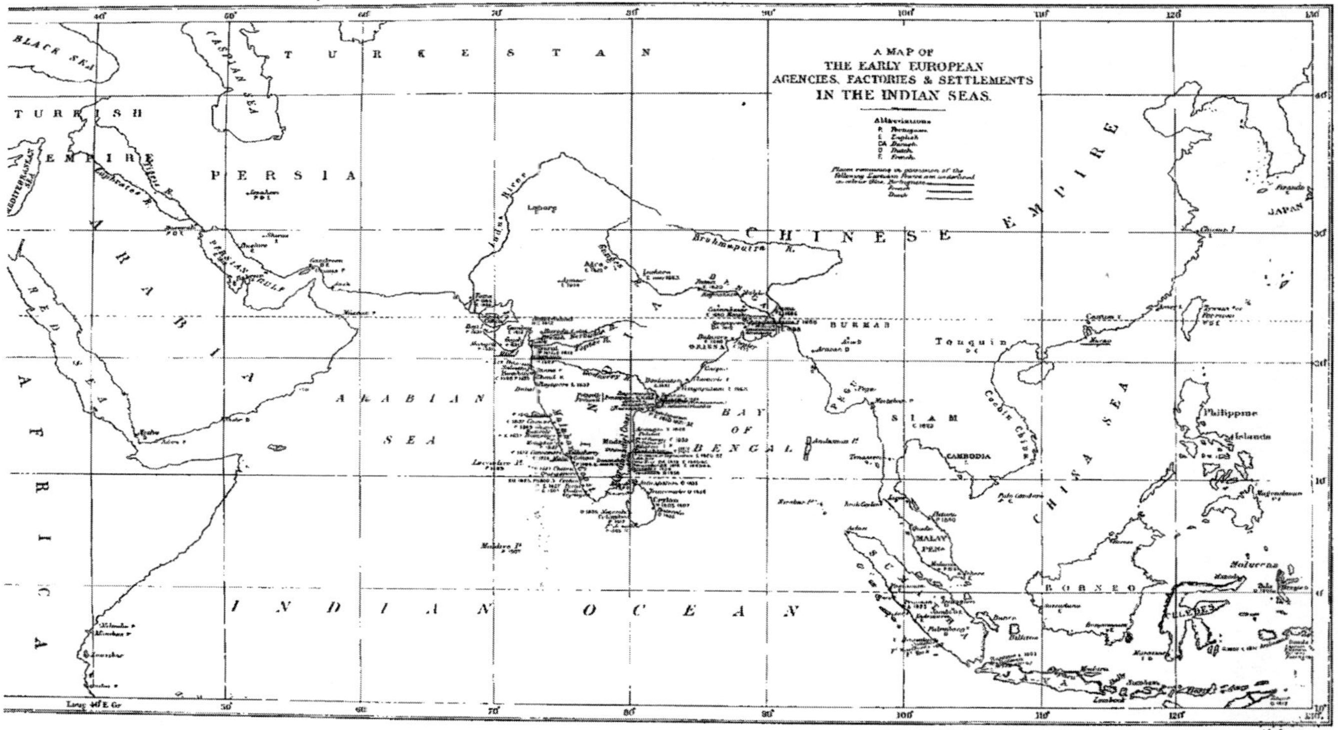

19097. I 2531. E. & S.

With his death, therefore, and the union of the two Companies, the annals of the English Factories end, and the history of the British Conquest of India begins.

I conclude this abstract and brief chronicle of the former period with an enumeration of the chief factories* established by the English from the commencement of their trade to the East until the union of the two Companies in 1702–8–9. Those mentioned in the deed of union, under the head of the "Old Company's" dead stock, are shown in italics; while those of which separate records are extant are denoted by an asterisk [*].

In the Red Sea, or Arabian Gulf.

Aden and Mocha.

In the Green Sea or Persian Gulf, and Persia.

Jasques or Jask, Bushire, Bassorah, **Ispahaun*, **Gombroon*, and *Shyraz*.

In Western India, and on the Malabar Coast.

Cutch, Cambay, Gogo, Rajbay or Rajbag, *Ahmedabad*, ['Amadavad'], *Broach*, **Surat* and **Swally*, Baroda ['Brodera'], **Bombay*, Rajapore ['Dundee-Rajpore'], *Carwar*, Baticola, Onore, Barcelore, Durmapatam, Cranganore, Mangalore, Cananore, Rattera, Brinjan, Porca, Carnoply, *Tellicherry*, *Calicut*, Cochin, Quilon, **Angengo*.

---

interest from that date added. The bribe pleased, quieted, and otherwise benefited the Scots,—

"And prosp'rous actions always pass for wise."

We may not therefore after so prolonged a period discuss either its policy or morality, any more than question the goodly fruit of a tree because of the unsavoury compost about its roots. But the memory of a transaction, profitable at once for doctrine, for reproof, for correction, and for instruction in state-craft, should not be allowed to perish.

* This list would be much more useful could the date of occupation of each place named be added; but I have not found it possible to do so in time for the present [1890] reprint.

In Southern India, on the Coromandel Coast, and in Orissa.

Tuticorin, **Porto Novo* [' Firingipet '], **Cuddalore*, **Fort St. George* [Madras, ' Chineepatam '], *Pulicat, *Armagaon [' Dasarapatnam '], Viravasaram [Verasheroon], Ingeram, **Pettipollee*, **Masulipatam* [' Metchlipatam '], **Madapollam*, **Vizagapatam*, *Golconda, *Tanjore, Bimlipatam, Biliapatam, Ganjam, *Conimero, **Fort St. David* [Tevnapatam], Chingee, Gingee, or Chingu, **Ballasore* [' Bulramgurry '], Pipley.

In Bengal and Hindustan.

**Hughley*, **Fort William*, **Chuttanuttee* [not yet merged in Calcutta], **Cossimbazaar* [' Castle Bazaar '], *Rajamaul*, **Maulda*, *Englesvad, *Patna*, **Dacca*, Lucknow, *Agra*, Ajmere, Lahore, Burhampur [' Brampore '].

In Further India, and the Malay Peninsula.

*Siam, Cochin China, Pegu, *Patany or Patania, Quedah, Johore, Cambodia, Ligore.

On the Island of Sumatra.

*Acheen, *Jambee, Passaman, *Priaman*, *Sillebar*, Ticcoo, **Fort York*, *Bencoolen*, *Indrapur* or *Indraporee*, **Tyamong* or *Tryamong*.

On the Island of Java.

Bantam,* Japara, Jacatra [afterward *Batavia].

On the Island of *Borneo.

Banjarmassin and Succadana.

On the Island of Celebes.

Macassar,* and a residency at Menado.

On the Moluccas, or 'Spice Islands.'

Factories on the island of Lantore or 'The Great Banda,' and on the islands of Rosengyn, Pulo Way, and

Pulo Roon, "their" [*i.e.*, the London Company's] "ancient inheritance," and on the island of *Amboyna.

IN THE YELLOW OR CHINA SEA.

Magindanao, *Tonquin*, *Pulo Condore*, *Amoy, *Tywan, *Macao, *Canton, Chusan.

IN *JAPAN.

Firando.

IN THE ÆTHIOPIC OR SOUTH ATLANTIC OCEAN.

**St. Helena*: appertaining, writes Herbert, "to *Afer* ". . . . [because it is nearest that Continent] rather "than *Vesputius*."

Such was the Factory Empire, extended through all the coasts and islands of Southern Asia, of the blue sea lions of the "Old" East India Company.

*Dutch, Italian, French, and English Books on the Factory Period.**

Jan Hugo van Linschoten travelled in India from 1583 to 1589, and Philip Baldæus about 1660; and the *Voyages into ye Easte and Weste Indies* [Dutch original, Amsterdam, 1596, and English translation, London, 1598] of the former, and the *Description of the Coasts of Malabar and Coromandel* [Amsterdam, 1672] of the latter, are two invaluable books for the information they give of the early days of the Dutch in the East, and their struggles with the Portuguese.

Cornelius Le Bruyn's *Voyage to the Levant*, of which an English translation was published in 1702, although it does not include India, and scarcely, therefore, comes within the scope of the present Note, is here mentioned on account of the excellence of its

* As in the case of the list of contemporary writers on the early Portuguese Period, this enumeration of works relating to the English Factory Period in the East is very incomplete, particularly in the important Dutch histories and narratives and collections of voyages and travels, of the time. It is a list simply of my own familiar books on the subject, and is quite long enough for all practical purposes. "Onerat discentem turba librorum, non instruit."

copper-plate illustrations, numbering 300, of the cities and people of the countries he describes, and particularly of the ruins of Persepolis, and other antiquarian remains, in Persia.

In 1563, Cæsar Frederick, a Venetian merchant, went by way of the Persian Gulf to India, and on to Pegu; and the account he gives of his travels was translated into English by Thomas Hichoch in 1588, under the title of *Voyage and Travaill into India, the Indies, and beyond the Indies.* He describes Cambay, where the commercial supremacy of the Portuguese was acknowledged, and Ahmedabad and Goa. He gives a very detailed account of the commerce of Pegu, visited by him in 1568. It had previously been visited by Antonio Correa, who, shortly after the occupation of Malacca by the Portuguese, was despatched thither with the view of establishing trade with Burmah. It was subsequently [1583] visited by Gasparo Balbi; and his *Viaggio dell' Indie Orientale* [Venice, 1590], and Cæsar Frederick's narrative, are the best notices we possess of the last-named country until the publication of the modern works of Symes and Phayre.

Pietro della Valle [*Viaggi in Turchia, Persia, e India*, Venice, 1650–58–63] travelled in Persia in 1614–26, and Adam Olearius [*The Voyages and Travels of the Ambassadors*, German ed., Schleswig, 1647, English trans. by John Davies, 1662 and 1669] was secretary to the Duke of Holstein's embassy to Russia and Persia in 1633–39; but neither of their narratives trenches on the proper ground of the Dutch and English factory period in India.

Mandelslo accompanied the Duke of Holstein's mission to Russia and Persia, to which Olearius was secretary, in 1633–39; and from Bandar Abbas went on to Surat, Baroach, 'Brodera' [Baroda], Ahmedabad, Cambay, Lahore, and Vizeapore, returning to Denmark, where he landed, May 1, 1640, from

Surat. The narrative of his *Voyage and Travels*, translated by John Davies, was published in England, in one volume with Olearius's account of the Duke of Holstein's mission, in 1662 and 1669, and gives a most interesting account of our factory at Surat, and of the manner of life of the factors there. They were the inventors of the potent Greekish poteen, punch [*Puntz* of Mandelslo, *Paunch* of Fryer], so called from the five [in Hindustani *panch*] ingredients, spirit, lemon or lime juice, spice, sugar, and rose-water, used in its composition. The πενταπλόα of the "merry Greeks" was composed of wine, honey, cheese, meal, and oil.

Jean Baptiste Tavernier [*Voyages en Turquie, en Perse, et aux Indies*, 1676, first English translation, 1677] travelled constantly in India between 1640 and 1667; Jean de Thevenot [*Voyages*, 1689] visited the East in 1655–63; François Bernier [*Histoire de la dernière Revolution des Etats du Grand Mogul*, 1670, translated into English with his *Voyage to Surat*, London, 1671 and 1675] lived at the court of Aurungzib for 12 years [1658–70], and accompanied that monarch to Cashmere; and "Sir John" Chardin [*Journal du Voyage*, 1st part published, London, 1686, and the 2nd and 3rd, Amsterdam, 1711], was in Persia and the East Indies from 1664 to 1681; and the works of these four accomplished Frenchmen rank among the most valuable records of travel in India that have ever been published.

Sir Thomas Roe's admirable *Journal of his Voyage to the East Indies, and Observations there during his Residence at the Mogul Court* [1615–18], originally given in Purchas [1625], was published separately in French, at Paris, in 1663.

Henry Lord's *Display of the Sect of Banians* and *Religion of the Parsees* were published in 1630.

Sir Thomas Herbert, descended from Sir W. Herbert, the ancestor also of the brilliant Pembroke family, travelled in the East as secretary to the English embassy to Persia, from 1627 to 1629. His book, entitled *A description of the Persian Monarchy now beinge, the Orientall Indyes, Isles, and other parts of the Greater Asia and Afrik*, was published in 1634. He pluckily contends that Prince Madoc ap Owen Gwynedd discovered America 300 years before Columbus. The 3rd edition, 1665, contains a beautiful etching of Persepolis by Hollar. Thomas Herbert is otherwise interesting as one of the Commissioners appointed to receive King Charles I. on his sale by the Scots to the English Parliamentarians in 1647.

Edward Terry's *Voyage*, published in 1655, gives a most interesting account of Surat and Swally, and of Thomas Coryate's travels in the East, and death at Surat in 1617.

John Ovington's *Voyage to Surat* was published in 1696.

John Fryer, surgeon to the Company, travelled in Persia and India from 1672 to 1681, and his *New Account of the East Indies and Persia*, published in 1698, is the most delightful book ever published on those countries, and invaluable for the graphic descriptions it gives of the factory life, and general condition of the people of India in his time.

Charles Lockyer was engaged in the Company's business in the Indian Seas about 1704, and his *Account of the Trade in India*, published in 1711, affords a complete account of the management of the commercial affairs of the English and Dutch East India Companies at that date.

Mr. Clements Markham, C.B., in the volume of *The Voyages of Sir James Lancaster to the East Indies*, edited by him for the Hakluyt Society [1877], has given abstracts of the journals of voyages to the East Indies by the Company's commanders during the 17th century. Lancaster's voyages are republished from Purchas and Hakluyt [1589], but the rest are from the India Office Records.

Among other books to which my acknowledgments are also due must be mentioned the following :—

Recueil des Voyages de la Compagnie des Indes Orientales des Hollandois, 10 vols. 12mo, 1730; Eden's *History of Travayle*; Alex. Hamilton's *New Account of the East Indies*, 1727 : Bruce's *Annals of the East India Company*, 1810; Peter Auber's various works on the East India Company, *circa* 1826; James Mill's *History of British India*, 1817; Milburn's *Oriental Commerce*, 1813; A. Anderson's *History of Commerce*, 4 vols. folio, 1787 [published anonymously]; the four volumes, edited by Mr. Noël Sainsbury, of the *Calendar of State Papers relating to the East Indies*, 1513 to 1629; Cooley's *History of Maritime and Inland Discovery*, 1830; and Lindsay's *History of Merchant Shipping and Ancient Commerce*, 1874–76. I have also derived great assistance from James Forbes's *Oriental Memoirs*, 1834; and Philip Anderson's delightful book, *The English in Western India*, 1856 [it is well worth republication, with the supplementary articles contributed by the author, subsequently to its publication, to the *Bombay Quarterly Review*]; and Mr. Talboys Wheeler's *Madras in the Olden Time*, 1862, and *Early Records of British India*, 1878.* Victor Jacquement travelled in India from 1828 to 1832, and Bishop Heber [who, before going to India, had visited Germany, Russia, and the Crimea] from 1823 to 1828; and the *Correspondence pendant son Voyage dans l'Inde* [1841–44] of the former, and the *Journal* [1828] of the latter, are two of the most instructive and important books ever given to the world on India.

---

* To this list I must now [1889] add, beside the recent works by Henry Stevens, Sir Henry Yule, and James Douglas [acknowledged at pp. 15, 23, and 228, respectively], Dr. John Anderson's volume ["Trübner's Oriental Series"] on *English Intercourse with Siam in the Seventeenth Century*; and the Rev. H. B. Hyde's [of St. John's Church, Calcutta], *First Bengal Chaplain* [John Evans], published in the "Indian Church Quarterly Review."

THE HISTORY OF "THE UNITED COMPANY," OR THE BRITISH CONQUEST OF INDIA.

The period of the conquest of India by the Company is beyond that covered by the general mass of the supplementary miscellaneous "Old Records" here reviewed, and all that is necessary to be given under the present head is a catalogue of the Company's conquests, in illustration of the original firmans and numerous copies of firmans ["translates of phirmands"] enumerated in my "Report on the Old Records." It will be convenient however, to preface this inventory with a slight sketch of the history of India from the appearance of the Portuguese off the coasts of the peninsula to the close of the Company's last Charter. Messrs. Fidler and Craufurd's "Memorandum" of 1873–75 affords an admirable index to the records of the later part of this period, from 1708–9 down to 1858, when the Honourable East India Company was extinguished as a political power, and the British Indian Empire was sequestrated to the Imperial Crown of the United Kingdom.

When the Portuguese first appeared in India, the seventh and last Afghan dynasty, of the House of Lodi [1450–1526], was the paramount power in Hindustan ["India alba"], while in the Deccan ["India nigra"] the Hindu Kingdom of Bijanagar, known to the earlier European travellers and settlers in India as "the Kingdom of Narsinga," still maintained its independence. A number of petty Hindu states also flourished along its westward borders, on the Malabar Coast, of which Calicut under its Zamorins [*i.e. Samudri*, Sea-Kings] was one. Baber, the Founder of the Mogul Empire of Delhi, the son of the governour of Ferghana, and descended from both Chingiz Khan and Tamerlane, seized on Cabul in 1504, conquered the Punjaub in 1518, and met and overthrew Ibrahim Lodi on the plain of Panipat, March the 5th, 1526.

It was under the fourth Afghan dynasty, of the House of Khilji [1288–1321], that the Mahomedans first invaded the Deccan in 1294. The Amirs established in the Deccan revolted against the House of Tuglak [1321–1412], the fifth Afghan dynasty of Delhi, in 1347, when Zuffir Khan the Afghan founded the Great Bahmini dynasty that ruled at Kulburga from 1347 to 1526. After this rebellion the rulers of Delhi [the Seiads, 1412–1450, and the House of Lodi, 1450–1526] never again crossed the Nerbudda into the Deccan until the reign of Akbar [1556–1605], the grandson of Baber. In 1526 the Bahmini Kingdom became divided into the Kingdoms of Bijapur [1489–1689], Baidar [1492–1609], Ahmednagar* [1490–1637], and Golconda [1512–1687]; and in 1565 the kings of these four Mahomedan States united against the Hindu Kingdom of Bijanagar, then ruled by Ram Raja, the seventh of the dynasts of Narsinga, and divided the bulk of it between them, the remainder falling to the Naiks, Zemindars, and Polygars of the Madras Presidency. It was then that Mysore [*i.e. Mahishasura*, the buffalo demon slain by Kali], hitherto tributary to Bijanagar, became independent, and the chief Hindu State of the Deccan.

It was during the wars caused by the efforts of Akbar [third Mogul Emperor, 1556–1605] and his successors to reduce the Mahomedan Kingdoms of the Deccan to subjection that the Mahrattas gradually rose to supremacy both in the Deccan and Hindustan. Sivaji was born in 1627, and died in 1680. After Aurungzib's death in 1707 the Mogul Empire fell into rapid decay, and the Punjaub, Rajputana, Oudh, Bengal, Behar, Orissa, Rohilcund, the Carnatic, and Hyderabad [under the usurping Nizam-ul-Mulk, Azef Khan, 1717–48] had already become virtually independent, when the whirlwind of Nadir Shah's invasion in 1739 swept over India. It was then that Baji Rao, the second Mah-

* The kingdom of Berar, founded by the Ummad Shahi dynasty which ruled at Ellichpur from 1484 to 1574, was in the latter year annexed to Ahmednagar.

ratta Peishwa, assembled the whole powers of the Deccan, and marched at their head to the relief of Delhi. As Baji Rao advanced Nadir Shah retreated, but in his army was Ahmed Shah Abdali [Durani], destined to overthrow the supremacy of the Mahrattas for ever, on the memorable plain of Panipat, in 1761.

Such was the political condition of India in the reign of the 12th Mogul emperor, Mahomed Shah [1719–1748], on the eve of the British conquest.

The French [Martin] had bought Pondicherry in 1672–74, Chandernagore in 1688, and Yanaon in 1706, Mahé was taken by them in 1725, and Carical ceded by the Rajah of Tanjore in 1739: and in 1741 Dupleix became, in succession to Dumas [1736–41], Governour General of the French possessions in India. In 1740 the Mahrattas invaded the Carnatic, then a dependency of the kingdom of Hyderabad, and the French, having given refuge to the Nawab's son, received the thanks of the Nizam-ul-Mulk [Azef Khan]. Dupleix now resolved to drive the English out of India, and the opportunity was afforded him in the war between England and France in 1744–48. Madras was surrendered to La Bourdonnais in 1746, and the English might then have really lost India but for La Bourdonnais' antipathy toward Dupleix, and the conclusion of the Peace of Aix-la-Chapelle, and the concurrent deaths of the Great Mogul [Mahomed Shah] the Peishwa [Sahu], and the Nizam-ul-Mulk [Azef Khan], all in the same year, 1748, before the situation compromised by La Bourdonnais could be recovered.*

---

* The subject of La Bourdonnais' [Bernard François Mahé de la Bourdonnais, b. at St. Malo 1699] bribery has always had an interest for minds given to searching out mean and sordid causes for the great results of history. Having carefully read through the "Law Case, No. 31, of 3rd March 1752," the only original document in this country, I believe, in the matter, and cited by Colonel Malleson, *History of the French in India*, page 157, note, I have been led to the opinion that it affords no conclusive evidence of the truth of

The death of the Nizam-ul-Mulk was followed by a disputed succession between his sons, in which the English and French took opposite sides, with the result

---

the charge. The capture of Madras by La Bourdonnais, its abortive ransom by Governour Morse and his Council—which, according to the charge against him, La Bourdonnais was induced to accept by a bribe of 100,000 pagodas (40,000*l.*),—and the annexation of the town by Dupleix, and its final restoration to the English, formed an unconsidered episode of the war of the Austrian Succession, 1744–1748. That war at once brought England and France into conflict; and the first hostile act of each country was to fit out a naval expedition for the destruction of the other's mercantile settlements in the Indian Ocean.

The English fleet was the first to arrive in the Bay of Bengal, in 1745, when Dupleix, the Governour of Pondicherry, in great alarm, sent a large present to the Nawab of the Carnatic, who replied, as desired, by forbidding the English, who up to that time were his tributaries, from engaging in hostilities within any part of his dominions. The English fleet in consequence left "the Bay and Coast" in 1746. They had no sooner disappeared than La Bourdonnais, with the squadron he had collected together with extraordinary energy from the Isles of France and Bourbon, entered it; and now Morse, the Governour of Madras, 1744–1749, in his turn applied to the Nawab of the Carnatic to restrain the French, as he had previously restrained the English, from hostilities, but, as Morse neglected to send a present with his application, it was left without an answer. In consequence, on 18th August 1746 [as this interesting Law Case, in correction and amplification of the vague statements of our standard histories, informs us], La Bourdonnais, with eight French ships under his command, appeared before the town of Madras, and fired a few shots into Fort St. George, and some broadsides into the *Princess Mary*, one of the English Company's ships then in the roads, and afterward lay to in the offing, or cruised up and down the Coromandel coast, in sight of the town and people of Madras. On 3rd September, Morse and his Council heard that La Bourdonnais had landed his men somewhere down the coast, and was marching on Madras; and the next day he opened his attack on the town. On 10th September, Morse and his Council, excepting Mr. Fowke, came to a resolution to capitulate, and treat for the ransom of the place; and for that purpose Mr. Monson, who was next to Morse in Council, and Mr. Hallyburton, an English gentleman of Madras, who spoke French, were deputed to wait on "Monsieur La Bourdonnais," and settle terms with him. These, in brief, were that the town should pay 1,100,000 pagodas for its ransom; and the charge of bribery and treason against La Bourdonnais is that he agreed to this ransom in consideration of a further sum of 100,000 pagodas, to be given to him for his own private use and gratification. Dupleix quashed the treaty, and confiscated all the Company's property in

that, in 1751, Salabat Jung, the third son of the Nizam-ul-Mulk, was installed at Aurungabad as Subadhar of

---

Madras, and all private property, excepting only personal apparel and jewelry, and carried off all the chief people of the place prisoners to Pondicherry, and annexed Madras [appointing Paradis Governour] to the French possessions on the Coromandel coast.

Had La Bourdonnais stood loyally by Dupleix at this conjuncture [after the example of our English officers in the early days of the Company's adventures in India] the future dominion of India would, as far as we can now judge, have passed away from us altogether, and "the trade, navigation, and conquest of the Indies" fallen into the hands of the French. But La Bourdonnais, in a huff, set sail from Madras 29th October 1746, leaving Dupleix in the lurch; thus throwing to the winds the greatest opportunity the French ever had of establishing their empire in the East. Dupleix fully understood this: and that La Bourdonnais did not, is the true secret of his strange conduct; and not that he took a bribe; or if he took it as a mere complimentary present [*dusturi*], that he was in the least influenced by it.

After this the operations of the French and English against each other dragged on in an ineffective manner for a year or two more; and on the conclusion of the Treaty of Aix-la-Chapelle in 1748, Madras was restored to the English Company.

On his return to France, La Bourdonnais was at once thrown into the Bastille, on the charge of collusion with the English in the matter of the ransom of Madras; but after a trial extending over three years [1748–51] was fully acquitted and set free. He died broken-hearted in 1755. His acquittal by his own Government, which was inspired by the deepest resentment against him, is a strong fact in his favour; and Colonel Malleson, a soldier as well as a historian, should at least have himself read the records of the case, not only in the India Office, but in the French Admiralty, before reviving so scandalous a charge against one of the noblest ornaments of the French Navy. La Bourdonnais acted with the gravest indiscretion, and that sufficiently accounts for his strange, and, in a political sense, culpable conduct. That he was a traitor is, for anyone who is acquainted with his character, an impossible assumption. He was a brave, ardent, and adventurous sailor, whose only idea, in fitting out his expedition from Bourbon and Mauritius, was to harry the English trade in Indian waters, and exact war prizes. Dupleix, on the contrary, was a prescient, calculating statesman, with a constitutional contempt for fighting [which he used to say "confused his thoughts"], whose far-reaching policy was directed to the complete expulsion of the English from India, and the raising of a great French empire on the foundations we had laid. From the moment, therefore, that these two men met they were in direct antipathy with each other, and in all these transactions at Madras in the autumn of 1746, La Bourdonnais' perverse part from the first was to withstand and disconcert Dupleix's political plans. He

the Deccan by Bussy, and the whole of Southern India virtually passed under French controul.

---

acted after the manner of all the French leaders in India in the last century, and it is the common-place moral of history that it was in this manner they lost India.

But to return to the evidence offered by Law Case, No. 31, of 3rd March 1752. Colonel Malleson merely refers to it, without quoting it. I will now quote every material passage of it bearing on La Bourdonnais' alleged bribery and treason; premising that the case arose from the objection of the Court of Directors of the East India Company to meet the bonds on which the sum required for the ransom of Madras was raised, on the ground that, in part at least, the bonds had been given, not to save the Company's property, but the private property of the Governour and his Council. Morse and the rest, excepting Fowke, examined by the Court, were really on their own defence, and it may be said that the only impartial evidence incriminating La Bourdonnais to the extent of his having received a complimentary gratification [*dusturi*] is that of Fowke.

Folio 3.—" Mr. Morse, late Governour of Fort St. George, in a letter to a Committee of the Court of Directors [18th January 1748], ... says :—' I ' take this occasion to advise you, apart, that in that transaction ' [ransom of Madras] ' we were under a necessity for applying a further sum besides that ' publicly stipulated by the articles ' [of ransom], ' which affair, as it required ' privacy, was by the Council referred to myself and Mr. Monson to be ne- ' gotiated.' "

" Mr. Monson, in a letter to the Court of Directors [21st December 1748], says :—' I am to acquaint you that, in treating for the ransom of the place, ' we were soon given to understand that a further sum was necessary to be ' paid beside that to be mentioned in the public treaty. You will easily ' imagine from the nature of the thing that it required to be conducted with ' some degree of secrecy. There was, however, a necessity for acquainting ' the Council with it, though for form's sake and to preserve appearances ' with the person [we were] treating with, it was referred to Mr. Morse and ' myself to settle the matter with him ; I can, nevertheless, with great truth ' assure you that all the gentlemen of the Council were constantly faithfully ' acquainted with every step that was taken in the matter, except Mr. Edward ' Fowke, who, from the beginning of the treaty about the ransom, declared ' that he would not join us in any of these measures, which by all the rest ' were thought absolutely necessary at that juncture. . . .

" ' It remains for me to acquaint you that we had no possible means for ' raising the money but by giving the Company's bonds for it ; and this nego- ' tiation was not kept secret from those who supplied the money on this occa- ' sion, as they were to a man informed of the use it was borrowed for, before ' they lent it, and thought by lending it they did a meritorious piece of ser-

The English having, however, through Clive, retrieved their position in the Carnatic, the French, in 1757, sent

---

'vice to the Company; bonds were accordingly given for so much as we 'could borrow under the Company's seal, and signed by Mr. Morse and all 'the rest of the Council, except Mr. Edward Fowke. Part of the money 'thus borrowed was actually paid to the person treated with, and the rest 'was disbursed in defraying the charges of the garrison until the French 'broke the capitulations and turned us out of the town.'"

Folio 4.—"Mr. Monson, in his letter [3rd May 1749] . . . after excusing himself from declaring to whom . . . this money . . . was given, says:—'I 'hope I shall stand excused if I declare no further than that part of the 'money was appropriated to pay six months' salary and two months' diet to 'your covenant servants, with a month's arrear to the garrison, besides 'sundry disbursements to the officers and sailors of the *Princess Mary*, to your 'officers and military that were going to Cuddalore, and some little advances we 'judged necessary towards our future re-establishment, the rest of the money, 'with the diamonds, was actually and *bonâ fide* applied to the purpose already 'mentioned' [the payment of "that person"], 'which, in the opinion of 'those who were concerned in this business, would have redounded very much to the honour, the credit, and the real advantage of the Company.'"

Folio 5.—"Mr. Edward Fowke . . . speaking [letter of 25th December 1746] of the ransom . . . says:—'In regard to ransoming of the town, after-'wards when Monsieur La Bourdonnais told us we might march out with 'our swords and hats, I thought it' [going out with swords and hats] 'much 'more to your interest than to accept the terms that were agreed upon. . . . 'I could have consented so far as five or six lacs. . . . Madras is but a tribu-'tary town . . . therefore for your Honours to be loaded with such a mons-'trous sum, and the Native Government not to feel any part of so severe a 'blow, would, I am afraid, in future have a very bad effect, especially with a 'little money laid out among the great men, which the French pretty well 'know how to place.'"

Again, 3rd March 1748:—'I can assure you, gentlemen, notwithstanding 'I may have appeared so lukewarm in defence of your town . . . I would 'rather have sacrificed my life than to have acceded to those terms of agree-'ment, I thought them as directly opposite to your interest, honour, and 'credit, as others thought them for it.' In the same letter he says one of the bonds was brought to him to sign, and he wrote on it:—'I acknowledge Mr. 'George Jones to have brought me the above-mentioned bond to sign, but as 'I do not approve the ransom, nor do I know whether I am now legally 'authorized' [being a prisoner of La Bourdonnais] 'to take up money on the 'Company's account, I refuse to sign it.'

out Lally expressly to expel them from India. Clive had been meanwhile called away to Bengal to avenge

---

Folio 10.—In the examination (1753?) of the bond creditors by interrogatories, Messrs. Abraham Franco, Jacob Franco, Aaron Franks, *inter alia*, say:—'That they heard and believe that the then President and Council of 'Fort St. George did, after the 10th September 1746, agree to give and pay 'to Monsieur de la Bourdonnais 88,000 pagodas, but that they did not know 'or believe that the said 88,000 pagodas, or any part thereof, were so agreed 'to be paid in order to free or exempt the goods and effects of the merchants and inhabitants . . . and particularly the goods and effects of the said 'Governour in Council, or the said Solomon Solomons' [one of the bondholders] 'in their private capacity, from being seized, taken, or plundered, 'but that the same was agreed to be given or paid to the said Monsieur de la 'Bourdonnais, as a *douceur* or present on behalf of the said East India Company, with a view to reduce the amount or value of the ransom insisted on 'by the said Monsieur de la Bourdonnais.'

And the same further say (folio 11):—'They do believe in their consciences that . . . the same and said present of 88,000 pagodas, as agreed to 'be given to the said Monsieur de la Bourdonnais, was entered into for the 'benefit and interest of the East India Company.'

Folio 12.—"Francis Salvadore, executor to Jacob Salvadore, says:—'He 'don't know, but hath heard and believes that the said President and Council 'did, after the said 10th day of September 1746, agree to give or pay to or 'to the use of the said Monsieur de la Bourdonnais the sum or value of '88,000 pagodas, as at present, but whether . . . in order to exempt or free 'the goods and effects of the merchants or inhabitants . . . and particularly 'of the proper goods and effects of the said Governour and Council, in their 'private capacity, or the said Edward and Joseph Fowke, or the said Jacob 'Salvadore, . . . he don't know nor has been informed.'"

Folio 21.—In reply to certain interrogatories, Mr. Monson says:—'He, 'the said Mr. Monson, having afterwards' [after the treaty of ransom had been settled] 'heard from Monsieur de la Bourdonnais that they must pay 'him down 100,000 pagodas, if they expected performance of the agreement, 'he communicated such his information to the Council, who after deliberation 'agreed to pay it, but says this money was not demanded for granting the '15th and 16th Articles.'

Again:—'No receipt was taken or required for the money privately paid, 'nor could any be insisted on in such a transaction, nor was any agreement 'made for returning the 88,000 pagodas in case the treaty was rejected by the 'Governour and Council of Pondicherry; and can't say whether the Governour 'and Council of Pondicherry were ever informed of this private transaction.'

Folio 23.—Mr. Fowke, in answer to the interrogatories, says:—'He is a 'stranger to the payment, but don't doubt the money being paid.'

the massacre of the "Black Hole" on the plain of Plassey; but in the course of the year Sir Eyre Coote arrived from England, and in December 1759 utterly

---

In folio No. 11, Francis Salvadore, executor to Jacob Salvadore, seems to prove that Mr. Morse and Messrs. Edward and Joseph Fowke advanced money on the Council bonds for the ransom; but I should like someone better acquainted with the phraseology of money dealings to examine this passage, before relying on it as of any pertinence in the present question.

In the whole Case the extract from folio 23 seems to me the only evidence that any money was ever paid to La Bourdonnais by the way of *dusturi*. Excepting Fowke, all the rest of the Council are out of court, *and so would Fowke be, if, while he disapproved of the capitulation, he yet joined with Solomons, Salvadore, Franco, and the rest of these extortioners, in advancing money on the Council bonds he would not himself sign.* Indeed, if Edward Fowke was personally interested, as a sleeping partner with his brother Joseph, in the prospective profits of an usurious advance of the kind, this of itself would be a sufficient explanation of his refusal to join with Morse and Monson in signing the bonds for the amount, on the plausible pretext of his disapproving of a capitulation that could not possibly have been prevented. Besides, if every one who advanced the money knew for what it was intended, Dupleix, through his half-caste wife, to whom he owed so much of the success of his intrigues in India, would easily have obtained sufficient evidence against La Bourdonnais to convict him when he was put on his trial for corruption and treason on his return to France. On the face of the Case also very little of the 88,000 pagodas could have gone to La Bourdonnais; and what Colonel Malleson states is that he received 100,000. La Bourdonnais was probably quite capable of accepting a *douceur* or *dusturi*. It was the universal custom of his time. It was one of the perquisites of public office. But this document, cited, without quotation, by Colonel Malleson, affords no evidence for reviving the charge of corruption and treason against La Bourdonnais after his acquittal by his own Government. It seems to me very probable that, in consideration of La Bourdonnais' "politeness and generosity in exempting Madras from pillage" [I am quoting from the Case from memory, for I cannot retrace the passage], the Governour, Nicholas Morse, and his Council, agreed to make him a private present, and raised 88,000 pagodas for the purpose; that this sum was mostly otherwise expended; and that difficulty having arisen with the Court of Directors about refunding this and other sums embraced in the ransom, it was plausibly pleaded that this particular sum was paid to La Bourdonnais to secure the execution of a treaty of ransom which was never executed but disavowed by Dupleix.

and for ever annihilated the French power in India on the famous field of Wandewash.*

Mir Jafir, whom we set up after Plassey as Nawab of Bengal, and from whom we obtained "the Zemindary of the 24 Pergunnahs," was deposed by us in 1760 in favour of his son Mir Kasim, but, owing to some disagreements with Mir Kasim, we reinstated Mir Jafir as Nawab Nazim. This led to "the massacre of Patna" [by Mir Kasim] in 1763, avenged by the battle of Buxar in 1764, and the annexation of Bengal, Behar, and Orissa to the Company's dominion.

Hindustan was swept clear of its Afghan pests during the Rohilla war of 1775.

---

* Bussy [Charles Joseph Patissier, Marquis de Bussy-Castelnau], who held a command in the French army under Lally in this battle, was taken prisoner and sent home. He subsequently returned to India, where it was his misfortune to again endure defeat at the hands of Sir Eyre Coote; when he retired to Pondicherry, where he died in 1785. Lally [Thomas Arthur] on surrendering Pondicherry to us 14th January 1761, was thrown into the Bastille until 1766, when he was executed. Dupleix [Joseph François], who was recalled in 1754, died of a broken heart in 1763. Such were the sad fates of the three Frenchmen who played so distinguished, albeit disastrous, a part in the critical campaigns of the last century in the Carnatic. Their high-bred courteous bearing made an indelible impression on the natives of India, with whom they identified themselves in a way that seems only possible, among Europeans, to Frenchmen. A countryman of theirs, Michael Joachim Marie Raymond, was, thirty years later, in command of the army of the Nizam of Hyderabad; and, notwithstanding that he suffered it to be annihilated by the Mahrattas [under Perron] at Kurdla in 1795, his memory is held in such affectionate reverence at Hyderabad, where he died in 1798, that to this day the anniversary of his death is celebrated by a general pilgrimage to his house and tomb. First his house is visited, and his uniform saluted, and then the people proceed, in crowds following crowds, to his tomb and adorn it with flowers, and fire volleys of musketry and salvos of artillery before it, and at nightfall light it up with lamps. It bears no inscription, but is known over all the country side as the tomb of *Musa Rahman*, "Moses the Compassionate"; and this popular corruption of the name and style of "Monsieur Raymond," in translating him to Mahomedan sanctity, serves to exalt the fascination of his fame. Paradis [p. 244, note] died early during the first siege of Pondicherry.

From the fall of Bijanagar in 1565 a Hindu dynasty reigned in Mysore until 1761, when Hyder Ali, an officer in the reigning Rajah's army, usurped his Sovereign's throne. This led to the four Mysore wars, viz., of 1766–69; of 1780–84, when Hyder Ali was defeated by Sir Eyre Coote on the very field of Wandewash where, 22 years before, he had gained his decisive victory over the French; of 1790–92, when half of Tippoo Sahib's dominions was divided between the English and their allies; and of 1798–99, when we stormed Seringapatam, and restored Mysore to the dynasty of its ancient Hindu rulers.

It remained only to deliver India from the predatory Mahrattas, whom it also took four wars to finally reduce; namely, those of 1775–82, 1803, 1804–5, and 1817–19.

After this there was no power left in India to oppose or disturb our supremacy, and the Afghan wars of 1839–42, although marked by untoward circumstances, and one great disaster, freed India from all fear of being again devastated by such barbarous hordes as were led to the sack of Delhi by Tamerlane, Nadir Shah, and Ahmed Shah Durani; while the third Afghan war, of 1878–81, enabled us to effect the strategic arrangements on the "North-West Frontier" that are believed to have rendered it impregnable against any civilized army likely to attempt an invasion of India from that quarter. Scinde was annexed in 1843, the Punjaub in 1848–49. Pegu [now Lower Burmah] in 1852, and Oudh in 1856.* The subversion of Turanian tyranny and the revindication of Aryan supremacy in India was now complete. The work of consolidation began with the famous reforms of Lord William Bentinck's administration in 1828; and was but confirmed, through the overruling Providence of God, by the terrible mutiny of the Bengal army in 1857;

* Upper Burmah was annexed in 1885–86.

the date of the beginning of the history of British India as an autonomous Empire; to which the preceding century of conquest from 1757, and the antecedent century, from 1600 to 1708–9, of merely trading relations, were but the prelude.

The Queen of the United Kingdom was proclaimed Empress of India [Kaisar-i-Hind] the 1st January 1877.

Inventory of the Company's Territorial Acquisitions.

1639,—Madraspatam [" Chineepatam," Fort St. George].

1668,—Bombay.

1690,—Thevnapatam or Tegnapatam [Fort St. David].

1694–95,—Angengo.

1700,—Calcutta.

1708,—Tellicherry, and Ennore near Madras.

1734,—Dharmapatam Island, Malabar.

1742,—Villages in Chingleput, near Madras.

1749,—St. Thomé [Maliapur], near Madras, and Devikota fort in Madura District.

1750,—Poonamallee, in Saidapet *taluk*, Chingleput District, Madras.

1756,—Villages in the Colaba and Ratnagiri Collectorates, Bombay.

1757,—" The 24 Pergunnahs," from the Nawab Nazim of Bengal.

1759,—Nizampatam, Masulipatam, and other towns in the Godaveri and Kistna Districts, from the Nizam.

1760,—Burdwan, Midnapore, and Chittagong, from the Nawab Nazim of Bengal.

1765,—Bengal and Behar, and Orissa, from the Mogul; and " The Company's Jaghire " in the vicinity of Madras, from the Nawab of Arcot.

1766–68,—The " Northern Circars," Vizagapatam, &c., from the Nizam.

1772,—Chunar and Allahabad forts.

1775,—"The Zemindary of Benares," from the Nawab Vazir of Oudh.

1776,—The Islands of Salsette and Karanjah, from the Mahrattas.

1778,—Nagore, from the Rajah of Tanjore.

1778,—The Guntoor Circar, from the Nizam.

1783,—Porto Novo [Firingi-pet], Palicole [Palakollu], and Cuddalore.

1786,—Paulo Penang, from the King of Queda.

1791,—Negapatam.

1792,—Malabar [including Calicut], Dindigul, parts of Salem, Madura, and North Arcot Districts, Baramahal, &c., from Tippoo Sahib.

1795–96,—Ceylon was taken from the Dutch, and annexed to Madras. It was established as a Crown Colony in 1801.

1799,—Coimbatoor, North and South Canara, Wynad, the Nilghiri Hills, and parts of Salem and North Arcot, &c., from Tippoo Sahib; and Tanjore, from the Rajah of Tanjore.

1800,—"The Ceded Districts," from the Nizam; and the city, fort, and territory of Surat, with Rander.

1801,—The Carnatic, from the Nawab of the Carnatic.

1801,—Goruckpoor, Lower Doab, Bareilly, &c., from the Nawab Vazir of Oudh.

1802,—Districts in Bundlecund, from the Mahratta Peishwa.

1803,—Cuttack and Balasore, from the Rajah of Berar; and the Upper Doab, Delhi territory, &c., from Scindia.

1805,—Districts in Guzerat, from the Guicowar, and Karnal, in the Punjaub.

1810,—Fatehabad.

1812,—The Ratnagiri Collectorate.

1814,—Cochin.

1815,—Kumaon, Dehra Dhun, Simla, and part of the Tarai, from Nepaul.

1817,—Saugur, Huttah, Dharwar, &c., from the Mahratta Peishwa.

1817,—" The Ahmedabad Farm," from the Guicowar.

1818,—Khandeish, &c., from Holkar; Ajmere, from Scindia; Poona, parts of the Concans, and Southern Mahratta country, from the Peishwa; districts of the Nerbudda, Sumbulpoor, Patna, &c., from the Rajah of Berar.

1820,—Southern Concan, from the Rajah of Sawuntwarree.

1822,—Beejapore and Ahmednugger, from the Nizam.

1824,—Sadras, in Chingleput District; and Singapore, purchased from the Rajah of Johore.

1825,—Bimlipatam, in Vizagapatam District; and Chinsurah and Malacca, from the Dutch, ceded in exchange for Bencoolen.

1826,—Assam, Arracan, Tavoy, Tenasserim, from the King of Ava.

1832,—Cachar, lapsed.

1834,—Coorg, from the Rajah of Coorg.

1835,—Jaintia, Darjeeling, Ferozepore, Muzaffarnagar, Meerut, Bulandshahr, Alighar, &c.

1839,—The Mandvi State, Surat, lapsed; Aden, captured.

1841,—The Dooars [*i.e.*, "Passes," from *dwara*, "a door," "gate," as in Dwaraka, ("the City) of Gates"] of Bhootan, from the Rajah of Bhootan.

1843,—Scinde.

1845,—The Jullunder Dooab; Serampore, and Tranquebar, from the Danes, purchased for 20,000*l*.*

1849,—The Punjaub and Sattara.

1850,—Sumbalpur, Sikkim, Sanawar.

1852,—Pegu.

1853,—The remainder of Cachar and Berar, lapsed.

---

* Tranquebar was the first possession [purchased in 1616 of the King of Tanjore] of the Danes in India. They also held Serampore in Bengal, Porto Novo [Firingi-pet] on the Coromandel Coast, Eddova, and Kolchery, on the Malabar Coast, and other forts and factories.

1853–54,—Nagpur and Jhansi.

1856,—Oudh and Tanjore fort.

1857,—Jhaijjar territory, Punjaub.

1858,—Bhanpur, Shahgarh, Central Provinces.

Subsequent Acquisitions of the Crown.

1860,—Upper Godavari Districts, Nimar, Harda, and Hindia.

1861,—The Panch Mahals, in Guzerat, and Shillong.

1865,—The Eastern Dooars, Dewangiri, and Bengal Dooars.

1878,—The Peint State.

1881,—The Afghan Passes from Central Asia into India.

1885–86, —Upper Burmah.

Australia and New Zealand were occupied as British territories in 1770, and Tasmania in 1803. Labuan was ceded in 1846, and Hong Kong in 1842. Cape Colony, captured in 1806, and the Mauritius, in 1810, were confirmed in our possession by the Treaties of 1814–15. Ascension was occupied in 1815, and the Falkland Islands [resigned to us by Spain, 1771] in 1833. Gibraltar was captured in 1704; and Malta, captured in 1800, was guaranteed to Great Britain by the Treaties of 1814–15. Cyprus was acquired in 1878, and a Convention with the Sublime Porte was signed, by which the English Government, guided by similar considerations to those which led to the temporary treaties of 1809 and 1814 with Persia, undertook also the conditional Protectorate of the Ottoman Empire. In 1882 we assumed the Protectorate and temporary military and political administration of Egypt, expressly as commanding the highway of the overland commerce between Europe and India.

Conclusion.

Such is the last result of that rivalry for the trade of the East, which began between Jerusalem, and Edom, and Tyre; was continued between Phœnicia and Egypt, and Assyria and Persia; and, after the disruption of the Roman Empire, was carried on in succession by Genoa and Venice, Spain and Portugal, Holland and England, and England and France. Ancient history is very much the history of the struggle for the transit trade of the East by the Persian Gulf and Red Sea; and the modern history of the Old World is almost altogether based on the opening up of the ocean-way to India round the Cape of Good Hope. The whole current of the commercial and political, social and religious history of Europe was changed by Da Gama's discovery. Venice was deprived of her mercantile supremacy; Italy lost the prosperity that had again returned to her; and Egypt, which for 2,000 years had commanded the most advantageous of all the overland roads to the East, was suddenly deposed from her position of incontestible superiority. The commercial monopoly of the Arabs in the Eastern seas, and of the Jews as the inheritors of the traffic of the Phœnicians and Greeks in the Mediterranean, was destroyed at a blow, and that re-arrangement of the mercantile and state systems of Europe was commenced which has subsisted to the present day. We have seen in our own time, since the opening of the Suez Canal, and the return of much of the trade of the East to its ancient route through Egypt, how greatly the social and political condition and international relations of many of the European States have already been modified. It has, indeed, been often said during the last two or three years [written in 1879] that Englishmen have become divided as to the policy this country should pursue in the so-called Eastern Question. But our apparent differences of opinion are founded simply on a fundamental change of circumstances that has not yet been popularly appreciated. While all our Eastern commerce went by the Cape of Good Hope we had little more concern in the affairs of Europe than of America. But no sooner was a practicable canal pierced through the Isthmus of Suez than the fact at once began to influence the course of our vast carrying trade, and our international relations with the countries lying along the new route opened to it. We may, therefore, the more readily understand the character of the revolution wrought, not only in the commerce and politics, but also in the whole moral and intellectual life of Europe, by Da Gama's discovery. Following immediately on the discovery of America by Columbus, it profoundly agitated the hearts and minds of the people of Europe. The rude multitude were stirred by an uncontrollable lust of riches* and spirit of adventure; and the cultivated by the sense of renewed faith and hope in the divine deliverance of the world, at the moment when Christendom was almost sinking into the old despair of human destiny and duty that marked the decline of Imperial Rome. For all men the sphere of human intelligence and sympathy was permanently and indefinitely enlarged. The Spanish and Portuguese discoveries of the Indies were, for Europe

---

* Ben Jonson has given expression to the covetous hunger of wealth, excited in the vulgar by the discovery of America, in the "*Alchemist*", [1611], Act II. Scene 1:—

Mammon. Come on, Sir. Now you set your foot on shore
In *Novo Orbe*. Here 's the rich Peru:
And there within, Sir, are the golden mines,
Great Solomon's Ophir! he was sailing to't
Three years, but we have reached it in ten months.
This is the day wherein to all my friends
I will pronounce the happy word BE RICH.
THIS DAY YOU SHALL BE SPECTATISSIMI.
You shall no more deal with the hollow dye,
Or the frail card . . .
. . . . . . No more
Shall thirst of satin, or the covetous hunger
Of velvet . . . . ,
. . . . make
The sons of Sword and Hazard fall before
The Golden Calf . . . . .
No more of this. You shall start up young Viceroys,
. . . . BE RICH.

indeed, nothing less than the revelation of a new moral world, and the definitive emancipation of the human soul from the ghostly trammels of its obsequious bondage to secular and religious dogmatism through all the dark centuries of the middle ages. Their quickening effect on the genius of Europe was at once made manifest. Camoens, the author of the first epic of modern times, was directly inspired by the discovery of India by his countrymen. He was rapidly followed by Tasso, Cervantes, Spenser, Shakespeare, Milton, Raphael, Michael Angelo, Titian, Luther, and Francis Bacon; and the wide moral gulf which separates the genius of these men from the certainly not lesser genius of Roger Bacon, Aquinas, Giotto, and Fra Angelico, Chaucer, Gower, and Dante,*

* There was a general looking forward to the discoveries of America and the Indies among the higher minds of Europe long before they were achieved by Columbus and Da Gama. The lines of Dante, in the *Vision of Purgatory*, in which he alludes to the "Southern Cross," are well known. Still more remarkable is the less generally known prophecy of Luigi Pulci [b. 1431, d. 1487], "sire of the half serious line":—

"Men shall descry another hemisphere;
Since to one centre all things tend,
So earth by curious mystery divine
Well balanced hangs amid the starry spheres.
At our antipodes are cities, states,
And thronged empires, ne'er divined of yore.
But see, the sun speeds in his western path
To glad the nations with unexpected light."

The leading minds of ancient Rome would seem to have had an equally clear, if not even a clearer, conception of the as yet unrevealed lands lying beyond the Atlantic and Indian Oceans. Pliny [II., 65] positively asserts the existence of the antipodes; and records [II., 67] the tradition of "certain Indians who sailing from India" for the purposes of commerce were driven by tempests to Germany. If the story had any foundation in fact, these Indians could only have been North American Indians, such as the Esquimaux. Seneca's hackneyed line, "Nec sit Terris ultima Thule," is not so vague a prophecy of the New World as it appears separated from the context [*Medea*, II., 376–80]; and reads like a positive indication of America when compared with a passage, quoted by me in the introduction to Stevens's *Dawn of British Trade in the East Indies*, from the *Quæstionum Naturalium Libri Septem*. Herein Seneca distinctly states that the distance from the west coast of Spain to the Indies was so short, that it could be sailed over, if the

is the measure of the spiritual freedom that was conquered for mankind by the discoveries of Columbus, Da Gama, and Magellan. The impression made by them on the English people was deep and abiding. It may be traced everywhere in the writers of the reign of Queen Elizabeth, particularly in Shakespeare and Ben Jonson, and in the elevation of character of the historical men and women of the age. Even in their infamies, they seem superhuman. Da Gama's discovery changed the face of Europe from the Mediterranean to the Atlantic; and the British Isles, which had before been wasting in the obscurity of their native fogs, were at once placed in the forefront of the new line of human advancement; and, as the geographical centre of the four continents of the globe, they became, in the course of the next two hundred years, the common emporium of the whole sea-borne merchandise of the world. The establishment of the East India Company was the first step in the prodigious political development of England under the rule of Oliver Cromwell and during the reigns of William III. and Queen Anne; and, all through the great wars that grew out of the French Revolution, it proved the chief corner stone of our unabated mercantile prosperity and naval supremacy. The possession of India, the command its possession gave us of the trade with the East, alone enabled us to contend victoriously against the European coalition with which Buonaparte threatened our industrial ascendency at the beginning of the present century; and the

---

wind was favourable, in a few days [*see* page 278, *note*]. It was always the quest and invention of the Indies that inspired Columbus and his English successors in their exploration of the New World; and they but picked up the Americas, and the greater part of Australasia, as unconsidered trifles by the way.

Plato's 'Island of Atlas' is more a name of fiction; a phantom land, like "Utopia," the "New Atlantis," and the "Terra Australis" of Bishop Hall's *Mundus Alter et Idem*, invented as the stage of a philosophical fable. Its only ground of fact was possibly the tradition, preserved in Egypt or at Carthage, of some remote Phœnician voyage beyond the "Pillars of Hercules" to the "Hesperidian Coast" of Africa.

peaceful possession of India is our chief stay in sustaining the preponderating productiveness and maritime pre-eminence of these islands in the crushing commercial competition marking its end.*

GEORGE BIRDWOOD.

---

* In the *Athenæum* of 28th January 1882 I wrote :—

"The rapid extension of the commerce of America is a never failing source of wonder. In round numbers the average values of the exports and imports of the United States for the five years ending with 1880 were 140,000,000*l.* and 106,000,000*l.* respectively. The foreign trade of India for the same period is almost exactly half this amount, showing a less proportionate excess of exports over imports. A more striking proof of the advancing prosperity of the country under our administration could not be adduced. It is an equally cogent proof of the close dependency of our commercial superiority on the prosperity of India. Every nation is essentially a shop, and oceans and rivers are the high streets of the nations. While the great traffic that has subsisted, and will always subsist, between the East and the West went by its overland routes, the nations situated along the Euphrates, the Nile, and the Mediterranean made the first and almost the whole profit of it. Then when at last it found its way round the Cape, the nations fronting the Atlantic, and particularly England, which fronts at once America and Europe, monopolised it, while the Mediterranean nations had, as it were, to put up their shutters and retire from business for nearly three hundred years. Now that trade is returning to its original overland routes, our disadvantage in relation to them is beginning to be seen, and would be seen still more clearly but for our immense dealings with America. But all the same the Eastern trade is the great trade current of the world; and France with her unique advantage of possessing a frontage both on the Mediterranean and the Atlantic, will, if she ever substantially competes with us in the trade of the East Indies, also draw to herself and away from us a proportionate amount of our American trade. The possession which she has just obtained of Tunis,—which is Carthage—the corner house of her Algerian shop frontage, gives her a commanding commercial position throughout the African side of the Mediterranean."

In short, our ever imminent danger lies not in the political rivalry of the aggressive military powers of the Continent, for if unsupported by industrial productiveness and mercantile activity, this is not to be too greatly feared; but is rather to be apprehended in the growing competition with us of the Mediterranean countries for the commerce of India. Since the opening of the Suez Canal the Eastern products formerly sent to Liverpool and London are being shipped in yearly increasing proportions to Havre, Barcelona, Marseilles, Genoa, Trieste, and Odessa. They are still carried chiefly in English bottoms, even when not consigned to English merchants; but the time must come when they will be borne in French, Spanish, Italian, Austrian, Greek, and Russian ships, loading at Karachi, Bombay, and Calcutta. There is no denying that just now America, North and South, has modified the old theory of the unequalled value to Europe of the trade with the East; for if in tea, silk, and spices the East still holds its own, in all the bulkier staples America seems, for the time, to have swamped both Asia and Europe. But the preponderance of America cannot continue for ever, and India is already beginning to show that she is capable of competing even with the United States in the exportation of wheat; and when India once begins to supply Europe with the food stuffs at present received from America, England will have to put forth her whole native force of enterprise to secure her traditional hold on the markets of the world. In this anticipation the immense importance of Egypt to this country, as securing to us some share of the profit on the transit of merchandise between the East and West, at once becomes obvious. Our whole future indeed seems involved in our right use of the opportunities afforded us by the protectorate we have established over Egypt.

APPENDICES.

Appendix A.

Report by Dr. Birdwood on certain documents relating to the East India Company discovered in 1875.

On my appointment to the Curatorship of the India Museum, Colonel Burne, C.S.I., sent me a box received by him from Sir John Kaye, on the retirement of the latter from office, with the statement that it had been lying in his room [Sir J. K.'s] from beyond the memory of anyone in the Political Department, and was said to contain very important documents. I found in it 51 tally-sticks,—a bag marked "fifteen pagodas," but which on being opened, I found to contain only two lumps of iron,—and forty parchments mixed up together in the greatest confusion.

The parchments all relate to the East India Company, and with two or three exceptions are under the Great Seal.

Several of the documents bear in the left-hand corner a vignette portrait, beautifully executed, of the sovereign reigning at the time of their engrossment. But in two or three instances they have been disgracefully mutilated by the cutting out of the vignette portraits. As a rule the Great Seal belonging to them is either missing or much damaged. There are, however, two or three fair specimens of it, and notably of that of the Lord Protector Cromwell, by Simon.

Finding these documents of such interest in relation to the East India Company, and that it was impossible for me to decipher many parts of them, I wrote and asked Sir Duffus Hardy if he would be good enough to allow a Calendar of them to be prepared by an expert in the Rolls Office. The Calendar thus prepared, by Mr. W. Noel Sainsbury, is attached.

I venture to suggest that the parchments should be carefully restored, and exhibited in this Office. I would not have them sent to the Museum. They are not idle curiosities to be toyed about in museums, but State Archives to be reverently kept in the India Office itself; and after restoration they should be rolled up, and put away in a glass cabinet in the Council Room. The [? draft] roll of the Original Subscribers of the 2,000,000*l.* stock, which contains the names of nearly the whole of the well-to-do middle class people of England a century ago, should never again pass out of sight.

The tally-sticks are mere curiosities, unless indeed, the fact of their not having been burnt is a proof of money still owing to the Indian Government by the Treasury. Tallies were, I believe, always kept until a debt was paid, and were then burnt.

(Signed) George Birdwood,
Curator of the India Museum.

17th April 1875.

Calendar of the aforesaid Documents prepared by Mr. W. Noel Sainsbury, C.B.

1. 9th August 1606 (4 Jac. I.).—The king's License to the Governor and Company of Merchants of London trading into the East Indies to utter, sell (and put to sale) spices, drugs, wares, and merchandises brought from the East Indies in whole packs or sacks unbroken, and to transport the same beyond the seas without loss, forfeiture, or penalty. *A fragment difficult to decipher, of which a transcript has been made. The Great Seal in fair condition is preserved.*

N.B. A Minute only of this License is in the Public Record Office. (*Grant Book, Jac. I., p.* 28.)

2. 22nd May 1609 (7 Jac. I.). Westminster.—The King's License to the Governor and Company of Merchants of London trading into the East Indies to sell any quantities of spices, wares, merchandises, and commodities in whole packs, sacks, or casks, ungarbled, to any merchant or other person, to be transported out of the realm, without incurring forfeiture for not garbling or cleansing them, upon payment of customs, notwithstanding any prohibition to the contrary. *With the Great Seal mutilated.*

N.B. There is a Minute only of this License, dated 11th May 1609, in the Public Record Office.

(*Docquet and Grant Book, Jac. I., p.* 15.)

3. 17th March 1610 (7 Jac. I.). Westminster.—The King's Commission to Sir Henry Middleton, appointing him principal Governor or General of all merchants, mariners, and others shipped in these ships to the East Indies (*the sixth voyage*). *With the Great Seal mutilated.*

4. 17th March 1610 (7 Jac. I.).—A duplicate of the preceding Commission. *With the Great Seal mutilated.*

5. 4th February 1623 (20 Jac. I.).—The King's Commission to the Governor and Company of Merchants trading into the East Indies, reciting a former Commission of 14th December, 13 Jac. I. (1615), giving them power and authority for punishing offences at sea, and granting, at the humble suit and intercession of said Governor and Company, power and authority to "make forth Commissions, Instructions, and Directions" to their President and Council of Defence in the East Indies to chastise, correct, and punish his Majesty's subjects employed on land by fine, imprisonment, or any other punishment, capital or not capital, as the laws of this Kingdom and martial law doth permit and require. *Injured by damp. With the Great Seal mutilated.*

N.B. There is a Minute only in the Public Record Office of a Grant of the date above recited, viz., 14th December, 13 Jac. I. (1615), but it has reference to transporting foreign bullion and other things.

6. 18th February 1628 (3 Car. I.).—Letters Patent to the Governor and Company of Merchants trading into the East Indies, reciting former Letters Patent of 16th January, 15 Jac. I., to transport

foreign coin, not to exceed 100,000*l.* yearly, without payment of custom or subsidy; also reciting further Letters Patent of 22nd March, 2 Car. I., to transport 20,000*l.* in gold or silver in English specie, on condition of their bringing into the Mint 25,000*l.* of foreign coin within three months; granting to said Governor and Company license to transport 60,000*l.* in foreign gold in their next intended voyage, and, if they cannot supply themselves with foreign gold to that amount, to transport 40,000*l.* in English gold, on condition of their bringing into the Mint 40,000*l.* in foreign gold within six months. *Injured by damp. With Great Seal mutilated.*

It appears by the endorsements that there were shipped upon these Letters Patent:—8th March 1627/8, in the *Expedition*, in foreign coin, to the value of 5,900*l.*; in the *Jonas*, in foreign coin, to the value of 18,050*l.* 24th March 1627/8, in the *Jonas*, in foreign gold, 4,780*l.*; in English gold, 15,000*l.* In all, 43,720*l.*

N.B. The License of 20th March, 2 Car. I., to transport 20,000*l.* above recited, and a License of 15th February, 3 Car. I., to transport 60,000*l.*, the foundation of the above Letters Patent, both under the King's Sign Manual, are in the Public Record Office.

7. 14th October 1627 (3 Car. I.).—The King's Commission to Robert Ducy, Ralph Freeman, Christopher Clitherowe, Sir Morris Abbott,* Henry Garway, Jeffrey Kirby, Robert Jeffreys, Humfrey Browne, Clement Harby, Job Harby, Henry Lee, William Cokaine, Robert Draper, George Strode, Thomas Mustard, and William Lee, of London, merchants, and John Barker, of Bristol, Abraham Jennynges, of Plymouth, Gyles Green, of Weymouth, and Peter Taylor, of Exeter, merchants, Robert Samon and William Case, Masters of the Trinity House, to inquire, search, discover, and find out what hath been disbursed, and in whose hands any part thereof remaineth undisturbed of the moneys collected by 1½ per cent. on tonnage of shipping towards the expedition for suppressing the pirates of Algiers. *In parts illegible. With Great Seal mutilated.*

N.B. There is another Commission on this subject in the Public Record Office (Sign Manuals, Car. I., Vol. 5, No. 12), dated 16th February 1628, with this memorandum:—"The like Commission did "lately pass the Great Seal, but it is now again prepared, with "addition of some Commissioners, and such further additions and "explanations as your Majesty under your Sign Manual hath been "pleased to direct."

8. 24th March 1629 (4 Car. I.).—Letters Patent to the Governor and Company of Merchants trading into the East Indies, reciting former Letters Patent of 16th January, 15 Jac. I., for transporting foreign coin, not exceeding the sum of 100,000*l.* yearly, without payment of custom or subsidy, and petition of said Company showing they have raised a stock of above 120,000*l.*, which is intended to be employed in a particular voyage this year for Persia, in cloth, tin, kerseys, and other native commodities and manufactures of this Kingdom, and that said Company have made a contract with the King of Persia to bring a fourth part of the value of their commodities in ready money, either gold or silver, granting to said Company license to transport the sum of 60,000*l.*, whereby to enable them to make good their contract with the said King of Persia. *Injured by damp. Without the Great Seal.*

---

* This is "the Honourable and Worthy Knight Sr. Maurice Abbot," to whom, with others, Henry Lord dedicates his *Discoverie of the Sect of the Banians*, and *Religion of the Parsees*, 1630.—G. E. S. B.

It appears by the endorsement that there were shipped upon these Letters Patents:—

In the *Discovery*, in foreign gold, 8,800*l.*;
In the *Charles*, in foreign gold, 20,000*l.*;
And in English gold, 16,900*l.*

9. 10th March 1630 (5 Car. I.).—Letters Patent to the Governor and Company of Merchants trading into the East Indies, reciting former Letters Patent of 16th January, 15 Jac. I., for transporting foreign coin, which "only extends to foreign silver and bullion of silver," and granting to said Company license to buy and take up in England the sum of 8,000*l.* in foreign gold, and to transport the same into the East Indies or Persia, without incurring any penalty, forfeiture, or other punishment, and without payment of custom or subsidy. *With the Great Seal Mutilated.*

10. 17th October 1629 (5 Car. I.).—Letters Patent to the Governor and Company of Merchants trading into the East Indies, reciting former Letters Patent of 16th January, 15 Jac. I., and petition of said Company that they have now enlarged their trade into Persia, where they shall have opportunity to vent yearly great quantities of cloth, kerseys, and tin, the commodities and manufactures of this Kingdom, and therefore shall have use of a greater proportion of gold, silver, and bullion than 100,000*l.* mentioned in said former Letters Patent, granting them license to transport 120,000*l.* yearly, whereof 40,000*l.* to be in foreign gold or bullion of gold. *The Great Seal to this Patent is wanting.*

11. 9th November 1630 (6 Car. I.).—Letters Patent to the Governor and Company of Merchants trading into the East Indies, reciting former Letters Patent of 16th January, 15 Jac. I., and granting to said Governor and Company license to buy and take up in England the sum of 30,000*l.* in foreign gold, and to transport the same in six ships which they intend to furnish and send from hence before the end of March next to the East Indies or Persia, without payment of custom or subsidy. *The Great Seal to this Patent is wanting.*

N.B. The License under the King's Sign Manual is dated 6th November 1630, and is in the Public Record Office.

12. 21st November 1631 (7 Car. I.).—Letters Patent to the Governor and Company of Merchants trading into the East Indies, granting them license to buy and take up in England the sum of 30,000*l.* in foreign gold, and to transport the same in their next intended voyage with seven good ships into Persia and the East Indies, without payment of custom or subsidy. *Without the Great Seal.*

It appears by the endorsement that there were shipped upon these Letters Patent:—

In the *Pearl*, one chest of foreign gold *ad valorem* 8,863*l.*
In the *Charles*, ditto, ditto, containing 8,000*l.*

N.B. The above License under the King's Sign Manual, dated 19th November, is in the Public Record Office (Vol. 13, No. 69).

13. 3rd March 1632 (7 Car. I.).—Letters Patent to the Governor and Company of Merchants trading to the East Indies, granting them license to buy, take up, and transport the sum of 20,000*l.* of foreign gold into the East Indies or Persia without incurring any penalty, forfeiture, or other punishment, and without payment of custom or subsidy; and in case said Company cannot supply themselves with said sum in foreign gold, then it shall be lawful for them to buy and take up and transport what shall be wanting in English gold. *Injured by damp. Without the Great Seal.*

14. 8th October 1633 (9 Car. I.).—Letters Patent to the Governor and Company of Merchants trading to the East Indies, granting them license, in regard by their Charter they have power only to transport foreign silver, to buy and take up, and to transport without payment of custom or subsidy in five good ships laden with tin, cloth, lead, and other native commodities of this Kingdom the sum of 40,000*l.* in foreign gold, and in case they cannot furnish themselves with so much in foreign gold, then to supply themselves with English gold, being no more than what hath formerly been granted them on the like occasions. *Injured by damp. Without the Great Seal.*

15. 30th November 1635 (11. Car. I.).—Letters Patent to the Governor and Company of Merchants trading into the East Indies, reciting former Letters of 16th January (15 Jac. I.), granting them license to transport a sum not exceeding 100,000*l.* per annum in foreign silver or bullion of silver, and granting them license on their petition to buy and take up and transport in their intended voyage to the East Indies and Persia the sum of 30,000*l.* in foreign gold, and what is wanting of said sum in English gold, without payment of custom or subsidy, in the *Mary, Hart,* and *Swan. Injured by damp,* and *without the Great Seal.*

16. 7th August 1655.—Warrant of the Lord Protector to the Commissioners of the Treasury and other Officers of the Exchequer to pay to the Governor and Company of Merchants trading to the East Indies the sum of 50,000*l.* in three equal portions, viz., one third part in one year's time from the date of these presents, a second third part six months after the termination of said year, and the third part, the full residue and remainder of said sum, at the end of one year to be reckoned from the termination of aforesaid year. *With the Great Seal, with the inscription* "In the third yeare of freedome by God's blessing restored."

17. 18th December 1660 (12 Car. II.).—Letters Patent to the Governor and Company of Merchants trading to the East Indies, granting them license to buy and transport the sum of 60,000*l.* in foreign coin and bullion in this their intended voyage to the East Indies or Persia. *With the Great Seal mutilated.*

N.B. A Petition of the East India Company to the King is in the Public Record Office, dated 8th October 1660, for a warrant to permit them to export 60,000*l.* in coin and bullion. Also the order for said warrant, dated 1st December 1661.

18. 14th November 1665.—Mandate of James, Duke of York, Lord High Admiral of England, to the Commissioners for Reprizals to sell the contents of the ship *Golden Phœnix* lately adjudged lawful prize by the Court of Admiralty. *Latin.*

N.B. There is a Warrant in the Public Record Office of the same date as the above confirming a contract between the Duke of Albemarle and the East India Company for purchase by the latter of two prize ships of the Dutch East India Company *Slothany* and *Golden Phœnix.* The contract itself is also among the State Papers.

19. 6th February 1668 (20 Car. II.).—Acquittance under the Great Seal to the Governor and Company of Merchants trading to the East Indies; recites the Articles of Agreement of 7th November 1665, between the Duke of Albemarle on the King's behalf, and Sir John Robinson, Lieutenant of the Tower, and others on behalf of said Governor and Company, touching goods taken from two Dutch East India Ships the *Slothany* and the *Golden Phœnix*, sold and disposed of for His Majesty's use for the sum of 154,969*l.* 13*s.* 5*d.*, the account thereof being examined and approved by the Commissioners for Prizes, and that the King doth by these presents remise, release, and for ever quit claim unto said Governor and Company and their successors the above said sum, and all actions, suits, accounts, processes, claims, and demands whatsoever of or concerning the same.

The vignette portrait of Charles II. has been cut out of this document, and the Great Seal is mutilated.

20. 7th October 1672 (24 Car. II.).—Letters Patent to the East India Company, who having promised to lend the King 20,000*l.* "for the supply of our occasions," and having been at great charge in fitting forth and keeping out at sea four ships to cruize to the westward for the security of trade, towards which the King has thought fit to allow them 2,000*l.*, and said Company having agreed to furnish the King with saltpetre to the value of 30,000*l.*, and saltpetre to the value of 40,000*l.* having been bought of said Company for satisfaction, of which an order was registered upon the King's revenue arising by fire hearths and stores, bearing date 13th November 1669, and said Company having made request that said 40,000*l.* may be satisfied out of customs for goods and commodities imported by said Company from 1st December next, the Commissioners of the Treasury are required to pay to said Company out of the receipt of the Exchequer said sum of 20,000*l.*, with interest at 6*l.* per cent. per annum from the time the same shall be paid into the Exchequer until the time of repayment, also said sums of 2,000*l.*, with interest at 6*l.* per cent. per annum from 29th September last, and of 30,000*l.*, with 6 per cent. per annum from 10th October instant, and 40,000*l.*, with interest at 6 per cent. per annum from 29th September last past. And for the better security of said Company to direct tallies to be levied upon the Receiver and Cashier General of Customs and new imposts upon wines and vinegar for said sums of 20,000*l.*, 2,000*l.*, 30,000*l.*, and 40,000*l.*, and interest as aforesaid, such Receiver General to discharge and satisfy said tallies for said sums of 20,000*l.*, 2,000*l.*, and 30,000*l.*, with interest as aforesaid, by six-and-twenty weekly payments of 2,000*l.* per week from 1st December next, and to discharge said tallies for said 40,000*l.*, with interest as aforesaid, out of the customs of such East India commodities as shall be imported by said Company after 1st December next according to their request.

With vignette portrait of Charles II., but without the Great Seal.

21. 7th October 1672 (24 Car. II.).—Acquittance under the Great Seal to the East India Company; recites articles of agreement between the Navy Commissioners and the East India Company, touching the setting forth His Majesty's ships *Dunkirk*, *Leopard*, *Mary Rose*, and *Convertine* to the East Indies at the King's charge to be freighted home by said Company, the return of said ships from the East Indies, and differences arising between said Company and Navy Commissioners occasioned by the return of the *Leopard* with much dead freight, the receipt by said Company of 1,000*l.*, for which they were to pay 4,153⅝ pieces of eight to Sir Gervase Lucas, the King's Governor of Bombay, but who died before they were paid to him, the misfortunes which befel the *Leopard* from the obstructions of the Dutch in India, who admitting the said Company's just demands for satisfaction, said Company were in a way of obtaining satisfaction when the Treaty of Breda was concluded, petition of said Company to be released from aforesaid articles of agreement, and from payment of said 4,153⅝ pieces of eight, said Company's present of 2,000*l.* money to the King, and bills of 282*l.* 13*s.* 6*d.* and 1,572 18*s.* due from the King to said Company for freight of the ship *London.* The King by these presents doth remise, release, and for ever quit claim unto said Governor and Company and their successors said articles of agreement and said pieces of eight, and all actions, suits, accounts, processes, claims, and demands in respect thereof.

With vignette portrait of the King and the Great Seal attached.

N.B. The King's letter to the Duke of York to order the Navy Commissioners to make above agreement is in the Public Record Office.

(*Dom. Entry Book, Vol.* 3, *p.* 11.)

22. 27th October 1673 (25 Car. II.).—Letters Patent ratifying an agreement between Prince Rupert, Duke of Cumberland, and others, His Majesty's Principal Commissioners of Prizes, and the East India Company, by which the Company are to sell the goods taken from the Dutch ships *Papenburgh, Alphen, Arms of Trewere,* alias *Camphire,* and *Europa,* on His Majesty's behalf, and pay the proceeds to Richard Mounteney, His Majesty's Receiver General of Prizes, after deducting customs, tare and tret, and charges of house room, management, &c. The Company undertake that the goods when sold shall amount to 33,700*l.* more than the above said rates (which are prescribed at length), and for the accommodation of His Majesty's occasions said Company will advance on account to said Richard Mounteney 50,000*l.* on 30th October instant, 50,000*l.* on 6th November following, and the remainder, whatsoever the sum may amount unto at the rates aforesaid, and the 33,700*l.* custom and charges provided for in these articles, and 6½ per cent. which they allow to their buyers, first deducted, on 18th of said November.

Injured by damp, with the vignette portrait of Charles II., but without the Great Seal.

23. 6th March 1674 (26 Car. II.)—Release from Prince Rupert, Duke of Cumberland, and others, His Majesty's Principal Commissioners of Prizes, to the East India Company. Whereas the said Company (in accordance with the articles of agreement under the Great Seal of 27th October 1673) have sold the goods taken in the Dutch ships *Papenburgh, Alphen, Arms of Treweer,* alias *Camphire,* and *Europa,* for 174,741*l.* 9*s.* 8*d.*, and paid thereof to Richard Mounteney, Receiver General of Prizes, 140,000*l.*, and have given an account of the expenditure of the residue in customs, expenses, and charges of management, &c., said Commissioners by these presents allow said account, and on His Majesty's behalf release and quit claim said Company from all demands on account of said goods or moneys. *Signed by* Rupert, Latimer, Ormonde, Craven, Henry Coventry, and (Sir John) Duncomb. *Much injured by damp.*

24. 13th March 1674 (26 Car. II.).—Acquittance under the Great Seal to the East India Company. That whereas in pursuance of articles of agreement under the Great Seal of 27th October 1673, between Prince Rupert, Duke of Cumberland, and others, His Majesty's Commissioners of Prizes, and the East India Company, touching East India goods lately taken from the Dutch in the four ships *Papenburgh*, *Alphen*, *Arms of Teweer*, alias *Camphire*, and *Europa*, which were put in the Company's hands to be disposed of to His Majesty's most advantage, said Company have disposed of said goods for the sum of 174,741*l.* 9*s.* 8*d.*, and have paid the same for His Majesty's use, or expended it in customs and charges, &c., His Majesty by these presents doth remise, release, and for ever quit claim unto said East India Company and their successors all suits, claims, and demands against said Company concerning said sum of money and goods.

With vignette portrait of Charles II.

Enrolled on the Patent Roll in the Public Record Office, Pat. 26, Car. II., Pt. 4, No. 4, 3159.

25. 21st October 1676 (28 Car. II.)—Warrant under the Great Seal to the Commissioners and Officers of the Treasury and Exchequer. Whereas the said East India Company have agreed to lend His Majesty the sum of 40,000*l.* on the credit of the customs payable by them for East India commodities imported, after satisfying the sum of 37,000*l.* and interest still unpaid for 700 tons of saltpetre by them formerly sold to His Majesty, His Majesty doth by these presents authorize and direct said Commissioners and Officers of the Treasury to cause payment to be made to said Company of said sum, with interest at 6 per cent., out of said customs aforesaid, and tallies to be levied accordingly upon the Receiver General and Farmers of Customs.

With vignette portrait of Charles II. and the Great Seal mutilated.

Enrolled on Patent Roll in the Public Record Office, Pat. 28, Car. II., Pt. 1, No. 4, 3180.

26. 24th January 1678 (29 Car. II.).—Warrant under the Great Seal to the Commissioners and Officers of the Treasury and Exchequer. Whereas the East India Company have agreed to lend His Majesty the sum of 20,000*l.*, and to furnish His Majesty's stores with 754¾ tons of saltpetre, which at the price agreed on amounts to 40,000*l.*, or 60,000*l.* in all, His Majesty by these presents authorizes and requires said Commissioners and Officers of the Treasury to cause payment to be made to said Company of said sum, with interest at 6 per cent., out of the customs payable by them for East India commodities imported after the 1st November last past.

With vignette portrait of Charles II., but the Great Seal is missing.

27. 22nd November 1678 (30 Car. II.).—Warrant under the Great Seal to the Commissioners and Officers of the Treasury and Exchequer. Whereas the East India Company have agreed to lend His Majesty 30,000*l.*, and furnish His Majesty's stores with 363 tons 12½ cwts. 25 lbs. of saltpetre, of the value of 20,000*l.*, making together 50,000*l.*, His Majesty by these presents authorizes and directs said Commissioners and Officers of the Treasury to cause payment of said sum, with interest at 6 per cent., to be made to said Company out of the customs on East India commodities by them imported, after the satisfaction of the sum of 60,000*l.* and interest mentioned in His Majesty's Letters Patent of 24th January last.

The vignette portrait of Charles II. has been cut out, and but a fragment remains of the Great Seal.

28. 18th September 1682 (34 Car. II.).—Warrant under the Great Seal to the Commissioners and Officers of the Treasury and Exchequer. Whereas the East India Company have furnished His Majesty's stores with 400 tons of saltpetre at the price of 15,372*l.*, His Majesty by these presents authorizes and requires said Commissioners and Officers of the Treasury to cause issue of said sum to be made to the Paymaster of the Ordnance, to be by him applied to satisfy said Company, payment to be made by tallies on the Receiver General and Farmers of the Customs of East India commodities imported after the 25th March next, with interest at 6 per cent.

With vignette portrait of Charles II., and a fragment of the Great Seal.

29. 5th July 1683 (35 Car. II.).—Warrant under the Great Seal to the Commissioners and Officers of the Treasury and Exchequer. Whereas the East India Company have agreed to furnish His Majesty's stores with 1,051 tons of saltpetre, which, at 38*s.* 6*d.* per cwt., amounts to 40,463*l.* 10*s.*, His Majesty by these presents authorizes and requires said Commissioners and Officers of the Treasury to cause issue of said sum to be made to the Paymaster of the Ordnance, to be by him applied to satisfy said Company, payment to be made by tallies on the Receiver General and Farmers of the Customs of East India commodities imported after the 29th September next, with interest at 6 per cent.

With vignette portrait of Charles II., and the Great Seal mutilated.

30. 12th November 1684 (36 Car. II.).—The King to John Petit, George Bourcher, Simon Cracroft, and Edward Littleton. Whereas His Majesty is informed by petition of the East India Company that they, being said Company's servants, under oath and security for their truth and fidelity, have notwithstanding for several years past manifestly injured said Company in their trade in those parts, by endeavouring to lessen their reputation with the Native Kings and Governors, and to break contracts with some of them, making others for the protection of interlopers, and labouring to promote their trade and interest and lessen the Company's, and that said John Petit is notoriously suspected to have been an encourager and adviser of the late rebellion at Bombay, His Majesty requires and strictly commands said Petit, Bourcher, Cracroft, and Littleton, within 14 days after His pleasure shall have been signified to them, to come for England to answer the premises and such other matters as by the said Company shall be objected against them.

31. 31st January 1688 (3 Jac. II.).—Acquittance under the Privy Seal to the East India Company and to the owners of the ship *Andaluzia*. Whereas the ship *Andaluzia*, John Jacob master, found trading between the Cape de Bona Speranza and the Straits of Magellan without license of said Company, was, on the 7th of April last past, condemned, and sentence passed that said ship and goods were forfeited, one half to his Majesty and the other to said Company, according to the Letters Patent of said Company of 3rd April 1661; and whereas His Majesty, at the instance of said Company, has consented that said ship be restored to the owners, and said goods sold, and the proceeds paid, one fifth to His Majesty and to said Company, and four fifths to the owners, which has been done accordingly, and the sum of 3,161*l.* 0*s.* 2*d.* paid into His Majesty's Exchequer; His Majesty is pleased to accept said sum, and by these presents doth exonerate, release, and discharge said Company and said owners from all claims and demands concerning the said ship and goods. *Injured by damp, and the Seal is wanting.*

32. 3rd October 1689 (1 Will. and Mary).—Warrant under the Great Seal to the Commissioners of the Treasury and Officers of the Exchequer. Whereas the East India Company on the 30th August last furnished Their Majesties' stores with 500 tons of brown saltpetre, which at 45*l.* per ton amounts to 22,500*l.*, and Their Majesties have agreed that said sum shall be paid out of the customs and duties of East India commodities since the 1st August last imported or to be imported, except the duties lately by Act of Parliament appropriated to the satisfaction of moneys due to the States General, and arrears due to the servants of the late King Charles the Second, Their Majesties hereby authorize and direct said Commissioners and Officers of the Treasury and Exchequer to cause payment to be made of said sum to the Paymaster of the Ordnance, to be by him paid to said Company as aforesaid, with interest at 6 per cent. per annum.

With vignette portrait of the King, but without the Great Seal.

33. 14th July 1698.—Roll of subscribers for raising a sum not exceeding two millions upon a fund for payment of annuities after the rate of 8*l.* per cent. per annum, and for settling the trade to the East Indies according to an Act made in the last Session of the last Parliament. Said subscribers undertake to unite their several shares and interests, and to be incorporated as a Company, and to trade in a joint stock to the East Indies.

The amounts of the several subscriptions vary from 20,000*l.*, the highest, to 100*l.*, the lowest. Henry Furnese, 15,000*l.*, is the first name on this roll, Jas. Courthop, 100*l.*, the last name. Among the subscribers are the following, viz:—

	£
John Smith, for Lord Portland	10,000
Sam Shepheard	20,000
Thos. Vernon	15,000
John Lloyd	4,000
Jas. Vernon, for Duke of Shrewsbury	4,000
Jas. Vernon, for himself	2,000
Theod. Janssen	15,000
Gilbert Heathcote	15,000
Ditto, for his brother John	3,000
Ditto, for his brother William	3,000
The Lord Chancellor	2,000
Henry Cornish	10,000
For His Majesty:—	
Chas. Montague, Ste. Fox, J. Smith, Tho. Littleton	10,000
Montagu	5,000
Ranelagh	3,000
Cha. Montague	5,000
Ste. Fox	4,000
J. Smith	2,000
Tho. Littleton	2,000

		£
Wm. Blathwayt	- - -	2,000
The Earl of Orford	- - -	6,000
Cha. Montagu	- - -	4,000
Thos. Clarke, for Jno. Bromley	-	7,000
John Chadwicke	- - -	3,000
John, Lord Culpeper	- - -	500
Duke of Devonshire	- - -	6,000
Gilbert Heathcote	- - -	2,000

This roll consists of fifteen skins of parchment.

34. 8th December 1703 (2 Anne).—Warrant under the Great Seal from George, Prince of Denmark, Lord High Admiral of England and Generalissimo of the Forces, granting letters of marque to Samuel Goodman in the ship *Martha* against ships, vessels, and goods belonging to France and Spain, their vassals, subjects, &c., Her Majesty having on 14th May 1702 declared war against France and Spain.

This document has suffered from damp, and only a fragment of the Seal remains.

35. 20th August 1705 (4 Anne).—Grant of pardon under the Great Seal to the Governor and Company of Merchants of London trading into the East Indies. Recites the substance of an Act of Parliament of 9 Will. III., intituled "An Act for raising a sum, not "exceeding two millions, upon a fund for payment of annuities after "the rate of eight pounds per centum per annum, and for settling the "trade to the East Indies," the incorporation of a Company by the name of the "English Company trading to the East Indies," the said Governor and Company being on 22nd July 1702 possessed of 315,000*l.* of said subscriptions, and an indenture tripartite made on said 22nd July 1702, between Her Majesty, the said Governor and Company, and the said English Company, for settling all disputes between the two Companies, whereby the said English Company doth covenant to assist said Governor and Company in bringing home their effects from the Indies, &c., and to pay to them so much of the additional duty of five per cent. payable by said Act of Parliament on goods brought from the Indies as shall be paid to such English Company for the goods, &c., of said Governor and Company, their agents and servants, and Her Majesty covenants to pardon both said Companies for all crimes, misdemeanours, &c., by either committed "from the beginning of the world" to the date of said indenture, except certain customs, duties, and saltpetre not yet paid or delivered. And whereas the said English Company, by deed of the 20th of July last past, have declared that certain informations in the Court of Exchequer in the name of Alexander Gawn and others, claiming that the ships *Regard*, *Howland*, and *Chambers* frigate (being the only ships of Governor and Company now abroad) were forfeited for certain seizures, were made without their direction or privity, and have released and quit claimed to said Governor and Company all causes of forfeitures and penalties which might arise by reason of said seizures or informations: Her Majesty by these presents pardons and quit claims to the said Governor and Company, their agents and servants, for all offences and crimes done on the 22nd of July 1702 and since, contrary to said Act of Parliament, except duties, customs, breaches of bond, &c.

Very much injured by damp, with the vignette portrait of Queen Anne, and the Great Seal, which is mutilated.

36. 20th October 1732 (6 Geo. II.).—Commission under the Great Seal to Robert Jenkins, commander of the ship *Harrington*, carrying thirty-four guns and ninety-eight men, empowering him to apprehend, seize, and secure all pirates, freebooters, and sea rovers, being His Majesty's subjects, or of other nations associated with them, with their ships, moneys, and goods, as he shall meet with on the coasts and in the seas of India (whither he is going), or in any other seas, and bring them to trial to the end they may be proceeded against with the utmost severity of the law, and enjoining him to keep a journal of said pirates' ships, goods, moneys, arms, &c., and to take care of the bills of lading and all other papers found in them.

This Commission bears the King's signature, but the Great Seal has been sadly mutilated.

37. 22nd August 1737 (11 Geo. II.).—Similar Commission under the Great Seal to William Jobson, commander of the *Royal George*, carrying thirty guns and ninety-eight men.

This Commission also bears the King's signature, but the Great Seal is mutilated.

38. 18th November 1745 (19 Geo. II.).—Letters of marque under the Great Seal to Harry Kent, commander of the ship *Dragon*, carrying twenty guns and ninety-nine men, against all ships and goods of France and Spain, their vassals and inhabitants.

There is a vignette portrait of George II., but the Great Seal is wanting.

39. 2nd July 1747 (21 Geo. II.).—Similar letters of marque under the Great Seal to Norton Hutchinson, commander of the *Swallow*, carrying fourteen guns and thirty-five men.

With vignette portrait of George II. The Great Seal is missing.

40. 16th October 1758 (32 Geo. II.).—Commission under the Great Seal to George Beamish, commander of the ship *Royal George*, carrying twenty-four guns and eighty men, to seize pirates.

This Commission is in similar terms to No. 36; it has the King's signature, but the Great Seal is wanting.

W. Noel Sainsbury.

P.S., 2nd Reprint.—The whole of the above 40 documents are now included in the new *Catalogue of Parchment Records* prepared under the direction of Mr. F. C. Danvers since the first reprint of the present Report was issued last year [1889]. See Appendix D.

Geo. B.

Appendix B.

Reprint of the Introduction to

THE DAWN OF BRITISH TRADE TO THE EAST INDIES,

As recorded in the Court Minutes of the East India Company,

1599—1603,

Printed from the Original Manuscript

BY

HENRY STEVENS of Vermont,

And published by
HENRY STEVENS and SON,
115, Saint Martin's Lane
[Now (1890) 39, Great Russell Street].
LONDON:

1886.

INTRODUCTION.

"Qui mare teneat, eum necesse rerum potiri."—Cicero, *Ep. ad Att.*, x.

The History of the East India Company is a work that has still to be written, although from its rise, at the close of the sixteenth century, to its disappearance thirty years ago, the Company was careful to provide all the necessary material for the task, and to place on formal record the simplest acts of its administration, and the reasons which prompted all its decisions. The value of these contemporary annals —for the Court Books, Factory Diaries, Consultations, and general correspondence, really constitute a continuous narrative—has been only in a small degree impaired by the ravages of time, and by the neglect of less careful custodians than the men who originally determined that their successors in office should gain by their example and experience, and that the Company itself should not suffer in the eyes of posterity from any ambiguity as to its proceedings. The present volume, printed as a labour of love under the direction and at the charge of the late Mr. Henry Stevens, is, so far as print can be made a facsimile of manuscript, identical with the first Court Book kept by the adventurers trading to the East Indies, who received from Queen Elizabeth in the last year of the sixteenth century a patent, or charter, recognizing them as the East India Company, with a monopoly of trade and specified privileges for a given term of years.

The first entry is of the names of those persons who subscribed on 22nd September, 1599, to "the pretended voiage to the Easte Indias, the whiche it maie please the Lorde to psper;" and the last is the report of a committee meeting on 28th June, 1603. Within those four years is contained the germ of every triumph subsequently achieved in the seas and lands of the East. The committees to which the adventurers entrusted the guidance of their affairs not merely laid down the countries with which it was desirable to trade, and the English commodities for which their markets might provide a vent, but they dwelt upon the inconveniences of the long sea route by the Cape of Good Hope to India, and listened with approval to any project, however visionary, for bringing London nearer to the wealthy kingdoms of Asia. As will be seen, their hopes centred in the North-West passage, which Robert Thorne had been the first to advocate in Henry VIII.'s reign as furnishing a road to Cathay and India, and which long continued to dangle before the eyes of the Company as a glorious possibility, never realizing its promise until in our time the discovery had been made, and the feat accomplished, not by naval skill and daring, but by the connection of the two great oceans of the world by a line of railway. The early references to America contained in this volume will be of peculiar interest to the descendants of the Pilgrim Fathers of the *May Flower*,* who have so rapidly spread themselves over that mighty continent, and who have so brilliantly carried on the commercial traditions of the Mother Country of us all.

The present volume, the first Court Book, furnishes irrefragable evidence that the managers of the East India Company began their undertaking in a thoroughly practical and businesslike manner. They encountered a rebuff, however, on the very threshold of their enterprise, for after three meetings they were obliged to postpone their first voyage until the following year in consequence of the negotiations then in progress with Spain for the conclusion of a peace. The active life of the Company, therefore, did not commence until the meeting at Founders' Hall, on 23rd September, 1600, whereat it was announced that "it was Her Ma[es] pleasure that they shuld proceade in ther purpose." The first steps taken were the appointment of committees to select and purchase suitable vessels for the voyage, as well as the necessary stores and equipment. The *Susan*, or more strictly the *Great Susan*, the *Hector*, and the *Assention*, were the first three vessels purchased, and then, after protracted bargaining with its owner, the Earl of Cumberland, the *Mare Scurge*, afterwards renamed the *Red Dragon*, was procured as the Admiral's ship. These four vessels constituted what is termed "the First Voyage," but a

---

* The East India Company possessed in 1659 a ship called the *May Flower*, which I believe subsequently foundered in the Bay of Bengal. In my *Report on the Miscellaneous Old Records of the India Office* [H.M.'s Stationery Office, 1879], I ask whether it could have been the same ship as the *May Flower* which landed the Dutch, Scotch, and English emigrants from Delft Haven, Southampton, and Plymouth, in New England, 25 Dec., 1620. See pp. 74-5.

fifth, and much smaller vessel, named the *Guift*,* was added to them for the conveyance of some of the indispensable supplies of the squadron, and it was to be cast adrift at the discretion of the commander. The committees had to report to the Court every particular of their transactions with the owners of the ships, and these form the substance of the first half of the present volume. The inventories of the four ships named, given at pp. 15–20, pp. 22–4, pp. 42–4, are exceedingly curious, and mention everything on board from culverins and masts to "1 pease pott & 2 gridirons." The *Mare Scurge*, of 600 tons burden, and twice the size of the next largest vessel of the fleet, the *Hector*, cost 3,700*l.* The *Susan* was purchased for 1,600*l.*; but the prices given for the others are not stated. The *Guift* cost 300*l.* These sums included everything on board, as well as the vessels themselves, and with regard to two of them it was stipulated that the seller should take back his ship at half price on its safe return.

The ships having been procured, the next thing was to make them ready for sea, and this was done with all dispatch; the workmen on the *Mare Scurge* being allowed a barrel of beer a day to prevent their running to the ale-house. They were then provided with their proper companies, the *Mare Scurge* having 200 men, the *Hector* 100 men, the *Susan* 80 men, and the *Assention* 80 men. The sailors received two months' wages in advance, and the officers were treated in an equally liberal manner. Great care was shown in the selection of the latter, and when the Lord Treasurer made a special appeal for Sir Edward Michelborne to be employed in the voyage the Court firmly refused "to imploy anie gent," and requested "leave to sort ther busines wth men of ther owne quality." Captain James Lancaster was appointed Captain of the *Mare Scurge*, and Admiral of the Squadron. Captain John Middleton commanded the *Hector*, with the succession to the chief command in the event of Lancaster's death. Both these officers were also appointed principal factors. The Master of the *Susan* was Samuel Spencer, and of the *Assention*, Roger Hankin.

The Company had difficulties of its own. Some of the adventurers were not prompt in paying up their instalments, and in April, 1601, the Company was 7,000*l.* in default, and had to appeal to the Lords of the Privy Council for special powers to deal with those that "shewe themselves remisse & vnwillinge to furnyshe there promyssed contribučons," and this request was granted. The order is a characteristic one, and will be found at pp. 165–6. The Company issued warrants against the defaulters in accordance with this order, and we may assume that this summary mode of dealing was attended with satisfactory results as the subject gradually disappears from the Court Minutes.

On 1st May 1601, the Court sanctioned the payment of "twentie merkes" to the King of Heralds for assigning Corporate Arms to the Company, but these were not the same Insignia† of Community, with the motto "Auspicio Regis et Senatus Angliæ," which, at a later date, became renowned throughout the East. Very stringent rules were also passed for the maintenance of order in the Court, and some of them would not be without their value in a more august assembly at the present day, as, for instance, the regulation providing that no

---

* The received names of the ships here called *Mare Scurge*, and *Guift*, are *Malice Scourge* and *Guest*. The name of the *Assention* is usually spelled *Ascension*.

† See pp. 21, *note*, and 222–3, *note*.

brother of the Company should speak to any one matter "above three sundry tymes." The penalty of doing so was 3*s.* 4*d.*, a considerable amount in those days. Penalties of different amounts were inflicted for uncivil or intemperate speeches and behaviour, for interruptions, such as private whisperings, &c., for breaking silence when enjoined by the Governour, for leaving the Court without permission, and the refusal to pay these fines or penalties entailed a term of imprisonment. For further information on these points the reader must be referred to pp. 201–4.

It was in June, 1603, that news was received through a Frenchman that left the English fleet at sea of its safe return to European waters, but the first Court Book contains only special reference to the arrival of the *Assention*, from the officers of which vessel several letters were read in the General Court held on 6th June, 1603. Ten days later the reward of five pounds was assigned to Mr. Midleton of Plymouth "for his paines ryding hether wth the first report of the coming of the "*Assention* out of the East Indies." Special orders were sent down to Plymouth that the ship was not to break bulk until anchored in the Thames. Warehouses suitable for the reception of its cargo were taken, tithes were paid to the Lord High Admiral for a prize captured at sea, and on the 16th June the entrance of the vessel into the river was publicly announced. Six pounds had then to be paid for pilotage and 917*l.* for customs to the King [for James I. had succeeded "Good Queen Bess"], before the adventurers were in a position to know how their first journey had prospered. The Court Book says modestly that it afforded encouragement for a second venture, but for more exact and detailed information concerning the return of the East India Company's first squadron from Asia the reader will refer to the passages themselves.

Very soon after the sailing of the first fleet for India by the Cape of Bona Speransa, the project of discovering a route to the East Indies by the North-West Passage was brought before the Court by "one George Waymoth* a navigator." The subject was considered in a dual form; first, whether the Company would take it up and be at the charge of fitting out two or three pinnaces, and secondly, if it would not accept this direct responsibility, would it leave the matter to private men, and reward their discovery by the surrender of the trade by this route for certain years? Whether from fear of losing any of the privileges and advantages of the monopoly of trade with China and the East Indies, or from pure public spirit, it was determined that "the findinge out of the Northwest passage" shall be "consented unto for a voyage." The readiness of the Court to undertake this quest, and to seriously take up George Waymouth's idea, can only be understood by realizing the state of geographical knowledge at the time, and the hopes of the commercial classes of the discovery of new and short routes to the Indies as well as of new countries.

The discovery of the North-West Passage had been the first ambition of English navigators. Henry VII.'s letters patent to John Cabot and his three sons in 1496 were for the discovery of this very route.† In the next reign Robert Thorne advocated the same project, which Sebastian Cabot revived under Edward VI. and Mary, and the expedition of Sir Hugh Willoughby and Richard Chancellor to the White

---

* His name is afterwards spelt Waymouth and Waymouthe.
† See pp. 193-5.

Sea, partly a failure and partly a success, was really another attempt to solve the same problem. The voyages of Martin Frobisher, in 1576–8, were the first to give any tangible ground of hope in the discovery of an inlet on the coast of Labrador running westward, and he was "highly commended of all men for the great hope he brought of a pas-"sage to Cathaia." These different attempts made in the course of a century were so many endeavours to realize the predictions of Seneca* and Pulci.† The latter clearly prophesied that across the Atlantic would be discovered not only a new world, but a new route to the East.

Political considerations confirmed the traditions kept alive by the bolder geographers and men of science of antiquity, and also of the Renaissance. Da Gama's discovery of the Cape route to the Indies had been to the benefit of a Portuguese monopoly, not of the commercial interests of Europe at large. For a century the Portuguese enjoyed as undisturbed a supremacy east of the Cape as the Spaniards had for three-fourths that period on the Spanish Main. When the English navy was in its infancy that of Portugal had reached its prime, and was, indeed, squandering the magnificent inheritance of Da Gama and Albuquerque. It seemed to English navigators and merchants that the only practical way of coping with the Portuguese in the Eastern seas was by the discovery of a new route thither of which England might claim and possess the sole right of usage. In the sixteenth century English naval enterprise found its chief impulse in this consideration, and when the next century was marked by the beginning of an East India Company whose programme was to compete with the Portuguese and Dutch—for the latter had also, and before us, embarked on the same undertaking—in a trade by the Cape route, there were many who turned with unconcealed longing to the earlier scheme, as holding forth the promise of easier and more complete success. It was in this hankering feeling after a monopoly and a sway not to be disputed that men like George Waymouth and other advocates of the North-West Passage found their best opportunity and argument.

Such were the prevalent views when Captain Waymouth proposed a fresh search for the North-West Passage, and obtained the sanction of the Court to his design. Although a fleet had sailed only a few months before by the Cape route, then new to Englishmen, the generality of the Company showed every disposition to patronise another attempt to open a route peculiarly dear to the English, and identified with their name. Yet even in this matter, an unexpected obstacle presented itself in the alleged prior rights of the "Muskovia Companie," the parent of the Russia Company of our time. Delays and objections

---

* See his *Medea*, II., 376–80:—

"Venient annis secula seris
Quibus Oceanus vincula rerum
Laxet, et ingens pateat tellus,
Tethysque novos detegat orbes,
Nec sit terris ultima Thule."

And again, his *Quæstionum Naturalium Libri Septem*:—"Curiosus spectator contemnit domi-"cilii angustias. Quantum enim est quod ab ultimis litoribus Hispaniæ usque ad Indos "jacet? paucissimorum dierum spatium, si navem suam ventus implevit." See pp. 257–8.

† Luigi Pulci, 1431–1487, "sire of the half-serious rhyme":—

"But see, the sun speeds in his western path
To glad the nations with unexpected light."

ensued as to the respective privileges of the two Companies, and the deliberations of chosen delegates did not greatly further any practical or definite conclusion. The discussion might have continued indefinitely had not the East India Company taken legal opinion as to their rights, and finding them ample for the purpose in hand, sanctioned the scheme as their "Second Voyage" to the Indies. Finding them so firm, the Muskovia Company waived their loftier pretensions, and proceeded to associate themselves in the enterprise. For the purposes of this voyage, a special levy of one shilling for each pound deposited by the adventurers for the Cape experiment was ordered, and special terms, mainly dependent, however, on the result of his voyage, were made with Captain Waymouth. The objects of the journey itself are well expressed on pp. 198–9, whereat are recited some of the chief passages of Elizabeth's patent, as well as the reasons which swayed the decision of the Court. The formal agreement between the Company and George Waymouth sets forth that the Governor and Company had deliberated on "the longe and tedious course wch hath benne "hitherto houlden by all such as do trade or sayle from these parts "of the world in to ye East Indies alonge the coast of Europe and "Africa by ye Cape of Bona Esperansa and of the great adventures "wch are borne in soe longe a viage by many kinds of daungers offered "therein, and beinge moved wth great hope that ther is a possibility "of discovery of a neerer Passage into ye said East Indies by seas by "ye way of the North-west yf the same were vndertaken by a man of "knowledge in Navigacõn, &c., &c.," and had in consequence entrusted the task to Captain Waymouth. In a subsequent passage further details are supplied as to how it was thought this would be effected, and these constituted what would now be termed Captain Waymouth's sailing orders. He was to "sayle toward the coast of "Groynland into that part of the open seas wch is described in sundry "generall mapps by ye name of fretum Danies and shall passe on "forward in those seas by ye northwest or as he shall fynd the Passage "best to lye towards the parts or kingedomes of Cataya or China, or "*ye backside of America*." Queen Elizabeth attached sufficient importance to the undertaking to write a special letter to the Emperor of China and "Kathai," the use of the double names for the one country implying rather the excess, or cautious completeness, of diplomatic courtesy than geographical ignorance.

Considering the great expense to which the Company went in the matter, the many hopes that were based on the enterprise, and the confidence of the commander himself, the speedy, not to say the ignominious, return of the expedition was extremely disheartening. The Court Book throws no further light on the cause of the failure of this well equipped expedition to achieve what was not then known to be impossible, than to attribute it to the intrigues of the minister or preacher, Mr. Cartwright. But Captain Waymouth endeavoured, and not unsuccessfully, to induce the Court to overlook his failure, and to take up new schemes for the discovery of another route, not by the North-west, but by the South-west, or round Cape Horn. There is little doubt that he would have carried his purpose had he not allowed himself to be drawn into litigation with the Company about what he considered his just claims in the matter of the abortive voyage. These were firmly resisted, with the consequence that he failed not only to obtain his damages, but also to induce the Company to employ him on a fresh voyage, as had been intended.

The opposition of the Court to Captain Waymouth's demands and propositions was made the more inflexible by the safe return of the ships that had sailed by way of the Cape of Good Hope. The arrival of the *Assention* showed where the practically useful route to the Indies lay. It had its difficulties, delays, and dangers, but in comparison with a mythical North-West passage it acquired greater substantiality as one prosperous voyage regularly succeeded another. Hudson, Button, and Baffin followed at short intervals, and with more favourable results, in the footsteps of Waymouth; but even their successes went to demonstrate the impracticability of the main purpose of their voyages, the opening of a North-West Passage. The first Court Book, characteristic in every particular and important in most, is historically curious as officially marking the first indication of the waning hopes of the school of Cabot and Frobisher, and the rising expectations, soon to be confirmed by facts, of that of Lancaster and Middleton, of Saris and Marlowe. The North-West Passage was a great idea based on an error of fact. The long and tedious route by the Cape was a magnificent certainty which supplied English naval skill and daring with their most profitable and glorious field of enterprise; for the pretensions of the Portuguese to a monopoly being steadfastly repelled, the opulent trade with the Indies became the prize in a fair and open competition of merit and energy. The present volume is evidence, not of the triumph of the English Company, but of the way in which they made up their minds to deserve and win it. The fruits of the victory they ultimately, after a contest of two centuries, secured over all rivals by the open ocean round the Cape of Good Hope, have been retained unimpaired now that the narrow seas from Gibraltar to Aden have become, since the piercing of the Suez Isthmus, the general thoroughfare to the Indies; and if the North-West Canadian Pacific Railway should realize the anticipations of its projectors, the practical solution of the old North-West Passage problem would leave the English-speaking races victors still in the secular and mortal struggle of the leading countries of the civilized world for commercial ascendency and political existence. The states which, through degenerate weariness and faint-heartedness in well-doing, failed in this implacable competition are foredoomed to wrested greatness and enforced decay.

Undying then should be our gratitude to the founders of the East India Company, for they were indeed the pioneers of the unparalleled colonial and mercantile prosperity of modern England: and we may be sure that wherever

"The strong hearts of her sons"

are not borne down, as they have been, for well nigh a whole generation among ourselves, by the miserable sense of constantly reiterated public shame, but are kept up by the high hopes on which they are perennially nourished in the invincible Republic of the West, and in the proud dominions of the British Crown in the great South Sea, there the names of these middle class Elizabethan merchant adventurers, who so well understood, when occasion called, how by transgressing, most truly to keep the moral law, will be for ever cherished and revered, as of "brave men, and worthy patriots, dear to God, and famous to all ages."

Our own destruction, as a beneficent power among the nations, may be as inevitable, as our peril, arising mainly from the weakness of the historical instinct in the English democracy, at the present moment seems imminent; but in the worst case we shall have bequeathed the secret of empire, in the New World and the Old, to more resolute inheritors of our common traditions and splendour.

GEORGE BIRDWOOD.

India Office, Westminster,
"Queen Elizabeth's Day" [*17th November**], 1886.

---

* The anniversary of the accession of "the Most Mightie and Magnificent Empresse Elizabeth" continued to be kept as a public holiday in England even within the last century, and it should still be so observed, at least in the India Office and in British India, and the State of Virginia, in praise perennial of Her imperious Majesty's heroic memory.

"Cynthia prima fuit, Cynthia finis erit."

"Her deeds were like great glusters of ripe grapes
Which load the branches of the fruitfull vine,
Offring to fall into each mouth that gapes,
And fill the same with store of timely wine.

* * * * * *

Her thoughts are like the fume of Frankincence,
Which from a golden Censer forth doth rise,
And throwing forth sweet odours mounts fro thence
In rolling globes up to the vauted skies."

Appendix C.

List of the East India Company's Charters found in the Accountant General's Department after the first reprint of my Report on the Old Records had nearly all passed through the press.

1. 3rd April 1661.—Charter to the Governor and Company of Merchants of London trading to the East Indies, dated 13th of Charles II. A copy also exists:—See No. 23 of *Catalogue of the Parchment Records* [Appendix D].

2. 27th March 1669.—Grant of the Island of Bombay, dated 20th of Charles II.

3. 16th December 1674.—Grant of the Island of St. Helena, dated 25th of Charles II.

4. 5th October 1677.—Charter confirming privileges and granting power to coin money at Bombay, dated 28th Charles II.

5. 7th October 1693.—Charter confirming privileges, dated 5th of William III. and Mary. A copy also exists:—See No. 47 of *Catalogue of Parchment Records* [Appendix D].

6. 11th November 1693.—Charter prescribing orders and directions, dated 5th of William III. and Mary. See also No. 49 of *Catalogue of Parchment Records* [Appendix D].

7. 3rd September 1698.—Charter of the "General Society" trading to the East Indies, dated 10th of William III.

8. 5th September 1698.—Charter of the "English Company" trading to the East Indies.

9. 14th July 1698.—Charter appointing Hugh Boscawen and others to take subscriptions for the General Society (English Company).

10. 22nd July 1702.—Indenture tripartite between Her Majesty Queen Anne, the Company of Merchants of London, and the English Company, dated 1st of Queen Anne.

11. Duplicate.

12. 29th September 1708.—Decree of Chancery on Lord Godolphin's award between the two Companies.

13. 24th September 1726.—Charter to the United Company for establishing Mayors' Courts at Madras, Bombay, and Calcutta, dated 13th of George I.

14. 8th January 1753.—Charter for erecting and holding Courts of Justice, dated 26th of George II.

15. 14th January 1758.—Constitutional grant of plunder taken since 19th September 1757, dated 31st of George II.

16. Duplicate.

17. 20th December 1760.—Charter to establish Courts of Judicature at Fort Marlborough, dated 1st of George III.

18. 2nd October, 1812.—Charter regarding property captured in war, dated 52nd George III.

GEO. B.

P.S., Second Reprint.—All the above 18 documents are now included in the new *Catalogue of Parchment Records*, prepared under the direction of Mr. F. C. Danvers since the publication of the first reprint of this Report in 1889. See Appendix D.

GEO. B.

Appendix D.

Catalogue of the Parchment Records,* prepared under the direction of Mr. F. C. Danvers, 23rd June 1890.

No.	Date	Description
1.	1498, 1st Sept. .	Deed relating to property in Lime Street Ward.
2.	1600, 31st Dec. .	Queen Elizabeth's Charter. [Copy only.]
3.	1606, 9th Aug. .	Royal License to sell spices, &c., in bulk, and to export the same. [Seal.]
4.	1609, 22nd May .	Royal Licence to sell spices, &c., for export in bulk, ungarbled. [Seal.]
5.	1609, 31st May .	James I.'s Charter. [Copy only.]
6.	1610, 17th March.	Royal Commission to Sir H. Middleton for the 6th voyage. [Seal.]
7.	1610, 17th March.	Duplicate of No. 6. [Seal.]
8.	1623, 4th Feb. .	Royal Commission granting judicial powers to the Company's servants in India. [Seal.]
9.	1627, 14th Oct. .	Royal Commision to Robert Ducy and others to enquire into the disposal of the monies collected for the purposes of an expedition against the Algerian pirates. [Seal.]
10.	1628, 18th Feb. .	Letters Patent for shipment of bullion. [Seal.]
11.	1629, 24th March.	Letters Patent for shipment of bullion.
12.	1629, 17th Oct. .	Letters Patent for shipment of bullion.
13.	1630, 10th March.	Letters Patent for shipment of bullion. [Seal.]
14.	1630, 9th Nov. .	Letters Patent for shipment of bullion.
15.	1631, 19th Feb. .	Counterpart of lease of a house in Bishopsgate Street.
16.	1631, 21st Nov. .	Letters Patent for shipment of bullion.
17.	1632, 3rd March.	Letters Patent for shipment of bullion.
18.	1633, 8th Oct. .	Letters Patent for shipment of bullion.
19.	1635, 30th Nov. .	Letters Patent for shipment of bullion.
20.	1655, 7th Aug. .	Cromwell's Warrant to the Commissioners of the Treasury for payment of 50,000*l.* to the Company. [Seal.]
21.	1660, 18th Dec. .	Letters Patent for shipment of bullion. [Seal.]
22.	1661, 3rd April .	Charter of Charles II., confirming and extending former charters. [Seal.]

* This Catalogue includes all the documents enumerated in the text and foot-notes of the present Report, pp. 18, 19, and 20, with the exceptions noted on page 19; and all the documents enumerated in Mr. Noel Sainsbury's Calendar [Appendix A, pp. 263–73]; and in the List of Documents found in the Accountant-General's Department [Appendix C, pp. 282–3]. And it further includes five documents, namely, Numbers 40, 41, 49, 50, and 51, not entered in my Report, Mr. Sainsbury's Calendar, or the Accountant-General's List.—Geo. B.

23.	1661, 3rd April .	Copy of No. 22.
24.	1665, 14th Nov. .	Mandate of James, Duke of York, Lord High Admiral, to the Commissioners for Reprizals to sell the contents of the prize *Golden Phœnix.*
25.	1668, 6th Feb. .	Acquittance under the Great Seal to the E. I. Co., with reference to the sum realized by the sale of the contents of two Dutch prizes, the *Slothany* and the *Golden Phœnix.*
26.	1669, 27th March.	Letters Patent granting the island of Bombay to the E. I. Co. [Seal.]
27.	1672, 7th Oct. .	Letters Patent for the payment, by instalments, of 92,000*l.* due to the E. I. Co.
28.	1672, 7th Oct. .	Acquittance under the Great Seal to the E. I. Co., remitting certain monies due from them. [Seal.]
29.	1673, 27th Oct. .	Letters Patent ratifying an agreement between Prince Rupert and others and the E. I. Co., for the sale of goods taken from certain Dutch prizes.
30.	1674, 6th March.	Release from Prince Rupert and others of any further sums due on account of the sale of the above goods. [Seal.]
31.	1674, 13th March.	Acquittance under the Great Seal to the E. I. Co., releasing them from all further claims on the same subject.
32.	1674, 16th Dec. .	Letters Patent granting the island of St. Helena to the E. I. Co. [Seal.]
33.	1676, 21st Oct. .	Warrant under the Great Seal to the Commissioners, &c. of the Treasury and Exchequer, for the repayment of 40,000*l.* to the E. I. Co. [Seal.]
34.	1677, 5th Oct. .	Letters Patent confirming former privileges and giving power to coin money at Bombay. [Seal.]
35.	1678, 24th Jan. .	Warrant to the Commissioners, &c. of the Treasury and Exchequer for the payment of 60,000*l.* to the E. I. Co.
36.	1678, 22nd Nov. .	Warrant to the Commissioners, &c. of the Treasury and Exchequer for payment to the E. I. Co. of 50,000*l.* [Seal.]
37.	1682, 18th Sept. .	A similar warrant for payment of 15,372*l.* [Seal.]
38.	1683, 5th July .	A similar warrant for payment of 40,463*l.* 10*s.* 0*d.* [Seal.]
39.	1684, 12th Nov. .	The King to John Petit, George Bourcher, Simon Cracroft, and Edward Littleton, requiring them to return to England to answer certain charges against them.
40.	1686, 12th April.	Letters Patent confirming former charters and authorizing the Company to establish Courts of Justice, to raise military and naval forces, and coin money in India. [Copy only.]

41. 1687, 30th Dec. . Charter establishing a municipality and Mayor's Court at Madras. [Copy only.]

42. 1688, 31st Jan. . Acquittance under the Privy Seal to the E. I. Co., and to the owners of the ship *Andaluzia*.

43. 1689, 5th Sept. . Hall and Wife *versus* Leigh and E. I. Co. Two decrees in Chancery. [Seal.]

44. 1689, 3rd Oct. . Warrant under the Great Seal to the Commissioners of the Treasury and Exchequer, for payment to the E. I. Co. of the sum of 22,500*l.*, for saltpetre purchased of them.

45. 1691, 19th Dec. . Atwood, Halford, and others *versus* Warr and the E. I. Co. Decree in Chancery. [Seal.]

46. 1693, 7th Oct. . Letters Patent confirming the E. I. Co. in their powers and privileges. [Seal.]

47. 1693, 7th Oct. . Copy of No. 46.

48. 1693, 11th Nov. . Letters Patent prescribing regulations for the conduct of the Company's business. [Seal.]

49. 1694, 28th Sept. . Letters Patent establishing further regulations, &c. [Copy only.].

50. 1695, 17th Jan. . Bye Laws. Approved by a General Court.

51. 1697-8. . . Act 44, 9 and 10 William III., for raising a sum not exceeding 2,000,000*l.*, &c.

52. 1698, 14th July. . Letters Patent appointing Commissioners to receive subscriptions for the "General Society"; with Schedule A., Draft Charter of General Society, and Schedule B., Draft of "the Charter for the Company to trade under a joint stock, which is to pass under the Great Seal" if the 2,000,000*l.* be subscribed. [Seal.]

53. 1698, 14th July. . Roll of subscribers to the 2,000,000*l.*

54. 1698, 14th–16th July. Two books of original subscriptions to the 2,000,000*l.*

55. 1698, 3rd Sept. . Charter of incorporation of the "General Society." [See Shaw's "Charters," Preface, p. 13.] [Seal.]

56. 1698, 5th Sept. . Charter of incorporation of the English Company trading to the East Indies. [Seal.]

57. 1698, 5th Sept. . Copy of No. 56.

58. 1698, 13th Oct. . Grant of Arms to the English Company trading to the East Indies.

59. 1702, 22nd July . Indenture Tripartite between Queen Anne and the two East India Companies, for uniting the said Companies. [Seal.]

60. 1702, 22nd July . Duplicate of No. 59. [Seal.].

61. 1703, 8th Dec. . Letters of Marque to ship *Martha*. [Seal.]

62. 1705, 20th Aug. . Grant of pardon under the Great Seal to the London E. I. Co. for all crimes, misdemeanours, &c., committed by them since "the beginning of the world." [Seal.].

63.	1708, 29th Sept. .	The Earl of Godolphin's award between the Old and New E. I. Cos.
64.	1709, 21st March.	Grant by the London E. I. Co. of their debts in Great Britain to Queen Anne for re-grant to Trustees.
65.	1709, 21st March.	Declaration of Trust of the London E. I. Co. as to bonds for 70,000*l.* which by Lord Godolphin's award were deposited in the hands of trustees appointed by the New E. I. Co.
66.	1709, 22nd April.	Grant to the United Co. of all foreign debts of the Old Company. [Seal.]
67.	1709, 7th May .	Queen Anne's acceptance of the surrender of the Charter of the London Co. [Seal.]
68.	1709, 15th Aug. .	Letters Patent re-assigning to Sir J. Andrews and others the debts in Great Britain due to the London Co. [Seal.]
69.	1720, 8th Oct. .	Apparently a record in an ejectment case.
70.	1726, 24th Sept. .	Letters Patent establishing Municipalities and Mayors' Courts at Madras, Bombay, and Calcutta. [Seal.]
71.	1727, 17th Nov. .	Letters Patent granting to the Company all fines imposed by the Mayors' Courts and Justices in India. [Seal.]
72.	1730, 26th Oct. .	Letters of Administration of the estate of Cæsar Burtou, late a factor at Angengo, granted to J. Spencer, Senior.
73.	1731, 10th Dec. .	Similar letters of Administration granted to J. Spencer, Junior, on the decease of his father.
74.	1732, 20th Oct. .	Commission to ship *Harrington* to seize pirates, &c. [Seal.]
75.	1737, 22nd Aug. .	Similar Commission to ship *Royal George.* [Seal.]
76.	1745, 18th Nov. .	Letters of Marque for ship *Dragon.*
77.	1747, 2nd July .	Letters of Marque for ship *Swallow.*
78.	1753, 8th Jan. .	Amended Charter of Mayors' Courts at Madras, Bombay, and Calcutta. [Seal.]
79.	1757, 19th Sept. .	Letters Patent granting to the Company a moiety of the plunder taken from the Nawab Nazim of Bengal. [Seal.]
80.	1758, 14th Jan. .	Grant to the Company of all booty or plunder taken by their ships or forces alone. [Seal.]
81.	1758, 14th Jan. .	Duplicate of No. 80. [Seal.]
82.	1758, 16th Oct. .	Commission of ship *Royal George* to seize pirates, &c.
83.	1760, 20th Dec. .	Letters Patent establishing Courts of Judicature, &c., at Fort Marlborough. [Seal.]
84.	1793, 25th March.	Grant to the E. I. Co. of the booty, &c., taken in the late war with Tippoo Sahib. [Seal.]
85.	1793, 5th Nov. .	Address to Lord Cornwallis on his leaving Calcutta.

86.	1796, 7th April .	Grant of an annuity to Warren Hastings of 4,000*l.* per annum for 18 years, commencing 25th Dec., 1795. [Seal.]
87.	1796, 8th April .	Assignment of the said annuity as security for the repayment of 36,000*l.* [Seal.]
88.	1796, 8th April .	Duplicate of No. 87.
89.	1800, 22nd Nov.	Grant to the E. I. Co. of booty taken from Tippoo Sultaun. [Seal.]
90.	1807, 21st March.	Grant of arms to Haileybury College. [Seals.]
91.	1812, 2nd Oct. .	Grant to the E. I. Co. of booty taken at Serhampore. [Seal.]
92.	Date indecipherable [? 5th June 1747].	(?) Commission to ship *Delawarr* to seize pirates, &c. [Seal.]

NOTE.—Besides the above there are a number of parchments (some of ancient date) in the custody of the Legal Adviser. These are, however, as far as is known, of no public interest, being merely title deeds and leases of properties held at different times by the East India Company.

INDEX.

NOTE.—*The letter* n *indicates that the reference is to a footnote.*

T

ERRATUM.

Page 26, *note*, line 5, *for* 18*d*. *read* 8*d*.
